Free Speech and Koch Money

"This deeply researched and urgent book reads like a detective mystery. A riveting self-defense manual for all who fear for the future of our country and our planet."

—Nancy MacLean, author of *Democracy in Chains: The Deep History of the Radical Right's Stealth Plan for America*

"Universities regularly conduct important discussions of free speech. And then there is the largely imaginary 'campus free speech crisis'. This book is a detailed and valuable guide to the shadowy right-wing financial networks irresponsibly stoking the latter to the growing detriment of the former."

—Hank Reichman, Professor Emeritus of History, California State University, East Bay

Free Speech and Koch Money

Manufacturing a Campus Culture War

Ralph Wilson and Isaac Kamola

First published 2021 by Pluto Press
New Wing, Somerset House, Strand, London WC2R 1LA

www.plutobooks.com

Copyright © Ralph Wilson and Isaac Kamola 2021

The right of Ralph Wilson and Isaac Kamola to be identified as the authors of
this work has been asserted in accordance with the Copyright, Designs and
Patents Act 1988.

British Library Cataloguing in Publication Data
A catalogue record for this book is available from the British Library

ISBN   978 0 7453 4302 0   Hardback
ISBN   978 0 7453 4301 3   Paperback
ISBN   978 0 7453 4305 1   PDF
ISBN   978 0 7453 4303 7   EPUB

Typeset by Stanford DTP Services, Northampton, England

Simultaneously printed in the United Kingdom and United States of America

Contents

Preface

We began writing this book a year after the 2017 Charlottesville Unite the Right rally, when violent anti-Black racists and antisemites imposed themselves upon the national stage in a way that the majority of Americans could no longer ignore. We finished the book during the months following the 2020 Black Lives Matter (BLM) protests sparked by the murders of George Floyd and Breonna Taylor. As millions of people from across American society came into the streets to demand justice, protestors were met with tear gas and pepper spray, run over by cars, and were abducted in unmarked vehicles. Far-right groups, including Republican politicians and the right-wing media ecosystem, diluted calls for justice, staging instead a dirge of white grievance and rekindled racist narratives of inner cities on fire. They rallied behind wealthy suburbanites who pointed guns at BLM protestors and behind a seventeen-year-old militia member who murdered two unarmed protestors. They demanded "law and order" and spewed culture-war fury over "socialism," "cancel culture," "snowflakes," and "social justice warriors." In 2021 they passed laws criminalizing protest as well as the teaching of critical race theory.

How did we get here? This book tells a small part of that larger story, a story about an organized counter-revolution seeking to reverse decades of progress made by movements for social justice.

Over the past 50 years the American libertarian movement—particularly those elements funded by Koch's growing network of corporate donors—has become a well-organized and well-funded political machinery. The Koch network seeks to fundamentally transform society in ways that reverse many of the progressive gains made during the middle of the twentieth century, especially those in the areas of civil and labor rights as well as consumer and environmental protections. Today this right-wing political infrastructure, which we term the Koch network, consists of academic centers, student groups, think tanks, policy mills, voter mobilization efforts, media outlets, legal organizations, and astroturf social movements (including the

Tea Party). This political machinery has attacked the Kyoto Protocol, smoking regulations, labor unions, Medicare expansion, and gun-control efforts. It has championed the deregulation of money in politics and undermined voting rights. Elements have helped spread the Big Lie of voter fraud in the 2020 election. Against all credible scientific opposition, the Koch network has made climate change a debatable topic in American life. It has groomed and successfully placed a generation of radically individualist and pro-corporate academics and judges in the academy and on the court, including a majority on the Supreme Court. Within higher education, the Koch network attacks affirmative action, harasses faculty who write about racial, gender, and economic justice, and undermines efforts to diversify faculty and make campuses more inclusive—all in the name of individual liberty.

This political operation has proven particularly successful precisely because it has not been built simply to elect politicians or advocate for specific policy preferences. Sure, anti-union and anti-climate legislation, rolling back affordable healthcare, privatizing education, and tax cuts for the wealthy are desired policy outcomes. However, these outcomes are achieved by the Koch network not only with successful corporate lobbying or lavish donations to political parties or candidates, but also with a well-funded ideological and political machinery that seeks nothing less than social transformation. To this end, the Koch network has long devoted considerable energy and resources to gaining footholds within the university, and thereby changing the ideas that are produced, taught, researched, and published therein. The resulting network of academic centers and think tanks reproduces an ideology that coheres around the language of "individual freedom" and "Western civilization," while denying the existence of actual material and historical legacies of racial, gendered, and class-based exclusions, marginalizations, and violences. Instead, this libertarian ideology holds that positive outcomes only follow from individuals maximizing utility within the freedom of immaculately self-regulating markets. The intellectual, ideological, and political infrastructure created by the Koch network seeks to remake the United States, and the world, in the image of this hardline libertarian worldview. Doing so, however, requires fundamentally remaking institutions of higher education, which have been a prominent source of intellectual criticism of the Koch network's preferred libertarian fantasy.

This book examines the Koch network's ideological and political machinery by exploring how it exerts power on college campuses through one particular strategy, namely manufacturing a campus free speech crisis. In the past few years, widely circulated examples of protests against Milo Yiannopoulos, Charles Murray, Ben Shapiro, Ann Coulter, and others have come to be taken as evidence that the academy is intolerant toward conservative views. *Free Speech and Koch Money*, however, demonstrates that these instances are neither spontaneous crises nor examples of a spirited debate about speech on campus. Rather, they are manufactured crises, funded by political operatives and intentionally designed to achieve specific political outcomes.

The book examines how and why the Koch donor network funds the vast political machinery driving the free speech movement on college campuses. We argue that what often appears as localized and spontaneous outrage among conservative students should instead be understood within the context of a larger strategy deployed by well-organized donors and political operatives seeking to fundamentally transform American society, including higher education. Understood as such, students, faculty, university administrators, journalists, and the general public should focus less on debating who does (and does not) have the right to speak on campus. We should instead be asking: "Who funds these speakers? Who brings them to campus? And why?" When we ask these questions, it becomes possible to take seriously the degree to which plutocratic libertarian donors value higher education as a cornerstone of social transformation.

We have written this book as a field guide to the Koch donor network's influence on college campuses. We hope that students, faculty, administrators, journalists, and concerned citizens will find it useful in contextualizing the seemingly random academic centers or oddly well-organized (yet often small) student groups that pop up on particular campuses, who all seem to be yelling in unison about "individual liberty" and "free speech." We hope the book is useful as an organizing tool to push back against dark money on college campuses, giving activists and academics an appreciation for the depth—but also the weaknesses—of this well-funded counter-revolution. While the various academic, political, media, and judicial organizations that the Koch donor network funds seem to enjoy a stranglehold on public discourse, their power stems from their seemingly bottomless funding and their highly networked nature—the combination of which makes plutocratic libertarian ideas appear more widely held than they actually are. This secretive strategy works by creating an echo chamber, whereby different academics, journalists, think tanks, and political groups all use the same vocabulary, and are easily misinterpreted as enjoying widespread public support. When ideas manufactured by a plutocratic libertarian minority are not taken seriously within the academy, media or wider public, these same actors weaponize free speech to demand that they nonetheless receive equal attention and consideration. We demonstrate that the so-called campus free speech crisis is not a spontaneous issue of great public concern. It is not an existential threat engulfing higher education. Rather, it is a well-funded political strategy. Understanding it as such also makes it much less effective.

We should stop entertaining the fabricated narrative that there exists an epidemic of persecuted conservative speech on college campuses. Or that free speech violations and cancel culture are endemic across higher education. Instead, we should follow the money. In doing so, we will discover a manufactured crisis.

The authors would like to thank the activists, journalists, researchers, and academics who have made the writing of this book possible. We would especially like to thank all those who helped build a student and faculty movement to protect academic freedom from undue donor influence.

Ralph: I would like to thank Kent Miller, Ray Bellamy, Jerry Funt, Lakey Love, and others from Florida State University. Invaluable help came from Lisa Graves, Connor Gibson, the Center for Media and Democracy, Greenpeace, and those in the American Association of University Professors and Protecting Dissent Network. I would especially like to thank my co-author Isaac, my family, and my partner Sarah for their tireless support.

Isaac: I came to this topic after Campus Reform attacked and slandered my colleague, Johnny Williams. I would like to thank Johnny and the countless academics who publicly and uncompromisingly condemn anti-Black racism and white supremacy in all its forms, often at great personal and professional risk. I have learned and grown so much because of your courage. I hope this book is a useful tool in that fight. Thanks to the many student activists at Trinity College whose work continues to inspire me, including Jederick Estrella, Brandon Herrera, Trinna Larsen, Sam McCarthy, Aaron Supple, and many others. Thanks to the national AAUP staff, the Trinity chapter of the AAUP, and my colleagues and friends who have been tireless defenders of academic freedom and faculty governance: Dina Anselmi, Stefanie Chambers, Dan Douglas, Diana Evans, Cheryl Greenberg, Josh King, Reo Matsuzaki, Alyson Spurgas, Mark Stater, Anna Terwiel, Kari Theurer, and many others. Finally, I want to thank Ralph for his unparalleled research and vision, and Serena Laws for her continued support (which often includes indulging my long harangues about the Koch network).

We would both like to thank Nancy MacLean, Jonathan Havercroft, and two anonymous reviewers who provided valuable feedback on the manuscript. Thanks also to the panelists and audience at the 2020 American Political Science panel (especially the discussant Mary Ryan), as well as Leigh Claire La Berge and others at the Social(ly Distanced) Theory Salon, Hartford, CT. We thank Jakob Horstmann at Pluto for conveying his enthusiasm so intently. Trinity College's Faculty Research Committee and the Dean's office provided necessary funding for manuscript completion. Jenna Leschuk, Tim Clark, Robert Webb, and Susan Storch performed much needed copy editing, production assistance, and indexing. And Jack Smyth designed the beautiful cover. Thank you.

Well, there's a lot to be done. We'd better get to it.

Introduction: Overview of the Koch's Campus Free Speech Machine

When people raise concerns that college campuses are hostile to conservative and libertarian perspectives, they often point to the same small handful of dramatic clashes over free speech. In February 2017 a riot shut down Milo Yiannopoulos's visit to the University of California, Berkeley, and the following month protestors prevented Charles Murray from speaking at Middlebury College. Far-right personalities like David Horowitz, Ann Coulter, Ben Shapiro, Laura Ingraham, Richard Spencer, Candice Owens, Gavin McInnes, Christina Hoff Summers, Heather MacDonald, and others have faced protests on college campuses, or have been disinvited. At Yale, students protested a professor who challenged an email from the administration requesting that students refrain from insensitive Halloween costumes. Students protested a faculty member at Evergreen State College who derided a request that white students and faculty vacate campus for the day.[1] These and other campus free speech incidents received considerable attention, and were often woven together as evidence of rampant left-wing "political correctness" and "cancel culture" in higher education. Administrators, some faculty, and public commentators seem engaged in a collective handwringing over the needs of aggrieved conservative college students, who claim that their right to free speech is being violated in the name of identity politics, political correctness, safe spaces, and preventing microaggressions.

These examples are taken as evidence that American colleges and universities are openly "leftist," hostile to conservative ideas, and eager to trample over the speech of those with whom they disagree. This narrative about a so-called free speech crisis helps justify the political claim that colleges and universities are primarily sites of political indoctrination, little more than willing participants in a broader culture war against conservatives. This general narrative helps explain why public support for higher education now breaks down along party lines. According to a 2017 Pew survey only 36 percent of Republicans view colleges and universities positively, compared with 72 percent of Democrats.[2] In 2019, President Trump amplified this campus-as-culture-war storyline by signing an executive order threatening a withdrawal of federal funding for those institutions that fail to protect free speech.[3]

In response to this supposed campus free speech crisis, many academics have responded by calling for more civil public discussion or by debating the proper balance between commitments to free speech, campus safety, and institutional inclusion.[4] The discussion treats these controversies as ethical conundrums that naturally emerge from campus life. Should someone with a history of writing books that endorse a notion of white racial superiority be invited to speak on campus? What about a homophobe? Or someone known for their transphobic rhetoric? What does such a speaker contribute to the educational mission of the institution? Shouldn't all sides be heard? Isn't more speech the best response to bad speech? Some argue that decisions to bar provocative speakers from campus are evidence of our highly partisan times. Others blame a generation of coddled and increasingly intolerant students.[5]

Often missing from these discussions, however, are questions about power and money: What explains the intensity and relentlessness of the recent wave of campus visits by highly provocative speakers? Who invites them? Who funds them? And why? This book argues that the major components of the so-called campus free speech crisis have been manufactured by a handful of wealthy political donors for explicitly partisan purposes. We show how a highly interconnected and well-funded political operation has instigated, amplified, and litigated what would otherwise be local debates over campus speech.

Beyond the same oft-cited anecdotal examples such as those mentioned above, there is very little actual evidence that conservative and libertarian voices are routinely stifled on college campuses. Georgetown University's Free Speech Project identified only 60 cases of speech violations on campuses between 2016 and 2018; with 4,583 colleges and universities in the United States, each year a serious violation of speech takes place on 0.65 percent of campuses.[6] It turns out that the imposition of safe spaces, speech codes, and trigger warnings has been dramatically overstated.[7] Most college students express strong support for free speech, and college campuses are generally more tolerant of conservative ideas than society as a whole.[8] Far from suffering left-wing brainwashing, students rarely feel pressured to change their political views based on ideas expressed by their professors. If anything, some evidence suggests that conservative faculty make greater attempts to sway students than liberal faculty do.[9] Furthermore, it is far more common for professors on the left—especially those who publicly criticize racism, sexism, homophobia, or who support Palestine—to find themselves threatened, harassed, and even fired.[10]

Higher education has long been the home of heated debates about free speech, free expression, and academic freedom. And examples of conservative voices being stifled do exist. Colleges and universities have also proven to be productive places for these contestations to be articulated, debated, and challenged. *Free Speech and Koch Money*, however, demonstrates that much of the contemporary outrage over a full-blown, nationwide campus free speech crisis has been largely manufactured as part of a well-funded and well-organized political strategy. Furthermore, this tactic of manufacturing a campus free speech crisis originates with the same funders, organizations, intellectuals, ideologues, and political operatives that form the core of the libertarian right.

As this book and others demonstrate, wealthy hard-right libertarian donors within the network built by Charles Koch have spent the past half century constructing a dense network of political organizations that seeks to remake society in line with their free-market fundamentalist views. Over the past five decades, a range of organizations funded by Koch and likeminded donors have worked in close collaboration to undermine environmental, health, and labor regulations, to attack unions, privatize education, reduce taxation, and dismantle the social safety net. This strategy has involved gaining greater footholds on college and university campuses, understood by libertarian donors and activists as strategic beachheads from which to train experts, legitimize their worldview, and recruit student activists into their political machinery. This plutocratic libertarian class sees university campuses as critical to their strategy for social change and as a pipeline of ideas and talent.

It is not surprising, then, that organizations created by the Koch donor network are also largely responsible for manufacturing the so-called campus free speech crisis.

This book is therefore less interested in debating "both sides" of the ethical and constitutional questions around particular issues of campus speech. Most commentators ask some version of "Should Milo Yiannopoulos or Charles Murray be allowed to speak on campus?" or "Should students be prevented from disrupting their talks?" These are important ethical, intellectual, and political questions upon which reasonable people can disagree. However, we instead ask: "How did these speakers end up at Berkeley and Middlebury in the first place?" This latter question does not settle the former. However, it does uncover the power and wealth that forces the public to obsess over those first questions. It also reveals the infrastructure that created a highly political framework for interpreting these controversies.

Free Speech and Koch Money examines how and why the Koch donor network funds the vast political machinery driving the free speech movement on college campuses. It argues that what often appears as spontaneous local outrage is actually the product of a larger strategy deployed by well-organized libertarian donors. The Koch donor network funds the student groups that bring provocative speakers to campus, as well as the careers of the speakers themselves. It funds the media outlets that amplify the outrage over protests as well as the lawyers who sue universities for denying the speakers platforms on campus. It even funds the politicians who pass campus free speech legislation that seeks to punish student protestors, as well as the academic centers and institutes in which allied faculty help instigate and leverage the looming free speech threat.

We also demonstrate that the broader political operation funded by the Koch donor network has an extensive track record of weaponizing free speech arguments more generally. Its members have long used the First Amendment to push back against civil rights, environmental and consumer protections, government regulation, and labor unions. Free speech arguments have been used to justify policies that shield wealthy political donors from campaign finance limits and transparency requirements, thereby maximizing their influence on the political process. For example, the Koch political operation has historically created phony grassroots movements on behalf of cigarette manufacturers and oil companies to insist that the public hears the "other side" of the story, arguing that free speech requires that smokers

4

and climate change deniers receive the same attention as public health officials and climate scientists.

Universities are central to the plutocratic libertarian project. They have also proven more resistant to donor control and influence than other organizations. Wealthy donors can easily gin up a tax-deductible non-profit organization committed to advocating climate denial or grooming the next generation of libertarian judges. However, norms around academic freedom, peer review, and faculty governance make it more difficult to persuade universities to generate research and train talent that legitimizes a specific ideological worldview. In this more challenging setting, free speech, combined with a narrative about the silencing of conservative voices, has become a political cudgel that donors have used to justify greater donor access to higher education. This helps explain why the Koch donor network has adopted the tactic of first provoking, and then leveraging, an illusory free speech crisis to gain greater say over who teaches, researches, and speaks on college campuses. It's ingenious, we must admit: a kind of jujitsu that enlists a core value of higher education—free inquiry—in order to crack open universities for corporate capture.

We hope this book serves as a useful tool for refocusing the debate about campus free speech. We recognize that navigating the complex intersection of free speech, academic freedom, campus safety, and institutional inclusion is not easy. What speech crosses the line? Who determines this? How does an institution protect a wide range of speech while also making sure that all students and faculty feel included and welcome within the campus community? These are difficult questions, especially in a deeply divided country. Asking these questions by themselves, however, also misses the fact that the growing outrage over free speech on campus is not a concern necessarily organic to the schools in question. It was—and is—intentional and manufactured.

Therefore, rather than litigating specific thorny speech issues on particular campuses, we propose that students, faculty, administrators, journalists, activists, and the broader public start by following the money. In doing so, we find, not a free marketplace of ideas, where all are equal, but rather a well-funded project to reproduce power, hierarchy, and exclusion. As P.E. Moskowitz points out, free speech is often used as a "smokescreen ... in a grossly unequal society, in which few corporations control the means of media dissemination and a small group of the ultra-wealthy bankroll entire political movements."[11] The same, unfortunately, is now true on college campuses.

HOW TO USE THIS BOOK

This book is designed as a field guide, useful to those seeking to better understand the integrated funding and political operation behind the so-called campus free speech crisis. As such, it does not provide a full account of the Koch donor network, or the influence "dark" and deliberately untraceable money plays in American politics more generally. A number of outstanding books, articles, and online resources already cover this material.[12] Instead, the book has three specific objectives.

First, it seeks to re-center the debate about campus free speech by following the money. Considerable funding and political mobilization have gone into creating a narrative about American universities as hostile to conservatives and beholden to a radical fringe of students and faculty who prevent supposedly mainstream conservative students, faculty, and speakers from sharing their ideas. This narrative of a virulent and closed-minded campus left censoring a victimized right misses the actual story. Rather than "the left" censoring the ideas of conservative students and faculty, the bigger story is that of a group of plutocratic libertarian donors engaged in a coordinated effort to make their free-market fundamentalist ideas more prominent on college campuses. The community standards of peer review and free inquiry that undergird academic teaching and scholarship are being challenged by a small group of ultra-wealthy donors with a particular ideological and self-interested agenda. Following the money makes it possible to have a clear-eyed conversation about whether or not academic communities should be forced to indulge speakers, student groups, and academic centers paid for by dark-money funders.

Second, this book examines the so-called campus free speech crisis as one example of how the Koch donor network operates in a coordinated and strategic manner. For those who have found themselves living through a Koch-sponsored campus free speech maelstrom, this book offers a case study in how this shadowy world of stealthy ultra-libertarian think tanks, academic centers, student organizations, legal advocacy groups, media outlets, and political networks collaborate to manufacture a controversy. Many of the lessons learned in examining the campus free speech issue can be applied to a whole range of Koch-funded initiatives, on and off campus. For example, similar networks, strategies, and even rhetoric are used to attack collective bargaining rights, climate science, public schools, affirmative action, anti-fracking legislation, and other policy areas where wealthy libertarian donors have a political, financial, and ideological interest. Even for readers not primarily concerned with the idiosyncrasies of campus free speech, the general lessons here are widely applicable to many other cases.

Third, and finally, this book is a resource for students, faculty, administrators, alumni, journalists, and members of the wider public who want to better understand—and push back against—the organizations and institutions that constitute the Koch donor network. As an easy-to-use field guide, it contains sections that readers can use to decode their particular situation. For example, if the Daily Wire writes a story about Speech First's threat to sue your school for not allowing the local Young Americans for Liberty chapter to host Ben Shapiro, the book provides an overview of these organizations, explains how they function, how they are funded, and the role they play within the overall Koch network. This information can hopefully empower you to understand the bigger, and often hidden, picture of what is taking place on your campus. Appendix 2 provides some useful research tools and organizing strategies as well.

The book is divided into eight chapters. The first examines the funders behind both the libertarian right and the campus free speech movement. It explains their broader political objectives and strategies, focusing on their keen interest in gaining access to higher education to advance their political agenda and their long track record of weaponizing free speech. The second chapter examines the student groups that bring intentionally provocative and partisan speakers to campus. Chapter 3 demonstrates how the Koch donor network funds the careers of many of the most prominent campus provocateurs. The following chapter illustrates how media outlets funded by the Koch donor network play an outsized role in amplifying the outrage over campus free speech. Chapters 5 and 6 demonstrate that the Koch donor network also funds the legal organizations that sue schools that deny campus access to speakers, as well as the politicians and legislative organizations that pass "Campus Free Speech" legislation at the state level. Chapter 7 examines the Koch-funded academic centers and programs that generate much of the academic argument about the supposed need to protect conservative speech on campus. Finally, Chapter 8 maps out how this integrated strategy is being exported abroad. Taken together, these chapters reveal a dense network of interconnected and well-funded organizations that have together manufactured all aspects of the so-called campus free speech crisis.

SOURCES AND METHODS

To make its case, *Free Speech and Koch Money* draws upon a wide range of sources, from academic articles and books, to investigative journalism, to a considerable amount of activist research and network tracing. As the creator of the Corporate Genome Project, Ralph Wilson has built a digital tool that aggregates data from 990s—the tax forms filed by non-profits with the Internal Revenue Service. This archive makes it possible to see where four of the largest funders within the Koch donor network—the Koch family foundations, Bradley Foundation (including the Bradley Impact Fund), DonorsTrust, and Donors Capital Fund—spend their higher-education-related money. This information is available in Appendix 1. We also draw upon the work of many activists and journalists who have done backbreaking research to uncover the intentionally secretive Koch network. Their findings include a number of leaked (and now publicly archived) documents and recordings from otherwise secret Koch donor summits, as well as excerpts from an unpublished book about Charles Koch's political operations, commissioned by Bill Koch and written by the George Mason University historian, Clayton Coppin. The unusually clandestine nature of the Koch donor network requires using a triangulation of evidence, and there is still much that remains unknown.

While we cannot see directly into the black box of the Koch-funded political and academic apparatus, this book engages in the method of what we call "operative tracing," which is well suited for understanding the Koch network. Operative tracing identifies the numerous connections and repeating patterns among a relatively small group of donors, activists, and academics. We draw upon investigative wikis and document repositories, such as those compiled by the Center for Media and Democracy and KochDocs, as well as research already done by groups such as DeSmog Blog and UnKoch My Campus. These sources are supported by material found on organizational websites, CVs, LinkedIn profiles, tax documents, annual reports, webpages, and YouTube videos. Useful tools for conducting one's own research into the Koch network can be found in Appendix 2.

We have written this book because we firmly believe that when the profound influence of dark money is revealed—whether in politics, in the courts, in elections, or on campus—most people are shocked and angered that a handful of plutocratic libertarian donors seek to disproportionately influence political, economic, and social life. It is important to have these conversations on campus, and in the classroom. Doing so requires protecting colleges and universities from the undue influence of well-funded provocateurs, lawyers, student groups, and partisan legislatures that seek to replace the pursuit of academic knowledge with greater donor influence.

Political operatives within the Koch network have long viewed higher education as a primary battlefield in the fight to remake the world according to their radical libertarian image. To see why, we first consider the scale of their overall investment and the audacity of their agenda.

1

The Donor Strategy

The vast wealth of Kansas billionaire Charles Koch flows from his second-generation privately held family business, Koch Industries. As of December 2020, Charles Koch enjoyed a personal net worth of $44.9 billion.[1] Despite the Koch family's pride in operating for decades as the "biggest company you've never heard of," they have recently garnered considerable national attention due to their outsized political activity, spending lavishly to support pro-corporate politicians and the Republican Party.[2] In 2016, the growing network of ultra-wealthy far-right donors led by Charles Koch pledged to spend nearly $900 million on their combined political efforts, compared with the $657 million spent by the Republican National Committee (RNC), the National Republican Senatorial Committee (NRSC), and the National Republican Congressional Committee (NRCC) combined.[3]

After the 2020 election, Charles Koch released a new book in which he mused that his funding of the Republican Party had been a "screw up." However, partisan spending on short-term electoral outcomes was never the most impactful element of his political investments. A considerable portion of Charles Koch's political expenditures has gone toward constructing and funding a dense and interconnected network of political organizations, each of which plays a specific strategic role in manufacturing social change.

Charles Koch and the wealthy arch-libertarian donors around him are known to fund a massive network of integrated pro-corporate organizations including academic centers, think tanks, legislation mills, political field operations, lobbying groups, and litigation outfits. Some of the most well-known organizations include the American Legislative Exchange Council (ALEC), which helps wealthy and corporate donors write and advance model legislation, and the Federalist Society, which grooms conservative judges. The Koch network also utilizes numerous front groups that mimic "grassroots" voter mobilization organizations, also known as "astroturf" groups, such as Americans for Prosperity. Depending on the issue, the Koch network also funds area-specific voter mobilization efforts, including Generation Opportunity (youth voters), and Libre Initiative (Latinx voters), as well as issue-specific advocacy groups, such as the 60 Plus Association (Social Security privatization), the American Energy Alliance (cap and trade opposition), the Center to Protect Patient Rights (health-care privatization), and organizations that help conservative candidates win elections, including Aegis Strategic (political consulting and candidate recruitment) and i360 (data analytics).

While these organizations attempt to appear independent from one another, they receive funding from the same small handful of ultra-wealthy donors and regularly collaborate to achieve the same political outcomes. Many of these organizations are formally networked together through the State Policy Network (SPN), an umbrella group that coordinates think tanks and other non-profits on the state level thereby solidifying a 50-state, Koch-funded "freedom movement." These organizations are also more informally networked through overlapping boards, events, and personnel. Together they push a plutocratic libertarian[4] agenda at the federal and state level, pursuing greater corporate deregulation, larger tax cuts for the wealthy, the privatization of schools and prisons, weaker unions, restricted voting rights, and drastic cuts to social spending—a set of economic policies described as "property supremacy," "hardline libertarian," and "ultra-free-market right."[5] This same network of organizations also manufactures the campus free speech crisis.

When compared to the substantial and transformative political and legal victories won by the Koch political network, campus skirmishes over free speech may seem fairly inconsequential. Why would such a highly effective billionaire-funded political operation take precious time and energy to focus on campus free speech? The answer lies in the fact that Charles Koch has long understood that the long-term strategy of social change runs through colleges and universities. Since the 1970s, he has argued that universities offer essential opportunities to recruit student activists, groom libertarian academics and policy wonks, and legitimize Koch's libertarian ideology.[6] This helps explain why, between 2005 and 2017, Koch-family foundations spent more than $256 million on donations to colleges and universities. More than half of that money went to one institution, George Mason University, and its affiliated Institute for Humane Studies and Mercatus Center.[7] In 2019 alone annual spending on higher education reached $112 million, up $23.9 million from the year before.[8] Unlike most philanthropic giving to higher education, these gifts are often explicitly designed to shape the content of what is researched and taught, and by whom.[9]

This chapter examines the origins of the Koch donor network's political operation and, in particular, the central role higher education plays in the theory of change that guides its political strategy. Understanding this long-term, integrated strategy requires situating the Koch donor network within the context of a right-wing response to the flourishing of social movements that erupted during the 1960s. In response to the Black freedom struggle, the anti-war movement, and gains made in the areas of consumer and environmental protections, wealthy businessmen and segregationists joined forces to create the political machinery necessary to roll back these progressive changes. "Economic freedom" and "individual liberty" became the rallying cries of this reactionary politics.

In short, the Koch donor network is reaping the rewards of a political operation built over the last 50 years—a project that constitutes nothing less than a multi-decade counter-revolution against the progressive changes made during the middle of the twentieth century. And as far back as the 1970s, Koch and like-minded donors had already identified universities as institutions that must be sieged and ultimately transformed into useful assets in the creation of their corporate utopia.

WHAT IS THE "KOCH DONOR NETWORK?"

So, what do we mean by the *Koch donor network*? Throughout the book we use this term as shorthand for a broad group of libertarian donors who have lavishly funded a well-integrated political operation designed to push their pro-corporate political and ideological agenda. We call the political operation these donors built the *Koch network*. Libertarian allies of Charles Koch—who later became critics—first branded this network "the 'Kochtopus.'"[10]

When discussing Charles Koch and his now deceased brother David, it is tempting to conflate their personal political spending with their private financial interests.[11] While Charles Koch does see the political operations of the network as a personal investment, and has profited handsomely from them,[12] we are more interested in understanding the ideological motivations that undergird and animate this network—not least because those are what it uses to recruit students. We therefore use the term Koch donor network in a broad sense, recognizing that the political strategy and vast infrastructure that largely originated with Charles Koch now operates in a plurality of ways, and with a significant number of prominent funders and strategists.

While the Koch donor network includes many individuals, foundations, and corporations loosely affiliated with one another, Charles Koch nonetheless remains a central node. Not only did he cultivate the general political strategy, but he also developed the sustaining funding mechanism. During the early 2000s, Koch realized that he could further magnify his political impact by bringing together other foundations, corporations, and wealthy individuals to finance a network far more extensive than what was possible through his own private investments.

To this end he convenes twice-annual donor seminars where wealthy individuals, politicians, lawyers, scholars, right-wing media personalities, and political activists are "exposed to ultra-free market and libertarian ideas as well as to practical political strategies."[13] Today more than 600 people regularly attend these events, with a minimum pledge of $100,000. Stand Together—formerly Freedom Partners Chambers of Commerce—oversees these events, collects the money, and distributes it across the network (which for a time was even known as the Seminar Network). Although the Koch summits are notoriously secretive, much has been learned from a handful of leaked documents and recordings, as well as from reporting by a few journalists recently granted very limited access. These hard-won materials reveal some of the regular figures at these events, including far-right multi-millionaires and billionaires like Robert Mercer, Foster Friess, Richard DeVos, and John Templeton Jr., as well as countless other still unknown wealthy individuals and their allies. One attendee, the late Whitney Ball, co-created the network's anonymizing donor-advised trusts, DonorsTrust and Donors Capital Fund, which one journalist called the movement's "dark money ATM."[14] Jane Mayer's 2016 book *Dark Money* identified many of the seminar attendees as a who's who of corporate white-collar criminals.[15] Like Koch Industries, many attendees have repeatedly run afoul of state and federal regulations and would profit from the repeal of key regulations. Also like Koch Industries, this political infrastructure is deliberately constructed as an opaque and diffuse network, with each organization feeding into the others but still playing a unique role.[16] It is an integrated entity organized by a centralized node.

As will be seen in the following chapters, many Koch seminar attendees have played an outsized role in the so-called campus free speech crisis. For example, the Lynde and Harry Bradley Foundation is a charitable foundation whose board members, including Diane Hendricks and board chair James "Art" Pope, are fixtures at Koch's donor summits. The Bradley Foundation has spent hundreds of millions of dollars on religious-right and free-market organizations, including campus-focused programs. Individual seminar donors also funded politicians such as Wisconsin Governor Scott Walker, who aggressively defunded state education and ended tenure across the University of Wisconsin system.[17] Some have used their political clout to shape policy directly. After the DeVos family helped elect Donald Trump in 2016, Betsy DeVos served as his Secretary of Education.[18] Likewise, after Art Pope bankrolled their electoral victories, North Carolina Republicans appointed him to the governing board of the University of North Carolina in 2020.[19]

The term Koch donor network, therefore, is an accurate and useful shorthand. We do acknowledge, however, that personifying the political success of this radical plutocratic libertarian movement in Charles Koch risks making him into a sort of conspiratorial mastermind while ignoring the disagreements and differences among this group of radical free-market corporate donors. That being said, we use the term Koch donor network to both describe the variety of individuals and organizations that directly participate in Charles Koch's secretive biannual donor summits and to acknowledge his foundational role in creating the integrated political strategy and infrastructure.

While some might accuse us of being conspiratorial, it should not be at all surprising that the ultra-wealthy regularly organize together to pursue their own political, economic, and ideological interests. After all, even the patron saint of free-market economics, Adam Smith, recognized that "The masters, being fewer in number, can combine much more easily … [and] whoever imagines … that masters rarely combine, is as ignorant of the world as of the subject."[20] Few masters of industry have done more to assemble a group of like-minded political operatives than Charles Koch. As such, it is necessary to understand the roots of his efforts.

MASSIVE RESISTANCE, AND THE MARKET SOLUTION TO MAINTAINING SEGREGATION

In 1951, four years before Rosa Parks helped ignite the bus boycott in Montgomery, Alabama, Barbara Rose Johns was a high school junior in the segregated community of Prince Edward County, Virginia. While white students attended properly resourced schools, many students at her overcrowded high school studied in tarpaper shacks often confused for chicken coops. Despite repeated requests by parents, white officials remained unwilling to renovate the school. To draw attention to their plight, Johns and her fellow students organized a student strike. The protest received attention from the National Association for the Advancement of Colored People (NAACP), which filed a lawsuit demanding integration of the Prince Edward County school system. This case eventually became bundled into the *Brown v. Board of Education*, in which the US Supreme Court ruled that racially segregated schools were "inherently unequal," and a violation of the Fourteenth Amendment guarantee of equal protection under the law.[21]

In the years following *Brown*, white segregationist lawmakers in Virginia responded with a package of "massive resistance" legislation including a plan to replace public schools with voucher-funded private institutions (which were free from the mandate to desegregate).[22] This segregationist plan came to be championed using the language of constitutional liberty and freedom of choice, carefully avoiding the explicitly white supremacist arguments of racial superiority common in the Deep South. James McGill Buchanan, hired as the new chair of the Economics Department at the University of Virginia in the midst of this fight, used his just-created Thomas Jefferson Center for Studies in Political Economy and Social Philosophy to provide an economic imprimatur to the State's defiance of the Supreme Court ruling.

Buchanan would go on to become one of the most significant Koch-funded academics.[23]

When the NAACP sued the Prince Edward County school board, the board turned to a corporate law firm to defend their segregationist practice. That firm's rising star, Lewis Powell Jr., became embroiled in Virginia's larger struggle to preserve as much segregation as possible in the new legal landscape. Following the Prince Edward County lawsuit, Powell ran for chair of his Richmond County school board, where he presided for nearly a decade before finding his way onto the Virginia Board of Education.[24] When the Prince Edward County school board shuttered its public-school system, Lewis Powell used his position on the state board of education to allow white parents to receive public money to cover private school tuition.

Powell was also a critic of New Deal governance. Rolling back the New Deal, he argued, required a vast corporate counter-mobilization. In public speeches Powell blamed American colleges and universities for incubating radicalism, calling college campuses "base[s] of revolution" where radicals manipulate non-radical students into sympathizing with "tactical" causes like the movement against the war in Vietnam, or the existence of "alleged racism." These dangerous campus elements, he argued, "inflame, confuse, exploit and even radicalize tens of thousands of fine young Americans" using "[f]ascist techniques" like "widespread civil disobedience." Powell saw civil disobedience, like that of sixteen-year-old Barbara Rose Johns, as an existential threat to American capitalism. He fretted over "New Leftists and black militant revolutionary groups" working together to attack the "free enterprise system."[25]

As a board member of the cigarette manufacturer Philip Morris he wrote the famous 1971 memo for the US Chamber of Commerce outlining how the social and legal success of "[l]abor unions, civil rights groups and now the public interest law firms" was coming "at business' expense."[26] The Powell Memo urged corporations not to underestimate the importance of grooming a pro-business sentiment on college campuses—strategic advice later taken up by Charles Koch. To this end Powell advocated for establishing a free-market speakers bureau, evaluating textbooks to ensure that they offered a "fair and factual treatment of our system of government and our enterprise system," ensuring equal time for conservative speakers on campus, lobbying trustees and

alumni for greater ideological "balance" within the faculty, and creating pro-market programing within high schools. Powell concluded
his memo with a call to action: "[T]he hour is late" and corporations
"should not postpone more direct political action." Their political
power should be "used aggressively and with determination."[27]

The Powell Memo became an open blueprint for an emerging free-market counter-offensive. It would also become the point
of departure for an even more radical and comprehensive strategy
pursued by Charles Koch and the plutocratic libertarian movement
he bankrolled.[28]

THE INTELLECTUAL LINEAGE OF
KOCH CAMPUS INVESTMENTS

Like Powell, Fred Koch (father of Charles and David) viewed the civil
rights movement as a communist front. His strident anti-communism
came from his experiences in the USSR, where his family company
survived the Great Depression by building oil refineries for Stalin.[29]
In 1960 Fred Koch laid out his anti-communist views in his self-pub-
lished pamphlet, *A Business Man Looks at Communism*, in which he
warned of an imminent communist plot to "take over America." By his
account, the "colored man looms large in the communist plan" to "stir
up racial hatred" and incite a "vicious race war."[30] It was this ardent
mixture of racism and anti-communism that had caught the attention
of candy-magnate Robert Welch in 1958, when he invited Fred Koch
to participate in the founding of the John Birch Society (JBS) along
with Harry Bradley, who would later go on to create the Bradley Foundation.[31] From 1961 to 1968, Fred Koch's son Charles was an active
member of the JBS.[32] Over time, however, Charles became disillusioned with the organization, eventually breaking with it over Welch's
autocratic leadership style and the reliance on conspiracy theories for
political mobilization.

In the 1960s, Charles Koch immersed himself in the writings of the
Austrian economists Ludwig von Mises and Friedrich Hayek, finding
the intellectual core of what would become his corporate-funded libertarian movement.[33] He would later credit Mises's *Human Action* as
having been central to his intellectual formation.[34] In that work, Mises
develops his theory of praxeology, a purported science of understand-

ing rational human action and individual choice. Rather than drawing economic arguments and conclusions from empirical studies, Mises used his theory of human action to intuitively reason how humans should act within particular circumstances. Embedded in this view of reason, however, is a deeply racialized worldview.[35] *Human Action*'s claim about the superiority of Western civilization, and about some races being culturally or intellectually "inferior," would become a major theoretical current within twentieth-century libertarianism, appearing, for example, in Charles Murray's 1994 *The Bell Curve* (funded by the Bradley Foundation).[36]

If Charles Koch was attracted to Mises's claim that Western entrepreneurs were the true heroes of history, he found in Friedrich Hayek a manifesto that appealed to corporate donors. Hayek refined and popularized the primacy of individual freedom and economic rationality, framing Western civilization as embattled by the forces of collectivism—equally evident, he maintained, in Nazism, Stalinism, and Roosevelt's New Deal.[37] The publication of his *Road to Serfdom* caught the attention of the Volker Fund and other anti-New Deal industrialists, who helped fund and disseminate Hayek's free-market ideas.[38] Mises and Hayek co-founded the Mont Pelerin Society in 1947, which would became the cradle of neoliberal economics and the growing economic and political movement that prioritized private property rights and unfettered individual economic freedom while disparaging government regulation and public goods.

Hayek also advocated for the creation of a pro-capitalist countermovement of intellectuals capable of carrying out long-term political change. In his essay "The Intellectuals and Socialism," Hayek argues that free-market ideas alone are not enough to defeat socialism. It was also necessary to cultivate "secondhand dealers in ideas" who could affect the "climate of opinion." Such operatives would play the role of the "intermediary in the spreading of ideas." They did not even need to be "particularly intelligent," just willing to espouse the principles of this new radicalism and "fight for their full realization, however remote" their chances were.[39]

During the mid-twentieth century, Austrian economics within the American academy was largely funded by corporate benefactors. The William Volker Fund, for example, financially supported many of the most significant figures and institutions in the early American libertarian movement, including James Buchanan's center in Virginia.[40] The Fund was responsible for securing pro-corporate intellectual footholds on campus, bankrolling Hayek's first years at the University of Chicago and Mises's position at New York University. Hayek's close relationship with the Volker Fund allowed him to use its considerable resources to bring together other corporate-friendly academics with supporters in the business world, empowering him to "supervise and develop the intellectual and political strategy" he had previously elaborated on in his writing on the political role of intellectuals.[41]

After the Volker Fund closed in the 1970s, the Charles Koch Foundation and the Harry Lynde Bradley Foundation took Volker's place as major funders of Austrian school economics, and of the American libertarian movement more generally. The Volker Fund's director, F. A. Harper, also founded the Institute for Humane Studies (IHS; see Chapter 7), which became one of Charles Koch's most heavily funded academic centers, now located at George Mason University.

Koch was clear from the very beginning that his funding of Austrian economics and the libertarian movement was done with the explicit intent of radically remaking society in accordance with his free-market absolutist vision. He laid out this strategy in a 1974 presentation before the IHS, in which he declared specifically that the Powell Memorandum did not go far enough. He questioned whether "the American business community actually believes in capitalism" given that it continued to accept taxation, support public universities, and perpetuate the claim that a corporation has a "social responsibility beyond its duty to its shareholder."[42] Rather than needing to protect free enterprise from progressive social movements, as Powell argued, Koch insisted that true free enterprise must first be created. Koch laid out four avenues that "pro-capitalist businessmen" might pursue in the "fight for free enterprise": "through education, through the media, by legal challenges, and by political action." He concluded with the observation that transforming society through education had the greatest "multiplier effect," and therefore could yield the greatest return on investment:

> The important strategic consideration to keep in mind is that any program adopted should be highly leveraged so that we reach those whose influence on others produces a multiplier effect. That is why

educational programs are superior to political action, and support of talented free-market scholars is preferable to mass advertising.

The development of a well financed cadre of sound proponents of the free enterprise philosophy is the most critical need facing us at the moment. And this task is not impractical.[43]

From the very beginning, underlying Koch's admittedly "radical" political strategy was a core belief that gaining footholds in colleges and universities was a necessary precondition for fundamentally transforming America—and the world.

DEVELOPING AN INTEGRATED STRATEGY
OF SOCIAL CHANGE

Two years after his IHS presentation, Charles Koch spent $65,000 to launch the Center for Libertarian Studies and their inaugural Social Change Conference.[44] This event brought together "several leading lights of the libertarian movement" to discuss "how the fringe movement could obtain genuine power."[45] The investigative journalist Jane Mayer notes that "the papers presented [at the conference] were striking in their radicalism, their disdain for the public, and their belief in the necessity of political subterfuge."[46] One paper by George Pearson, Koch's longtime political collaborator and a JBS member, argued that the libertarian movement not only needed considerable investments in the academy but that such donations should be focused on creating stand-alone programs—rather than giving to college endowments, over which donors had very limited control. Leonard Liggio presented a paper arguing that the Nazi youth movement offered the model that libertarians might emulate to build power.[47]

Charles Koch's own paper examined what lessons libertarians might draw from the John Birch Society. On the one hand, he argued that the JBS was an organization to emulate; after all, it claimed 90,000 members, 240 employees, $7 million in annual expenditures, and a political reach that allowed for meaningful policy impact. On the other hand, the organization was hobbled by autocratic leadership, conspiratorial paranoia, and a lack of intellectual and ideological coherence. Koch argued that the libertarian movement should instead focus on grooming leaders who are entrepreneurial, while keeping leadership "limited to a small group of sound, knowledgeable and dedicated people." He insisted on "public statements being carefully controlled," while concealing how their organizations are "controlled and directed" thereby "avoid[ing] undesirable criticism." The libertarian movement should deploy "all modern sales and motivational techniques to raise money and attract donors," including "work[ing] with, rather than combat[ing], the media and people in the arts." And it should be led by leaders who are "attractive, articulate, knowledgeable, and well-trained."[48] Murray Rothbard, who at the time was also co-founding the Cato Institute with Charles Koch, summarized the conference's strategies as an anarcho-capitalist revolution to abolish the state. This revolution required a "cadre that will control and direct the libertarian movement," and the kind of covert "movement building solution that Lenin adopted." Rothbard emphasized that "ideas are important, but action is what is required ... The libertarians need a dedicated cadre which is committed to victory."[49] This cadre would be found on college campuses.

Richard Fink was one such example. He became a disciple of Austrian economics while an undergraduate at Rutgers and would gain a Ph.D. in economics from New York University. He joined the economics faculty at George Mason University, and would become vice-president of Koch Industries and president of the Charles Koch Foundation. As an insider, he helped develop the theory of social change, which became the Koch network's guiding organizational strategy. Fink retooled Hayek's model of industrial production to explain how organizations can produce not commodities but social transformation. Fink's "Structure of Social Change" (see Figure 1) was the theoretical model for how Koch-funded libertarians could ensure that their "ideas are transformed into action" with industrial efficiency.[50]

Fink described the first stage of manufacturing social change as requiring an "investment in the intellectual raw materials"—those "abstract concepts and theories" produced by academics on college campuses.[51] However, to ensure that they "have consequences," the raw ideas are passed into a "middle stage" where they are "molded into needed solutions for real-world problems." This is the role of think tanks "such as the Heritage Foundation, the Reason Foundation, [and] the Cato Institute." However, think tanks were less well-equipped to "implement change," and this is where the final stage comes in:

namely, "[c]itizen activist or implementation groups," which includes Citizens for a Sound Economy, the National Taxpayers' Union, and Defenders of Property Rights. Each organization should focus on one stage, Fink explained, undertaking specific activities in which it has a "comparative advantage," while also creating integrated "pipelines or connections between the stages," with the output of one stage becoming the input for the next (see Figure 1).

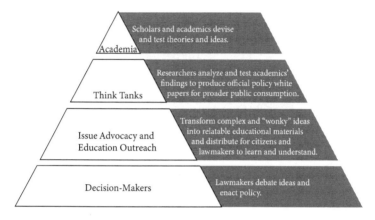

Figure 1   Structure of Social Change Diagram

Author's rendition of "AFP's Place in the 'Structure of Social Change'—Issue Advocacy and Educational Outreach." Originally published in: Americans for Prosperity (2015) Partner Prospectus, Winter, 14. Made public in: Vogel, Kenneth (2015) "Secret Koch Memo Outlines Plans for 2016," *Politico*, April 22.

The Koch Foundation had long prioritized the first stage, cultivating a "market-oriented intellectual framework."[52] During the 1970s and 1980s that focus expanded to include the middle stage, namely the creation of think tanks. By the 1980s and 1990s the focus expanded further to include political mobilization. In the decades since then, this integrated strategy for social change—carried out by a now vast network of specialized but interconnected organizations—has only become more robust, more integrated, and more reliant on access to academic institutions. It has also become more successful at fundamentally transforming all aspects of American politics.

The overwhelming effects of this political machinery were clearly visible during the Obama presidency, and especially after the 2010 *Citizens United* Supreme Court decision. In the years since, Koch-funded groups like Americans for Prosperity and FreedomWorks bankrolled the Tea Party, providing the funding and infrastructure to harness otherwise disorganized grassroots discontent into a laser-like assault on Obama's policy agenda. At the federal, state, and judicial levels the Koch network has secured a whole litany of corporate libertarian victories, including environmental deregulation, tax cuts for the wealthy, right-to-work legislation, and preventing Medicare expansion.[53] They have also proliferated socially regressive policies like school privatization and vouchers, stand-your-ground gun laws, prison privatization, and voter suppression laws.[54]

One of the well-honed strategies used by this integrated network is the weaponization of free speech. Consistent with Charles Koch's free-market extremism, operatives have become increasingly savvy at expanding the definition of free speech (for example, to include money spent on political campaigns), while also expanding who can claim speech rights (for example, corporations). The end result has been a fundamental reframing of important questions about collective rights and responsibilities in a democracy, effectively reducing complicated social questions to an absolutist dogma of individual (and therefore also corporate) liberty. This weaponization of free speech arguments has become a widely shared and integrated strategy used to achieve hardline libertarian political and legal victories. It has proven especially useful in pushing back against progressive victories in areas such as civil rights, labor protections, affirmative action, gun control, consumer protection, environmental regulation, and campaign finance reform. We should not be surprised, therefore, that free speech libertarianism is being replicated on college campuses, and used to gain even greater donor influence over the production of the "raw material" needed to fuel the structure of social change.

THE WEAPONIZATION OF FREE SPEECH

The political machinery assembled by the Koch donor network has effectively used free speech arguments to achieve its political and ideological objectives. This strategy dates back to Lewis Powell who, as a board member and attorney representing the interests of numerous corporations, including Philip Morris, engaged in fierce warfare with government regulators and scientists who were then starting to publicize the science concerning the health risks associated with smoking. Powell himself argued before the Federal Communications Commission that cigarette companies should be allowed "equal time" to counter their critics. While the judge ultimately rejected his arguments, Powell asserted that emphasizing the harms of smoking, while failing to also "compel pro-smoking announcements," violated corporate freedom of speech, and created a "coerced presentation" of the official government view.[55] Since at least the 1980s, cigarette companies have "work[ed] to create the appearance of broad opposition to tobacco control policies" by manufacturing a seemingly "grassroots smokers' rights movement." The seemingly grassroots advocacy group that orchestrated this work, Citizens for a Sound Economy (CSE), was created by Charles Koch and Richard Fink.[56]

In a 1995 action plan, for example, Philip Morris laid out the long-term goal of creating a "political environment where 'moderates' of both parties" would be primed to support tobacco deregulation. The Koch-funded CSE—the precursor to Americans For Prosperity and FreedomWorks—was contracted "to quarterback behind the scenes, third-party efforts" that were designed to delegitimize the US Food and Drug Administration. According to internal documents, CSE was meant to "help direct a multi-front action plan" that would "launch, publicize and execute a broad non-tobacco-based attack" questioning the legitimacy of the government's claim that smoking causes cancer. Citizens for a Sound Economy mapped out a multi-million-dollar campaign to "educate and mobilize consumers, through town hall meetings, radio and print ads, direct mail, patch-through calls to the Capitol switchboard, editorial board visits, polling data, meetings with Members and staff, and the release of studies and other educational pieces."[57] As a sign of what would come, CSE and tobacco companies developed a "coherent strategy," seeking to influence public policies "from multiple directions." They "fund[ed] multiple think tanks, within a shared network, [to] generate a conversation among independent policy experts, which reflected its position in tobacco control debates."[58]

Such corporate onslaughts—what some have called "discourse sabotage"[59]—would become a major feature of the Koch political machine: namely, creating multiple, distinct-yet-overlapping organizations working together to manufacture the appearance of broad-based public opposition. A network of cooperating organizations creates a cacophony of seemingly competing positions, when in reality these groups offer minor variations on the same basic extreme policy. For those seeking to prevent tobacco regulation, free speech became a particularly useful lever for demanding that this manufactured position, which only exists because of corporate interests, receives the same time and attention as scientists, public health officials, and widely popular social movements.

It is not surprising, therefore, that many of the same groups using free speech to defend corporate tobacco have also advocated climate denial on First Amendment grounds. Funded by Koch Industries and Exxon, a network of corporate-funded, libertarian, anti-regulation organizations have filled this policy space with multiple parallel voices, spreading misinformation in the name of free corporate expression and ensuring that the corporate (and anti-science) position has equal access to the public square.

This effort began in earnest in 1997, as the climate negotiations leading to the Kyoto Protocol were heating up. Charitable foundations within the Koch donor network spent more than $140 million on 90 groups that sought to delegitimize climate science and derail policy solutions. In 2020, Minnesota Attorney General Keith Ellison sued Koch Industries, ExxonMobil Corporation, and others for having "lied, deceived, muddled the facts, and created a false controversy [over climate change] where there wasn't one."[60] The suit details a "multi-pronged campaign of deception,"[61] alleging that these groups "knowingly directed, conducted, and funded a campaign to deceive and defraud" the public by making "facts and science seem controversial when they really weren't."[62] Other large foundations within the Koch donor network have also actively funded climate denial groups, include the Anschutz, Bradley, Coors, DeVos, Dunn, Howard, Pope, Scaife, Searle, and Seid foundations.[63]

The Koch political machinery has also used free speech arguments to attack public sector unions. The Koch-funded National Right to Work Committee, whose officials have led sessions at Koch's donor seminars, orchestrated a series of lawsuits claiming that collecting union dues constitutes coerced political speech and therefore violates the First Amendment. A similar case in 2018, *Janus v. AFSCME*, the US Supreme Court sided with the Koch-backed plaintiffs. Newly appointed Justice Neil Gorsuch wrote the opinion for the majority of five justices closely tied to the Federalist Society.

Janus was initially brought in 2015 by Illinois Governor Bruce Rauner, who regularly attends Koch's secretive donor summits.[64] The lawyers who tried *Janus* came from the Illinois Policy Institute and the National Right to Work Legal Defense Foundation—both members of the Koch-funded State Policy Network (SPN) and both receiving funding from the Bradley Foundation ($170,000 and $840,000, respectively) and DonorsTrust/Donors Capital Fund ($1.7 and $1.2 million, respectively).[65] Of the 18 organizations that filed amicus briefs in *Janus*, all but five are current or former SPN members.[66] After the decision, the American Legislative Exchange Council disseminated toolkits, designed to help state legislatures use *Janus* to further undermine unions at the state level.[67]

The Koch network's weaponization of free speech received a steroid injection following the 2010 Supreme Court's *Citizens United v. FEC* decision. During the 2008 primaries, the Robert Mercer-funded production company, Citizens United, sought to advertise its Hillary Clinton "documentary" at a time when the FEC forbade election advertising by non-campaign entities.[68] The conservative majority court, including Justices Antonin Scalia and Clarence Thomas who had just recently attended Koch seminars,[69] ruled that corporations are individuals with free speech rights, affirming a hardline libertarian free speech argument. They further ruled that corporations cannot be regulated in how they spend money during elections, since doing so would infringe upon their speech rights.

Citizens United handed the Koch network an unbridled opportunity to invest even more lavishly in its political operations. Since the ruling, corporate money has flooded local, state, and federal elections at unprecedented levels. In 2010, Koch's secretive donor summit raised $30 million for their activities.[70] Two years after the ruling, Freedom Partners Chamber of Commerce raised $240 million at these summits. In 2015, the network announced a two-year plan to spend $900 million, collected from 450 donors associated with the semi-annual donor summits. Of this haul, $300 million would be spent on the 2016 elections and the rest would go into university grants, non-profits, and other priorities.[71] Prior to the 2020 elections, the Koch network disclosed plans to compete in "nearly 200 federal and state races," compared to 64 races in the 2018 midterms.[72]

Free speech arguments are also used to justify continued donor anonymity, keeping the wealthy Koch network donors largely secret. In 2018, a California court ruled that Americans For Prosperity (AFP) must submit a list of its donors to the state. AFP responded, arguing that revealing donors "imperils people's First Amendment right to freedom of speech."[73] But the six-judge Federalist Society majority on the Supreme Court ruled in favor of AFP in July 2021. Of the 22 amicus briefs filed supporting AFP, 15 were written by groups "closely tied to Koch and his political influence and funding network," including: the Cato Institute, Institute for Justice, Institute for Free Speech, Philanthropy Roundtable, Public Interest Legal Foundation, Pacific Legal Foundation, National Right to Work Legal Defense Foundation, People United for Privacy Foundation, Judicial Watch, and others.[74] The American Legislative Exchange Council's Center to Protect Free Speech, as well as the Institute for Free Speech and the New Civil Liberties Alliance, are Koch network organizations that specialize in using free speech arguments to protect plutocratic libertarian donors from revealing their sources of funding.

The Koch network has also found the strategy of weaponizing free speech particularly useful because it helps construct a political narrative about conservatives as victims of out-of-control universities and governmental institutions—a narrative that has unfortunately gained considerable sympathy and traction far beyond conservative audiences.

According to Richard Fink, the Koch network sees the United States as broken into three parts: one third who are "very conservative libertarians," and who they have been successfully mobilizing; the "collectivist third" who believe in expanding government; and a "middle third" that is "not ideologically unified." Fink told a roomful of donors that "[t]he battle for the future of the country is who can win the hearts and minds of that middle third," because whoever can "mobilize a majority of that 30 percent will determine the direction of the country."[75] The manufacturing of culture war narratives about "radical left-wing professors," student "snowflakes," "social justice warriors," and "critical race theory"—like those about "urban youth," "eco-terrorists," and "union thugs" before them—serve to spread a moral panic that helps polarize the middle third against the "collectivist" third.

Situating current efforts to weaponize free speech as part of a broader corporate and Koch-funded political machinery lends much needed context to a full understanding of why today's so-called campus free speech crisis has reached such a fevered pitch. The same motivated donors and political operatives who use free speech arguments to defend plutocratic spending in elections, to break unions, deny climate change, and shield wealthy donors from scrutiny, have also invested heavily in manufacturing campus free speech controversies.

Students for Liberty, Young Americans for Liberty, Young Americans for Freedom, and Turning Point USA often appear on campus as fairly traditional student organizations, run by undergraduates who happen to share a common interest in individual freedom and free markets. However, when situated within the Koch network's broader integrated structure of social change, it becomes clear how and why these groups—often with access to undisclosed amounts of external funding, training, and legal support—are so successful at spreading the narrative of a campus free speech crisis.

2

The Student Groups

As discussed in Chapter 1, participants at the first meeting of the Koch-funded Center for Libertarian Studies in 1976 submitted papers strategizing the future of the US libertarian movement. Charles Koch presented a paper stating that a "major portion of a movement's efforts needs to be directed toward attracting youth since this is the only group that is largely open to a radically different social philosophy."[1] The young Koch network already recognized that capturing the state required providing students with more than ideas and opportunities for action. They needed the incentives necessary to create a pipeline of committed talent that could feed into Koch's Structure of Social Change.[2]

As recently as 2014, leaked recordings from a Koch donor summit revealed that this remains the Koch network's strategy. The recording captures officials bragging to a roomful of corporate donors that their youth recruitment created a "culture of freedom that will not just change the policies of those states, but also have a significant impact on the federal government." The "students that graduate out of these higher education programs also populate the state-based think tanks and the national think tanks," as well as the "major staffing for the state chapters" of their "grassroots" organizations. Kevin Gentry went on to explain that their "network is fully integrated" thanks to the construction of the "talent pipeline."[3]

To build this talent pipeline, the Koch donor network invests heavily in student groups on college and university campuses and in high schools. On the surface, groups like Students for Liberty (SFL), Young Americans for Liberty (YAL), Young Americans for Freedom (YAF), and Turning Point USA (TPUSA) look like many other campus groups, providing intercollegiate opportunities for students to pursue areas of common interest. However, unlike most campus organizations, these groups exist within a broader political network and enjoy considerable external attention and financial support. Furthermore, student groups within the Koch network often obscure the origins of their funding as well as the broader political network in which they operate. By appearing as traditional campus organizations, while covertly benefiting from considerable external connections and funding, these groups are able to enjoy an outsized impact.

Most student groups—even national groups representing labor and environmental interests, such as United Students Against Sweatshops (USAS) or Public Interest Research Group (PIRG)—succeed by organizing large numbers of students to gain political traction on campus. In contrast, a small handful of Koch-backed campus activists often receive support for inviting high-profile speakers, campaigning for campus elections, starting campus newspapers, and suing their schools. In a form of asymmetrical campus warfare, external organization and funding makes it possible for these student groups to amplify minoritarian views well beyond their actual representation on campus.

Some groups at the center of the talent pipeline were explicitly created by Koch-funded adherents of Austrian economics, while others are legacy conservative student groups happily acquired or co-opted. As demonstrated below, a number of student organizations in this so-called liberty movement have also proven to be fertile recruiting grounds for hate groups and white nationalists. This is not entirely surprising given that, despite other ideological differences, both Austrian school and alt-right ideologies marshal the language of free speech and perceived victimization to advance highly moralized anti-egalitarian ideals.

Examining these four student groups reveals a well-coordinated, well-funded and top-down strategy that relies on pre-packaged activism. The student groups help manufacture raw outrage that others process into political change.

APPLIED HAYEK: STUDENTS FOR LIBERTY (SFL)

Students for Liberty defines itself as a "rapidly growing network of pro-liberty students from all over the world."[4] Unlike other Koch-funded student groups within the libertarian youth movement, SFL claims an international focus, with a thousand chapters around the world. Their organization "educates young people about the philosophy of liberty ... develop[s] the leadership skills of those who support liberty ... [and] empowers students and alumni to make the world a freer place."[5] SFL has chapters in North America, Europe, Latin America, Africa, South Asia, and the Asia Pacific, and focuses on training students to become advocates in the so-called liberty movement. In addition to leadership trainings, they host the SFL Academy, which offers online courses such as Liberty 101, Freedom of Expression, Liberty in Africa, Introduction to Objectivism, and other "classes" taught by professors at institutions with strong Koch backing, including Creighton University and George Mason University (GMU).[6] SFL's CEO Wolf von Laer, writing for the DonorsTrust website, boasts of hosting 1,000 events, for 43,000 people, in 100 countries, and "spreading pro-liberty literature on campuses that desperately need ideological diversity. They're fighting for our ideas on the front lines."[7]

Students for Liberty was founded in 2008 by students attending the Koch Summer Fellows Program, supported by the Institute for Humane Studies.[8] SFL vice-president Clark Ruper got his start working with FreedomWorks (formerly Citizens for Sound Economy) and his local State Policy Network think tank (the Mackinac Center). SFL's board includes Tom Palmer, who, like Leonard Liggio, is an officer at the Atlas Network and former vice-president of the Institute for Humane Studies. Other board members are closely affiliated with IHS, Atlas, and the Cato Institute as well as GMU, Koch Summer Fellows, the Libertarian Party, and other Koch-funded libertarian organizations.[9]

Charles Koch and Richard Fink's influence on the organization is clearly evident. For example, an early blog by an SFL Campus Coordinator shows that staff are explicitly trained in their Hayekian role as "second-hand dealers in ideas." Staff are encouraged to embrace their specialized niche among the stages of Fink's social change pyramid: "Intellectuals," "Think Tanks," "Communicators and Actuators," and "Voting Blocks." Student leaders are not expected to be "original thinkers" who produce ideas, or think-tank members who refine them, but rather the "communicators and actuators" that help libertarian ideas "take hold in society." They are expected to amplify the ideas and mobilize students to form a pro-liberty "voting block."[10]

SFL's recently discontinued handbook uses a variation of Richard Fink's model to detail how the organization understands "produc[ing] value" through social change. Their mission to "educate, develop, and empower" refers to their three-stage process, where the end product is a cadre of activists ready to feed Koch's talent pipeline. The "raw materials" that SFL mines on campus are the students they identify who "believe in liberty" or can be persuaded to believe. Some of these students are converted into "intermediate goods," namely the "leaders of liberty on campus." SFL then provides resources for students to "become more effective in their organizing and holds leaders accountable to a high level of professionalism." This ensures efficiency in the creation of the "final product," namely "alumni who support liberty both on campus and in the real world." Even SFL's "theory of volunteering" uses a Fink/Hayek diagram to describe cultivating individual activists. SFL looks to develop volunteers into the "highest level" of volunteerism where, unlike in the lower tiers, they "go from just donating time, body and mind, to developing identity with the organization," and being "capable of making their identity the organization."[11]

Involving students in pre-packaged campus campaigns, including free speech initiatives, is therefore an explicit strategy for grooming professional communicators and highly motived libertarian activists. SFL founder Alexander McCobin told an audience at the Conservative Political Action Conference (CPAC) in 2010 that SFL organizes "protest activities to defend liberty on their college greens" including "student protests in favor of free trade, against smoking bans, and in favor of their university's free speech."[12] SFL also offers "activism kits," with themes like "Less Marx, More Mises" designed to promote the Austrian school and "help our leaders make these ideas compete in colleges' marketplace of ideas." SFL provides a number of different campaigns since "[s]ome activists may be more interested in regulation reform, while others might be more interested in free speech efforts on campus." The Free Expression kit contains ready-made corporate activism merchandise including high-quality T-shirts, posters, stickers, books, and fliers, all for students who plan on "kicking it old school through [the] inspiration of the 1964–65 Berkeley free speech protests."[13] These supplies equip students to engage in out-of-the-box "activism," including instigating campus conflicts around university speech policies.

In 2015, Students for Liberty also announced the creation of campus "Strike Teams," including Campus Disorientation (to "reach new students on campus before statist professors and administrators did") and Constitution Day events (for which chapters could receive a $100 grant to purchase copies of the Constitution to distribute and a "Free Speech Ball" to roll around campus).[14] Participating SFL chapters could win a $1,000 "activism prize."[15] By encouraging students to hand out copies of the Constitution outside areas generally reserved for tabling and leafleting, these campaigns intentionally put students into conflict with administrators over free speech. SFL therefore also offers training sessions on "When to Sue Your University" over administrative interference.[16]

SFL draws upon a stable of provocative campus speakers as well as literature developed by key Koch network organizations. An associate member of the State Policy Network, SFL received $3,437,213 from Koch family foundations, the Bradley Foundation, DonorsTrust, and Donors Capital Fund between 2009 and 2019.[17]

In addition to supporting this start-up student group, the Koch network has also successfully co-opted several legacy conservative and libertarian campus groups. Making inroads into Young Americans for Liberty and Young Americans for Freedom has vastly expanded the network's recruitment activities and multiplied their efforts on many campus issues, including around issues of free speech.

APPLIED ROTHBARD:
YOUNG AMERICANS FOR LIBERTY (YAL)

Students drawn to the liberty movement often initially embrace the defiant individualism that libertarianism affirms. However, the Austrian-school framework also cultivates a radical distrust of government into a fiercely principled belief that any government action is coercive and inherently immoral, including civil rights protections for minorities, women, and LGBTQ+ communities. This explains why some libertarian and alt-right circles have considerable overlap.[18] This is especially true for strands of the libertarian movement drawn from Murray Rothbard, who explicitly brought libertarianism together with "racial science."[19]

After the 1976 kickoff of the Center for Libertarian Studies, many attendees went on to establish several key well-funded organizations designed to make their political vision manifest. Charles Koch, Ed Crane, and Murray Rothbard created the Cato Institute. Within a few short years, however, Rothbard became disillusioned with Koch's motives and methods, criticizing his focus on electoral politics and policy change as contrary to a principled anarcho-capitalist approach. Rothbard also resented the undue influence Koch enjoyed within the libertarian movement—a movement Rothbard had a legitimate claim to have built organically through grassroots organizing, rather than through corporate funding. According to Rothbard, Koch would "go to any end to acquire/retain control" and had a "practice of misusing non-profit foundations for his own personal ends."[20] Following the 1980 defeat of the Ed Clark/David Koch Libertarian Party ticket, Charles Koch relocated the Cato Institute from San Francisco to Washington, D.C., leading Rothbart to write: "The massive shift of the Kochtopus to D.C. symbolized and physically embodied the shift of the Kochtopusian Line towards the State and toward Respectability."[21]

After being kicked out of Cato in 1981, Rothbard and several others from the Center for Libertarian Studies continued developing the Austrian school's far-right elements with the help of Texas politician Ron Paul. Lew Rockwell and Joseph Stromberg teamed up with Rothbard and Paul to form an Austrian school think tank called the Ludwig von Mises Institute for Austrian Economics, located at Auburn University in Alabama. Frustrated by the direction of the Libertarian Party and the libertarian movement more generally, Rothbard and Rockwell cultivated a theory of "paleolibertarianism," seeking to reground libertarianism in traditional conservatism. In *Liberty Magazine*, published by the Mises Institute, Rockwell argued that true libertarianism recognized the state as the "institutional source of evil throughout history" whose moral alternative is private property and the "unhampered free market." Egalitarianism is "morally reprehensible and destructive of private property" and therefore a threat to "Western civilization." True libertarianism, in contrast, requires returning to "[o]bjective standards of morality, especially as found in the Judeo-Christian tradition."[22] This civilizational-libertarian ideology was expressed in a number of openly racist, anti-gay, and anti-abortion newsletters, including the Rothbard-Rockwell Report. During the late 1990s Rothbard used this venue to openly promote anti-Black and neo-confederate causes.[23] He referred to this as "outreach to rednecks."[24]

In 1988, four years after becoming the first chairman of Charles Koch's burgeoning corporate front group Citizens for a Sound

Economy (later Americans for Prosperity/FreedomWorks), Paul launched a particularly lucrative newsletter called the Ron Paul Political Report (allegedly written primarily by Rockwell under Paul's name).[25] During Paul's presidential campaigns, these newsletters were widely publicized and criticized. Critics pointed, for example, to a special issue about the 1992 Los Angeles riots where Paul told his readers that they can "safely assume that 95% of the black males in [major US cities] are semi-criminal or entirely criminal," and because the "animals are coming," readers should seek urgent advice on how to get away with murdering "urban youths."[26] These political reports "brimmed over with virtually every far right obsession and hatred." And as one ex-staffer stated: "The wilder they got, the more bombastic they got with it, the more the checks came in."[27]

During his 2008 presidential run Paul built a large campus following motivated by his anti-war policies and support for the legalization of marijuana. After Paul failed to win the Republican nomination, student organizers refashioned Students for Ron Paul chapters into Young Americans for Liberty (YAL). YAL members were consistently exposed to Austrian economists like Ludwig von Mises and Murray Rothbard, who Ron Paul repeatedly championed as his personal inspirations.[28] Their founding mission is thoroughly Rothbardian, decrying the "corrupt, coercive world that has lost respect for voluntary action" and declaring that "government is the negation of liberty."[29]

YAL establishes high school and college campus chapters to identify, train, and deploy conservative talent. They describe a four-stage process of campus recruitment: "Identify Youth Leaders through YALS's National Campus Program," then "Educat[e] through On-Campus Activism Events," then "Train YAL Members in How to Make Liberty Win," and finally mobilize these activists to help get "liberty candidates" elected.[30] YAL president Cliff Maloney described the organization as providing trained campaign staff that can then hold elected officials "accountable" and "give them model legislation they can propose."[31]

Shortly after its founding, this proudly grassroots movement was largely co-opted by the very influence Rothbard had warned against. By 2009, YAL's strategic partners included the standard gamut of Koch network groups, including the Charles Koch Institute, Americans for Prosperity, FreedomWorks, the Cato Institute, the Institute for Humane Studies, State Policy Network, and the National Right to Work Legal

Foundation.[32] In 2014, YAL's executive director Jeff Frazee presented at the Koch network's secretive donor summit. In leaked documents from a session titled "Educating and Engaging the Next Generation," Frazee is flanked by two staff members of Generation Opportunity, the millennial front of Americans for Prosperity.[33] Young Americans for Liberty received $5,920,023 from Koch and DonorsTrust/Donors Capital Fund from 2012 to 2019.[34] In 2015, YAL and SFL announced the joint venture Alumni for Liberty, to "build up the largest network of pro-liberty individuals possible."[35]

In synch with other Koch network organizations, YAL's campus operations involve top-down "activist" kits designed to agitate around campus free speech. Begun in 2015, YAL's campaign "Fight for Free Speech" organizes students to protest free speech zones. As with SFL, YAL also provides a $100 "activism grant," as well as a "recruitment kit packed with materials, clip boards, sidewalk chalk, books, flyers, and everything else you'll need to get students to support free speech and attend your event."[36]

While Chapters 5 and 6 discuss more fully the legal and political debates over campus free speech zones and speech codes, we should point out that nuanced arguments exist for and against using campus regulations to balance free speech protections against the institutional interests in—and commitments to—equal access, safety, and inclusion. Supporters of hate speech bans, for example, argue that such regulations enable students from diverse backgrounds and marginalized identities to feel safe on campus. Likewise, free speech zones limit the influence of outside groups and seek to balance free speech rights with the realities of a residential institution. Arriving at a fair balance between speech, safety, and inclusion is difficult, and organizations like the American Civil Liberties Union (ACLU) and American Association of University Professors (AAUP) have varying, yet thoughtful, positions concerning if, when, and how to regulate campus speech.[37] Many libertarian student groups, however, receive considerable support to weaponize this issue in ways that feed into a very particular partisan narrative of conservative students as victims of oppressive (often state) institutions. In doing so, they claim that speech rights are absolute and therefore should be completely deregulated. As discussed in Chapter 6, these arguments rely on, in the words of legal scholar Mary Anne Franks, a "simplistic orthodoxy built around the narrative of white male victimhood, the mythology of the free market, and populist and often patronizing clichés to ensure that the interests of white males, often extremely wealthy, are protected above all others."[38]

To promulgate their highly ideological campus free speech narrative, YAL, like SFL, distributes pre-packaged campaigns involving handing out pocket Constitutions, erecting a "free speech wall," or rolling an inflatable "free speech ball."[39] These activities, often located outside of designated free speech zones, are designed to provoke pushback from campus administrators. YAL instructs students to record "video footage of an encounter with the administration" in order to ensure "legal standing," and then to "contact YAL's Free Speech Director, your Regional Director, or the State Chair in your area."[40]

YAL groups then use these manufactured controversies to sue colleges and universities. For example, at Modesto Junior College, YAL members were prevented from distributing pocket Constitutions without permission outside of designated free speech zones.[41] At Kellogg Community College, YAL students were arrested after refusing to stop distributing copies of the Constitution and recruiting members.[42] At both schools, YAL sued with the help of Koch network legal groups (Chapter 5), and administrators at both schools settled out of court for at least $50,000. YAL has filed similar lawsuits, taking up aggressive litigation over free speech policies nationwide, including at the University of Cincinnati (2012), the University of Georgia (2015), and the University of Massachusetts, Amherst (2018). By February 2018, YAL claimed to have challenged nearly 200 campuses and forced policy changes on 31.[43] By the end of that year, YAL claimed to have changed campus policy on 50 campuses, leading one right-wing media outlet to proclaim that "nearly 1 million students may now be exposed to the ideas of liberty, not just the usual leftist talking points typically presented in the classroom."[44]

Drawn from the Austrian school and paleolibertarianism, YAL's rhetoric of liberty and anti-state moralization has regularly comported comfortably with individuals holding full-blown white nationalist ideas. By 1994, Rockwell and several founding Mises Institute figures helped launch a militant "Southern nationalist" group called the League of the South, which advocates a neo-Confederate secession of Southern states.[45] Despite denials by most of the individuals involved, archived versions of the League's own website identify at least ten current Mises Institute staff and scholars involved in the League and its educational arm, the League of the South Institute. Murray Rothbard, who passed away one year after the League's founding, is listed as a charter member.[46] Longtime YAL Outreach Director, Jack Hunter—a blogger for Ron Paul's 2012 presidential campaign and Rand Paul's senatorial aid—resigned from his Senate position when it became public that he also masqueraded as the Southern Avenger (a far-right personality whose identity was obscured by a Confederate flag wrestling mask). Hunter led the Charleston, South Carolina chapter of the League of the South, and once praised John Wilkes Booth for assassinating Abraham Lincoln.[47] Hunter is a longtime YAL staffer, who has visited campuses on YAL's speakers circuit and attended YAL conferences. YAL's conferences routinely include scholars affiliated with the Mises Institute, including those who were also members of the League of the South Institute. The Southern Poverty Law Center credits the Mises Institute for helping to mainstream the League of the South.[48]

Individual campus YAL chapters have also been unmasked as racist and civilizationist hotbeds of paleolibertarianism, and often overlap with alt-right and white nationalist groups. One group in particular, the American Identity Movement (AIM, formerly Identity Evropa), is a designated hate group responsible for an explosion of white nationalist fliers on campuses.[49] In 2017, they co-organized the deadly Charlottesville Unite the Right rally with the League of the South. In subsequent years, AIM's chat logs were leaked, allowing researchers to identify numerous YAL officers who were also members of AIM. At the University of Nevada, Reno, for example, one AIM member and YAL officer bragged about his flyering and recruitment efforts while extolling nations for expelling Jewish populations.[50] Another AIM member, Derek Magill, was president of the YAL chapter at the University of Michigan during a time when the group successfully sued the university—supported by Alliance Defending Freedom (Chapter 5)—for not providing a $1,000 reimbursement for their visiting anti-affirmative action speaker. Magill was a featured author and speaker at YAL's "strategic partner," the Foundation for Economic Education (FEE), and was featured at an IHS seminar in 2017.[51]

It is important to note that journalists and activist researchers are just scratching the surface of this opaque organization. Still, what is known so far is worrisome given the degree to which the Koch network and far-right hate groups often recruit from the same populations of students holding principled anti-government positions.

In addition to the relatively recent organizations like SFL and YAL, the Koch network has also been highly successful at co-opting legacy right-wing infrastructure already on campuses.

THE OLD RIGHT: YOUNG AMERICANS FOR FREEDOM (YAF)

Young Americans for Freedom is a 60-year-old student organization founded in 1960 by Conservative icon William F. Buckley, Jr. This group grew rapidly around the effort to secure the Republican presidential nomination of segregationist Barry Goldwater and support his 1964 presidential campaign. Many of the prominent leaders of the conservative movement and the Republican Party in the 1980s cut their teeth with Young Americans for Freedom.[52]

A separate organization, launched by conservative activists in 1969 and eventually called the Young America's Foundation, focused on bringing conservative speakers to campus. In subsequent decades the Foundation engaged a number of programs to spread conservative ideas on college campuses and in public policy. The group had close ties to Ronald Reagan, who regularly spoke at events. In 1998 the Young America's Foundation purchased Reagan's Rancho del Cielo, converting it into a conference and event venue, which includes running "training seminar(s) focused on hosting conservative speakers on ... campuses."[53] In 2001, the Young America's Foundation merged with the National Journalism Center, cementing its commitment to training conservative journalists. In 2011, it merged with the Young Americans for Freedom to form a unified entity. The Young America's Foundation remains the parent entity, with student chapters operating under the name Young Americans for Freedom.[54]

YAF's mission includes "ensuring that increasing numbers of young Americans understand and are inspired by the ideas of individual freedom, a strong national defense, free enterprise, and traditional values."[55] YAF exists to train "activists, authors, and tacticians in the Conservative Movement" and "prides itself on the people that have made an impact on our young leaders and conservatism."[56] YAF alumni include authors, journalists, pundits, columnists, and producers within the conservative news ecosystem, including Ann Coulter;

top leaders of Koch-funded political organizations; as well as elected politicians and White House staffers such as former Attorney General Jeff Sessions and White House advisor Steven Miller (the architect of Trump's anti-immigrant policies).[57]

By 2007, however, YAF had lost momentum and existed primarily as a legacy brand. The "essentially moribund" group consisted of "a loose and decentralized network of campus chapters, each one appearing to act independently," and amounting to little more than a "brand name for radical right-wing student activism."[58] YAF's website around this period complained that other national conservative student groups were taking credit for YAF's grassroots organizing efforts.[59]

After the 2011 merger with Young America's Foundation, however, the newly conjoined organization began receiving considerable donations, many from the Koch donor network. YAF received more than $124 million in gifts between 2010 and 2017, making up the majority of its operating budget. Donors included Vice-President Mike Pence, Secretary of Defense Donald Rumsfeld, Steve Forbes, Wheel of Fortune host Pat Sajak, Tom Clancy, and others. In 2013, a $16 million bequest from Robert Ruhe enabled YAF to double its outreach programs, making it possible to send 111 speakers to 77 campuses in 2016 alone (Chapter 3). YAF also receives funding from prominent attendees of Koch's donor summits. The DeVos family, who gave approximately $10 million to purchase their Reagan Ranch, also donated an additional $15 million between 2003 and 2012. YAF received $100,000 from hedge fund billionaire Robert Mercer in 2016, and his daughter Rebekah Mercer sits on the board of the Reagan Ranch.[60] YAF received $3 million from Koch family foundations, the Bradley Foundation, DonorsTrust, and Donors Capital Fund between 1998 and 2019.[61] The Young America's Foundation is also a member of the Koch-funded State Policy Network.[62]

This influx of funding has allowed YAF to become a major player in libertarian-funded free speech activism. YAF frequently runs con-ferences for college and high school students to train them in campus activism and journalism. During YAF training sessions students learn "when it is legal to record a conversation with a college administrator; how to press schools to cover some of the security costs [of a con-troversial speaker]; regulations on sidewalk chalking, fliers and other forms of promotion and whether they can be challenged; and when to call the foundation's legal staff for help."[63] Like SFL, YAF also provides its campus activists with pre-packaged campaigns. Students can order a "Free Speech Box," supposedly valued at $270 but free to high school and college students, and introduced with the following warning: "Are your free speech rights being curtailed on your campus? Of course they are! Most schools infringe on students [sic] free speech rights, especially if you want to promote conservative ideas. Well, we can help you push back at a moment's notice." The box includes a "Free Speech Quick Action Plan," along with buttons, stickers, T-shirts, pocket sized copies of the Constitution, and posters featuring the slogan "I Support Free Speech, Not Political Correctness."[64]

In addition to training and supporting campus activists, YAF also specializes in developing a vast infrastructure to bring conservative speakers to campus, touting campus speaking tours and a large speakers bureau consisting of a hundred individuals—including Ben Shapiro—many of whom can be booked directly through the Young America's Foundation's website.[65] Between 2005 and 2017, YAF spent roughly $54.3 million on its campus conference and lecture programs alone.[66] In addition to bringing often-controversial speakers to campus, YAF's Censorship Exposed program engages in legal action against colleges and universities that deny or place limitations on the Foundation's speakers. As part of this effort, the YAF has sued California State University, Los Angeles, the University of California-Berkeley, Kennesaw State University, Oxnard Union High School, the University of Texas, Austin, Virginia Tech, University of Virginia, University of Florida, and the University of Minnesota over free speech issues (Chapter 5).[67]

In addition to succumbing to the ever-widening influence of the Koch network, even this principled legacy conservative group has not been impervious to more radical far-right elements. After Michigan State University's YAF chapter invited the white supremacist Jared Taylor, British fascist and Holocaust-denier Nick Griffin, and others, the group became one of the only student organizations designated a "hate group" by the Southern Poverty Law Center. The chapter's president, Kyle Bristow, later went on establish the Foundation for the Marketplace of Ideas, providing legal support to the alt-right and filing lawsuits supporting Richard Spencer's efforts to speak at Michigan State, the University of Cincinnati, and Ohio State.[68] YAF's national chairman has since denounced Bristow.[69] This is not an isolated incident, however. YAF was forced to fire Michelle Malkin from their speakers bureau after she openly praised the white nationalist Nick Fuentes during a YAF speech at UCLA.[70] Matthew Heimbach, who founded the Montgomery College chapter of YAF, went on to create the neo-Nazi group Traditionalist Worker Party. YAF chapters sponsor events such as "Catch an Illegal Immigrant," a "Koran Desecration" competition, "Affirmative Action Bake Sales," and a "Hate Speech is Free Speech" event.[71] And YAF board members have held leadership positions in groups promoting white nationalism.[72] It is not entirely surprising, therefore, that YAF chapters are also known to regularly bring hateful speakers to campus in the name of promoting free speech (Chapter 3).

It is not only the traditionally conservative political organizations that have been increasingly co-opted by corporate and far-right interests, however. Turning Point USA emerged in the wake of the Occupy movement to catalyze a new wave of far-right campus organizing. This group is also well integrated into the larger libertarian-funded free speech efforts.

THE NEW RIGHT: TURNING POINT USA (TPUSA)

Turning Point USA claims to be a "501(c)3 non-profit organization whose mission is to identify, educate, train, and organize students to promote freedom,"[73] but its funders and tactics come from the worst of far-right corporate politics. Eighteen-year-old Charlie Kirk created TPUSA in 2012 to organize conservative college students, focusing on combating so-called liberal bias in colleges, calling universities "islands of totalitarianism."[74] In his book, *Campus Battlefield*, Kirk—who never went to college—writes that universities "have become leftist echo chambers that reinforce an anti-American, anti-freedom, pro-Marxist worldview."[75]

TPUSA's ideology and tactics have made the organization very popular among far-right students. As many former members have revealed, there is a culture of overtly racist, alt-right leanings among the group's leadership at all levels, including numerous instances that garnered national attention—often involving staff losing their job when their use of blatantly racist slurs, praise of Nazis, or circulation of anti-immigrant or antisemitic memes becomes public.[76] Similar

to YAL, TPUSA has become a convenient vessel for white suprem-
acist groups like the American Identity Movement (AIM). Leaked
AIM chatlogs describe the group's efforts to "[t]urn your local Turning
Point USA chapter into a de-facto [AIM] chapter."[77]

Despite these controversies, TPUSA has maintained a robust fundraising effort among traditional conservatives and corporate interests.
The most recent study of TPUSA's financing identified the source of
roughly 43 percent of their revenue, over $11.1 million, between 2014
and 2018.[78] Much of this budget comes from individual and foundation donors tied to the Koch's donor network, including the Bradley
Foundation and DonorsTrust, which provided $2.3 million.[79] Several
other key donors are family foundations tied to individuals that have
been invited to attend Koch's secretive donor seminars, like Thomas W.
Smith, Illinois Governor Bruce Rauner, and the DeVos family. Foster
Friess, an attendee of Koch's summits, provided the seed money for
TPUSA in 2012.[80] FreedomWorks president Adam Brandon sits on the
group's advisory board along with Friess, Deason, and Ginni Thomas
(the wife of Koch summit attendee and Supreme Court Justice, Clarence Thomas).[81]

Funding from Rauner and Friess appears largely responsible for
the group's budget increases from $52,000 in 2012 to $5.5 million in
2016.[82] By 2017 the budget reached $8 million, and according to Kirk
that included funding from donors "in the fossil fuel space." This may
explain why TPUSA chapters have led fights against carbon divestment efforts on college campuses.[83] In 2018 TPUSA had 322 employees
and revenue of $10.8 million.[84] In 2016 TPUSA served as the unoffi-
cial campus organizing effort for the Trump campaign and claimed to
have footholds on more than 1,000 campuses.[85] Since then, the group
has also been caught engaging in illegal campaign activity on behalf of
Texas Senator Ted Cruz, facilitated by Ginni Thomas.[86]

To combat the so-called radical left on college campuses, TPUSA
staffs a National Field Program and sends paid organizers to campuses. This program is designed to "[r]e-brand free market values on
college campuses," and "push back against intolerance and bias against
conservatives." It pledges "to educate students about the benefits of
limited government, capitalism, and freedom" and to unite "like-
minded" groups to increase the impact of their "activism initiatives."[87]
TPUSA claims that its field program is "the largest and most pow-

erful campus activist program in America."[88] In addition to its field program, TPUSA also provides student groups with "educational" resources and publications as well as libertarian and pro-corporate branded materials, such as posters and flyers bearing the messages: "Big Government Sucks," "Commies Aren't Cool," and "Fossil Fuels Save Lives."[89] It hosts a number of activist conferences, such as the High School Activist Conference, Young Latino Leadership Summit, Young Women's Leadership Summit, and Winter in West Palm Beach Activist Retreat.[90] TPUSA also gained notoriety for publishing the online "Professor Watchlist," which states as its mission: "expos[ing] and document[ing] college professors who discriminate against conservative students and advance leftist propaganda in the classroom."[91]

TPUSA actively engages in taking over student governments at colleges and universities across the country. Appearing before the (anti-immigrant/anti-Muslim) Horowitz Freedom Center in 2015, Kirk described TPUSA as involved in combating "the radical left and its Islamist allies," admitting that "you would be amazed ... You spend $5,000 on a [campus] race, you can win. You could retake a whole college or university." For example, at the University of Maryland in 2015, the College Republicans president emailed out a call: "Anyone who wants to run for SGA president, Turning Point is offering to pay thousands of dollars (literally) to your campaign to help get a conservative into the position." Examples such as these have led Kirk's critics to label Turning Point the "super PAC for student government." At several schools, candidates were removed from ballots after these contributions became public, as many schools have clear campaign finance regulations that forbid undeclared contributions from outside groups.[92]

Despite this criticism, TPUSA has only doubled down on its investments in college elections. In a brochure pitched to potential donors, TPUSA claims that the student government candidates "we have supported and financed will have direct oversight and influence over more than $500 million in university tuition and student fee appropriations."[93] Their "Campus Victory Plan" has pledged to "commandeer the top office of Student Body President at each of the most recognizable and influential American universities." The goals that TPUSA "hopes to achieve by spending big on student-government races" include "block[ing] all boycott, divestment and sanctions" efforts on campuses, defunding progressive groups, and promoting a "national speaker's circuit and tour and forums using student resources to message American Exceptionalism and Free Market ideals on campus."[94]

In the section titled "What Happens When We Win," the brochure retells the story about the University of Colorado, Boulder, where TPUSA elected the entire executive ticket and a majority of the Senate. The student officials subsequently passed a pro-free speech resolution and lobbied the state legislature to eradicate free speech zones on all public Colorado university campuses (Chapter 5). The brochure lays out a three-stage plan to "target every Division I school in the country and over 100 critical universities in 'swing states' before 2020."[95]

As we demonstrate in the next chapter, these student groups not only provide a talent pipeline to the corporate-funded liberty movement, they also become the point of access for inviting a whole host of professionally provocative speakers to campus. The resulting outrage and protest becomes the raw material used to produce not only a culture war narrative, but also lock in social change through lawsuits and legislation.

3

The Provocateurs

In recent years US college campuses have witnessed a resurgence of grassroots anti-capitalist and anti-racist student activism, inspired by Occupy Wall Street, Black Lives Matter, and Standing Rock, and including student and faculty efforts to end rape culture, secure LGBTQ+ protections, halt climate change, seek justice for Palestinians, and secure economic equality and labor protections. During the same period, an increasing number of high-profile controversies have also shaken American colleges, often as a result of non-academic provocateurs booking space on campus or being invited by student groups, only to be protested or disinvited. Unlike in the past, today there exists a whole infrastructure designed to court student protest by inviting highly controversial speakers to campus. Provoking outrage has become an end in itself.

In his 1971 memo, Lewis Powell sketched a strategy to gain a foothold in the academy by increasing the number of pro-business college speakers appearing on campus. Drawing on arguments he used when litigating on behalf of the tobacco industry, Powell claimed that campuses will only host free-market groups if conservatives "aggressively insisted upon the right to be heard" and the right to be given "equal time." Such efforts would "require careful thought" and were not "for the fainthearted," but they would ultimately succeed because good faith academic communities would want to avoid the optics of "refusing a forum to diverse views."[1]

Five decades later, campus student organizations funded by the Koch donor network regularly impose speakers upon a college campus and demand they receive equal attention, regardless of qualifications or academic merit. The most successful speakers in this army of "second-hand dealers" are not those who offer academic arguments about the virtue of free market economics but rather those operating at the intersection of libertarianism and the racist, misogynistic, Islamophobic, transphobic, and otherwise hateful rhetoric of the alt-right and paleolibertarianism. While Powell proposed in 1971 that corporations fund highly respected scholars as pro-business campus speakers, Charles Koch challenged his colleagues five years later to consider whether the libertarian movement could attract the necessary adherents with something "other than the highest scholarship," including "non-intellectual motivations" like "short-term self-interest." For a movement whose ultimate objective was to "destroy the 'legitimacy' of the [present political] system," Koch asked, "[u]nder what conditions should radical ideas be introduced gradually and tactfully, and when should they be advocated starkly for shock value?"[2]

The strategic deployment of shock value has made it possible for the Koch network to manufacture polarizing outrage at an industrial scale. In fact, a number of Koch-funded organizations specialize in targeting disciplines and scholars for advocating academic arguments they disagree with.[3]

During the 1980s and 1990s the anti-tax right effectively stoked the campus culture wars, sowing outrage over multiculturalism and "postmodernism" as an explicit strategy for undermining support for publicly funded universities.[4] Today similar attacks on "radical professors," "social justice warriors," "snowflakes," and "critical race theory" seek to similarly discredit higher education. Unlike in the 1980s and 1990s, however, these new culture wars are aided by a greatly expanded web of well-funded campus student groups creating favorable conditions for the Koch network to fully leverage the shock value of its brand of far-right provocateurs. Chapters of national student groups have platformed some of the most controversial figures, specifically for the purpose of triggering protest, manufacturing crises, and elevating radical notions of individual freedom and unregulated markets over the protection of civil rights.

Examining the financial support received by speakers like Milo Yiannopoulos, Ben Shapiro, and Charles Murray helps demonstrate the unequal influence that the Koch donor network exerts over the campus free speech debate. Namely, that the Koch network funds both the speakers *and* the student organizations that invite them to campus. In many instances career Koch network provocateurs have little-to-no academic training, no interest in contributing to scholarly discourse, and often situate themselves as openly hostile to the academy itself.

They often rail against culture war tropes, such as "liberals," "socialists," "postmodernists," and "feminists," without engaging the actual academic arguments (much less scholarship) of those they ridicule. In doing so, they seek to score political points and "trigger the libs" rather than engage in a meaningful academic discussion. Unlike the many other partisan provocateurs who never get the chance to speak on campus, Koch-funded speakers routinely find themselves invited to colleges and universities. They arrive based not on the merit of their ideas, the quality of their research, or their curricular contribution, but solely because a well-funded political organization platforms them. In this highly unequal "marketplace of ideas," money really is speech.

THE LIBERTARIAN TO ALT-RIGHT PIPELINE

Many of the most controversial conservative speakers that come to campus specialize in railing against feminism, Muslims, affirmative action, campus equity initiatives, and gay and trans people. They jeer at "liberal professors," and caricature "snowflake" students who demand "safe spaces" and "trigger warnings." Most arrive on campus at the invitation of Koch network student groups.

Because of its fiercely principled belief that governmental and institutional action is coercive and inherently immoral, Austrian economics has provided numerous onramps for anti-egalitarian "paleolibertarian" ideals. Commentators note that key figures in neo-Nazi, white nationalist, and alt-right circles have tended to arrive at their beliefs through libertarian ideology, and particularly the work of Austrian school economists. One journalist called this tendency a "libertarian to alt-right pipeline."[5] For example, the white nationalist podcaster Mike Peinovich, aka Mike Enoch, noted that everyone involved in producing his programs started off as Ron Paul libertarians.[6] White nationalist Richard Spencer cited Ron Paul as his initial political inspiration, and Spencer's mentor Paul Gottfried is a scholar at the Ludwig von Mises Institute.[7] Co-founder of the neo-Nazi Traditionalist Worker Party Tony Hovater cited the Mises Institute's Murray Rothbard and Hans Hermann Hoppe as informing his "anarcho-capitalist" beliefs.[8]

Many of the student groups within the Koch network's "talent pipeline" invite fairly run-of-the-mill conservative speakers to campus: politicians, libertarian economists, and think-tank members. However, alongside these speakers—and often listed in the same speaker's bureau or campus tour—are also provocateurs who specialize in anti-feminist, anti-LGBTQ+, anti-immigrant, white nationalist, and alt-right ideology. These speakers routinely argue against civil rights protections for marginalized groups on campus, often in the name of individual liberty, free markets, free speech, and against "collectivism."

The Koch network's campus infrastructure offers speakers regular access to colleges and universities, empowering them to manufacture off-the-shelf controversy on an industrial scale. It has further supported this campus infrastructure with legal and political institutions (Chapters 5 and 6) that weaponize, defend, and legitimize campus provocateurs under the banner of "free speech." On many campuses, this machinery has effectively chastened college administrations and potential student protestors, making it too costly to speak out against the onslaught of extreme speakers.

A number of prominent speakers on the campus tour who have drawn considerable protest include:

- Heather MacDonald, who draws a six-figure salary from the Manhattan Institute, a far-right think tank that received $15,046,602 from Koch family foundations, the Bradley Foundation, and DonorsTrust/Donors Capital Fund between 1998 and 2019.[9] MacDonald has attracted protests for alleging that Black Lives Matter is a violent murderous movement, and that universities are corrupt for implementing diversity and inclusion efforts on campus. At Claremont McKenna, five students were suspended after protestors blocked the entrance to her talk.[10] MacDonald's travel expenses are often covered by the Intercollegiate Studies Institute, one of the groups that spun off from the Volker Fund.[11]
- Candice Owens—who attacks #BlackLivesMatter and #MeToo protestors as victims who fail to take personal responsibility—was originally employed by Turning Point USA before her current job at Prager U (which, funded by prominent Koch

donors as well as DonorTrust, creates right-wing online video content).[12]

- David Horowitz (of the Horowitz Freedom Center) and self-described Islamophobe Robert Spencer (of Jihad Watch) have come to campuses to give anti-Muslim and anti-immigrant talks.[13] At a May 2017 talk at the University at Buffalo, Spencer was drowned out by protesters critical of his Islamophobic stances. YAF covered his $2,000 speaking fee, but also trained the students who organized the event during YAF's National Conservative Student Conference and provided literature for the group to distribute.[14]

- Ann Coulter is a prominent right-wing pundit who is regularly invited to speak on campus. In April 2017 her talk at UC Berkeley was canceled due to threats of violence. The YAF chapter announced that it had provided "a large portion of the funding to bring Coulter to Berkeley," including "logistical support before the event as well as on-the-ground support from experienced staff."[15] Like many prominent campus provocateurs, Coulter started her career within the right-wing talent pipeline, having entered conservative media as a college intern at YAF's National Journalism Center.[16]

Turning Point USA also spends lavishly to bring speakers to campus. By 2018 TPUSA had spent $3.6 million on conferences featuring former Wisconsin Governor Scott Walker, Education Secretary Betsy DeVos, former US Attorney General Jeff Sessions, and others.[17] TPUSA's high-profile national speaking circuit also features Trump administration officials, Fox News commentators, billionaire donors, as well as corporate economists and CEOs, many of whom draw protesters.[18] The group's founder Charlie Kirk is now infamous enough to draw a counter-protest himself. His events are promoted in ways designed to trigger their intended outcome, with names like "Melting Snowflakes & Smashing Socialism," "Campus Clash," and "Culture War."[19]

This infrastructure of well-funded campus speakers has been incredibly effective at empowering often small groups of conservative and libertarian students to drive campus conversation. For example, Young Americans for Freedom spent roughly $54.3 million on its campus conference and lecture program between 2005 and 2017.[20] YAF chapters can apply to bring a speaker to campus simply by filling out an online form.[21] In addition to making it easy to invite controversial speakers, YAF's Censorship Exposed program files public records requests to "expose" the deliberations of colleges and universities that deny or place limitations on YAF speakers.[22]

As a consequence, Koch network student groups—sometimes with no more than a few students—have the access, resources, and support to bring big-name and highly disruptive speakers to campus. Sometimes these speakers are traditional libertarians, economists, politicians, or pundits. However, the speakers who generate the most shock value not only promote free-market ideas but also stoke culture war social issues.

Many of the campus speakers most successful at sparking free speech outrage have been longtime beneficiaries of the Koch donor network. In addition to the examples above, this chapter focuses on three of the most prominent, controversial, and highly leveraged campus speakers: Milo Yiannopoulos, Ben Shapiro, and Charles Murray. All three blend libertarian economics with stridently anti-egalitarian—and often hateful—rhetoric. They also owe their entire careers to funding provided by the Koch donor network.

MILO YIANNOPOULOS

At the peak of his career in 2017 Milo Yiannopoulos was the best-known speaker provocateur, whose campus appearances drew large crows of protestors and counter-protestors. A major player in the misogynist online movement Gamergate, Yiannopoulos earned a following among young conservatives and libertarians with his inflammatory speeches and writing, full of racist, misogynistic, anti-immigrant and anti-LGBTQ+ rhetoric. As a columnist for Breitbart, Yiannopoulos produced a steady stream of disjointed ramblings in which he frequently gloated about helping to get "Daddy"—Donald Trump—elected, railed against "political correctness," and made spurious, racist, and sexist claims about Islam, feminists, and racial minorities. He stated, for example, that contraception gives women "cottage cheese thighs" and makes them fat and ugly. Elsewhere he claimed that "feminism attracts ugly women" and that Lena Dunham is a "typical feminist rape-hoaxer."[23] His writings are those of an internet troll and a narcissistic, alt-right social media personality, devoid of any academic content. Leaked chats also suggest that an army of more than 40 paid and unpaid interns wrote most of his articles and speeches.[24]

Between 2015 and 2017 Yiannopoulos gave a large number of confrontational talks on college campuses. At a 2016 talk at the University of Oregon, co-hosted by chapters of Young Americans for Liberty and Students for Liberty, Yiannopoulos proclaimed, "I don't want any Muslims in the country" and railed about free speech being restricted on campus. The SFL campus coordinator proudly defended the decision to bring him to campus, "not for his criticisms of college campuses, but for what he represents: The idea that no topic is taboo," that there is "nothing we cannot question and discuss and make better," and that only through "questioning the unquestionable we can live in a freer society."[25]

Although many stops were ultimately canceled, Yiannopoulos's "Dangerous Faggot" tour kicked off with a contentious event sponsored by Young Americans for Liberty at Rutgers University where Milo railed against feminism, Black Lives Matter, and protestors in the room while decrying the lack of free speech on campus.[26] YAL also hosted Yiannopoulos at Michigan State University where seven protestors were arrested for attempting to block the entrance to the venue. He expressed disappointment that "the angry, frightened, social justice posse they whip up against me doesn't exceed two hundred" people, before going on an Islamophobic rant about the "clash of western civilization with radical Islam."[27]

In January 2017, a Yiannopoulos supporter at the University of Washington shot a student protestor.[28] At Berkeley the following month, Yiannopoulos reportedly planned to expose the identities of undocumented students.[29] The campus community pushed for the event to be canceled, with more than 1,000 students demonstrating peacefully. When the administration caved to the right-wing provocateur rather than listening to the protestors' peaceful demands, local anti-fascist activists arrived on campus, throwing fireworks, starting fires, and smashing windows until the talk was canceled. On September 24, Yiannopoulos returned to Berkeley for his so-called "Free Speech Week," having promised to bring a slate of speakers including

Steve Bannon, Ann Coulter, Blackwater founder Erik Prince, Conservative Political Action Committee (CPAC) organizer Lisa De Pasquale, David Horowitz, and many others. In the end, the multi-day event collapsed and only Yiannopoulos, anti-Muslim blogger Pam Geller, and misogynist rape apologist Mike Cernovich arrived for a poorly attended 20-minute appearance at Sproul Plaza. The event cost the school $800,000 in security.[30]

At the University of California, Santa Barbara, MAGA-hatted YAL chapter members carried Yiannopoulos on stage in a regal procession chair, setting him beside a cardboard Trump cutout, where he ranted about feminism and made rape jokes.[31] Also in January 2017, TPUSA chapters hosted Yiannopoulos at the University of Colorado, Boulder and at Cal Poly San Luis Obispo. During his talk in Colorado, Yiannopoulos called "feminism 'cancer' and Islam a 'lifestyle choice.'"[32] The Cal Poly stunt cost the school $86,200 in security.[33]

Like other provocateurs who specialize in spewing hate while demonstrating no interest in academic engagement, Yiannopoulos had billionaire funders who provided the institutional and financial backing needed to access the audience and the legitimacy that colleges campuses provide. In fact, Yiannopoulos's whole career has been funded by these plutocratic libertarian donors.

Yiannopoulos first came to prominence as a senior editor at Breitbart News (2015–17), where leaked emails show him strategizing with neo-Nazi and white supremacists to guide Breitbart's efforts to "become the platform of the alt-right."[34] Robert Mercer, the billionaire backer of Cambridge Analytica, poured $10 million into Steven Bannon's Breitbart News, enabling the platform to grow into one of America's most visited sites on the internet, reaching 2 billion page views annually.[35] While not always in lockstep with the Koch brothers in terms of candidate and policy preferences, Mercer began attending Koch's secretive donor summits in 2011, donating at least $1 million each year.[36] The billionaire gave $2.5 million to the Koch network's Freedom Partners Action Fund in 2014 before eventually leaving the network over policy differences. Mercer has adopted many of the strategies developed by the Koch network, funding a whole host of media and political operations designed to push his political agenda.[37] For example, Mercer financed Citizens United, the film production company at the heart of the Supreme Court's decision to deregulate campaign financing. He also backs numerous free-market think tanks and bankrolled Trump's 2016 campaign.[38] His daughter, Rebekah Mercer, is also highly politically active and sat on the board of the Young America's Foundation.[39]

In addition to funding Yiannopoulos's career at Breitbart, the Mercers also provided the resources necessary to bring Yiannopoulos to dozens of college campuses. For example, his University of Washington talk was funded by Glittering Steal, a production company owned by Mercer and Steve Bannon.[40] Leaked emails suggest that Mercer likely backed the entire 2017 college tour. As one reporter for the Berkeley student paper noted, Yiannopoulos "backed out of an interview with the Los Angeles Times in July when they started asking about the Mercers."[41]

At the end of February 2017, Yiannopoulos resigned from Breitbart when his views on pedophilia became public. Groups such as the American Conservative Union that once denounced college campuses for disinviting Yiannopoulos, suddenly barred him from their events.[42] But the Mercers only severed their financial backing after videos surfaced of Yiannopoulos singing karaoke with Richard Spencer, as members of the audience gave Nazi salutes. In a tweet, Yiannopoulos stated: "I am grateful for Bob [Mercer]'s help in getting me this far in my career."[43]

By the end of 2017, Koch network student groups had also cut ties with Yiannopoulos. The SFL blog post that had praised Yiannopoulos's free speech principles as justification for bringing him to University of Oregon had been deleted, replaced by a new post proclaiming that "Milo's tactics are hardly a good defense of free speech, especially when there are so many better examples to point to," such as those provided by YAL. The revisionist blog post stated: "[M]isogyny and transphobia, for many conservatives, are ideal ways to advocate for the advancement of free speech," but Yiannopoulos's despicable remarks "didn't do much to turn our favor against Milo because there was never much favor there to begin with. Milo has never been on the side of libertarians."[44]

BEN SHAPIRO

Ben Shapiro is another regular campus speaker with a strong libertarian bent, who has also been protested for bringing hate to college campuses. Not as incendiary as Yiannopoulos, Shapiro is considered a "conservative wunderkind" and the "cool kid's philosopher" among conservative millennials.[45] Entering UCLA at age 16, and graduating from Harvard Law School at age 23, Shapiro fashions himself as the young, hip alternative to the older conservative talk radio personalities. He has a strong media presence as a syndicated columnist, author of seven books, editor-in-chief of the conservative media platform The Daily Wire, host of a daily podcast, and formerly editor-at-large at Breitbart. Shapiro left Breitbart in 2016 following the website's failure to support its reporter, Michelle Fields, after she was assaulted by Trump's campaign manager Corey Lewandowski. Since then his criticisms of both Trump and the rampant antisemitism among the alt-right occasionally place him at odds with right-wing activists, including the Groyper Army.[46]

In practice, however, Shapiro is primarily a partisan provocateur, described by critics and supporters alike as "part of an industry that whips up conservatives against the left" and "just one more partisan mobilizing his troops."[47] Like Charlie Kirk, Shapiro launched his career around an explicit antipathy toward higher education, starting with his first book *Brainwashed: How Universities Indoctrinate America's Youth*. As an undergraduate, Shapiro claims to have witnessed "brainwashing occurring on campus on a daily basis" as leftist professors "plant those rancid seeds in the minds of their students."[48] Shapiro prides himself on getting under the skin of "leftists," whom he dismisses as intolerant, stupid, hypocritical, dangerous, and corrosive to American values. For example, in his book *Bullies: How the Left's Culture of Fear and Intimidation Silences Americans* he writes: "Leftists think and act like protofascists. Control is the key. And control through fear, threat of force, and rhetorical intimidation is the modus operandi."[49]

In his commentaries, political writing, and campus presentations, Shapiro uses pseudo-intellectualism and spurious logic to belittle those he sees as ideological opponents. For example, when challenged by one student about his transphobia, Shapiro asked the student her age. When she said 22, Shapiro responded: "Why aren't you 60? ... You can't magically change your gender. You can't magically change your sex. You can't magically change your age."[50] Shapiro is a regular speaker on the campus circuit, having presented at 37 colleges between 2016 and 2017.[51] In 2018–19 Shapiro received a purported 1,500 inquiries about speaking on college campuses, and spoke at 12.[52]

As with Yiannopoulos, Shapiro's career has been largely funded by plutocratic libertarian donors. After leaving the Mercer-funded Breitbart in 2016, he briefly joined the right-wing website Truth Revolt, bankrolled by the David Horowitz Freedom Center.[53] After the website went under, Shapiro helped create the online conservative media platform, The Daily Wire. The website was launched with the financial support of Farris Wilks, a billionaire who made his fortune in fracking.[54] Wilks has contributed tens of millions of dollars to key Koch network organizations. For example, just between 2011 and 2012 he gave $50 million to a number of organizations within the network, including the American Majority ($2.1 million), the State Policy Network ($1.5 million), the Franklin Center ($1.3 million), and the Heritage Foundation ($700,000).[55] Wilks claims his libertarian economics are "grounded in the Bible" and regularly donates to Republican candidates, the religious right, and a network of misleading "pregnancy centers" (often near campuses) that steer women away from abortion and contraception.[56] Wilks and his brother Dan have bought up hundreds of thousands of acres in the American West, including in Montana, Idaho, Texas, Kansas and Colorado, and closed them off to the public.[57]

In addition to the direct largesse of billionaires, Shapiro is platformed as a regular speaker at events funded by Young America's Foundation and Turning Point USA.[58] Shapiro's visit to Berkeley, for example, was ostensibly hosted by the College Republicans, who received the necessary $16,000 from the Young America's Foundation.[59] YAF also funded Shapiro's Spring 2019 campus tour titled "Facts Don't Care About Your Feelings."[60] At California State University, Los Angeles, Shapiro's YAF-hosted lecture "When Diversity Becomes a Problem" drew protests and was ultimately disrupted after students pulled the fire alarm.[61] In November 2016, shortly after the inauguration of Donald Trump, the YAF chapter at the University of Wisconsin, Madison invited Shapiro to give a speech titled "Dismantling Safe Spaces: Facts Don't Care About Your Feelings." He set out to "debunk three favorite terms of the left," namely "social justice, white privilege, and safe spaces." Protestors chanted "shame" and lined up in front of the podium, while Shapiro asked the police to intervene. He explained that "social justice" meant that people could abdicate individual responsibility if they were "the right race, or the right gender, or the right sexual orientation. You get to do these things without punishment," like disrupting his lecture. His crowd chanted "Free Speech Matters!"[62] In September 2017, YAF also brought Ben Shapiro to the University of California, Berkeley, which spent $600,000 on security for the event.[63] Berkeley charged YAF and the college Republicans $16,000 in security fees. Outraged, YAF declared it a tax on conservative speech and refused to pay;[64] a laughable indignation given that YAF annually spends millions of dollars to bring speakers to campus.

Shapiro is also on the TPUSA speakers bureau.[65] In February 2018 TPUSA hosted him at Creighton University, which maintained a police presence including officers on horseback and on rooftops, despite drawing only two protestors.[66] Shapiro called TPUSA "indispensable," shortly after headlining TPUSA's 2016 Women's Leadership Summit, an event he regularly headlines.[67]

CHARLES MURRAY

In addition to funding the careers of online media personalities and conservative journalists, the Koch donor network has also funded the careers of a number of fringe academics who have become a staple of the campus free speech circuit. Charles Murray has emerged as a prominent campus speaker and shares particularly close ties with the Koch donor network. Murray is most notable for making arguments about how races and genders vary in levels of intelligence due to genetic differences. These arguments were then weaponized to advance libertarian attacks on welfare and other social policies perceived to primarily help African Americans and other minority groups. His first book *Losing Ground* (1984), which served as an intellectual justification of the Reagan-era welfare cuts, regularly conflates Black with poor and blames Black culture for poverty. He constructs a moral argument about the problems that occur when "we" assist "them." Murray claims that public assistance programs not only create short-term incentives that keep Americans poor, but that they essentially amount to "bribes" that the civil rights movement extorted by rioting and fomenting "White confusion and guilt."[68] His book proposal explained that publishers would find a market for the book because "a huge number of well-meaning whites fear that they are closet racists, and this book tells them they are not. It's going to make them feel better about things they already think but do not know how to say."[69]

Murray is best known for his infamous co-authored book *The Bell Curve: Intelligence and Class Structure in America*, which, building on his previous work, uses eugenicist claims to conclude that white men have higher average IQs than minorities and women. This argument is used to explain and naturalize social stratification along gender, race, and class lines.[70] Shortly after its publication, the book was resoundingly discredited when it was revealed that its core findings draw heavily upon the work of white supremacists and Nazi sympathizers supported by the Pioneer Fund, which bankrolled eugenicist research.[71] The Southern Poverty Law Center calls Murray's work "racist pseudoscience."[72]

Since 2012 Murray has been touring the country to talk about his book *Coming Apart: The State of White America*, which argues that a growing level of social segregation is resulting from different IQ levels, amplified by declining levels of honesty, religiosity, "industriousness" (i.e. lack of employment), and marriage rates.[73] The tour for this book landed him at the center of a number of deeply contentious campus visits, including at the University of Wisconsin, Madison (November 2016), Middlebury College (March 2017), Indiana University (April 2017), Harvard University (September 2017), and the University of Michigan (October 2017). The most notable incident was at Middlebury College, shortly after Milo's appearance at the University of California, Berkeley. The common narrative told about this altercation is that a mob of violent students prevented Murray from speaking and then attacked him as he was leaving the venue. As with most campus speech controversies, the actual story is much more nuanced than the "liberal mob attacks conservative" headline widely circulated in the right-wing media ecosystem (Chapter 4).

What really happened? Murray's visit took place in the context of a considerable uptick in racist incidents aimed at Black, Muslim and Jewish students at Middlebury, including swastikas painted on the door of the Jewish center, racist slurs, cultural appropriation, and a general lack of support for students of color. So, in the spring of 2017, when it was announced that Murray was invited to campus and the college president would introduce him, many saw the move as another example of the college "signaling that students of color, who already felt isolated and underserved by the institution, and sometimes even unsafe, were less of a priority than presenting racist ideas as worthy of debate."[74] Many students felt outraged. They planned a protest, wrote opinion letters to local press, and launched a petition. Allison Stanger, who was an IHS research fellow in Summer 2019,[75] agreed to moderate the event, and deflected accusations of racism by puzzling how Murray could "be a white supremacist when he married an Asian woman"?[76] Middlebury students organized a large peaceful disruption, an example of organized "good" speech confronting "bad" speech. Students and community members stood with their backs to the stage reading in unison from a statement about the dangers of academia legitimizing eugenics, including Middlebury's own former eugenics program. "This is not respectful discourse, or a debate about free speech... There are countless groups of people affected because of what claims to be academia, which then makes its way into the public, which then makes its way into the White House chair."[77] After the students had finished, Murray tried unsuccessfully to deliver his speech over student chanting. After 20 minutes he was ushered into a room where he delivered the rest of the talk via video. As Stanger and Murray left the venue, police began pushing a path through a crowd of student protestors outside. In the ensuing tussle, Stanger was shoved, resulting in whiplash and a concussion.[78]

While much of the public discussion has focused on whether or not Murray warranted being no-platformed, far less attention has been paid to the financial backing that made his career—and visit to Middlebury—possible. During the early 1980s, Murray was languishing as an obscure libertarian academic in Washington, D.C., until he received a grant from the Manhattan Institute to write *Losing Ground*.[79] The publication of that book attracted the support of the Bradley Foundation, which provided annual support of $100,000 per year during the period he wrote *The Bell Curve*.[80] As his work veered more explicitly in the direction of eugenics, the Manhattan Institute disaffiliated with Murray, citing publicity concerns.[81] The American Enterprise Institute (AEI) quickly took Murray in, along with his Bradley funding, and the Bradley Foundation president called him "one of the foremost thinkers of our time."[82]

In recent years, as with AEI president Arthur Brooks, Charles Murray has been a regular presenter at Koch's donor summits. From leaked documents and the limited reporting allowed in these meetings, we know that Murray headlined the June 14, 2014, dinner and led the breakfast book discussion the following morning.[83] Two of Murray's books appeared on the recommended reading list distributed to donors at Koch's 2016 donor summit.[84] In February 2017, Murray headlined Koch's donor summit, which drew 550 donors who each pledged $100,000 to the political operation.[85] Murray has claimed that he began a friendly acquaintance with Charles and David Koch during the early 1990s, the same time he was writing *The Bell Curve*.[86]

This proximity is not accidental. As a fellow at AEI, Murray works at the center of the Koch network. AEI received an astonishing $44,110,272 from Koch family foundations, the Bradley Foundation, DonorsTrust, and Donors Capital Fund between 1998 and 2019.[87] Many members of the Koch donor network sit on AEI's board, including Ravenel Curry, Clifford Asness, William Walton, and Richard DeVos.[88] Unsurprisingly, Murray's most recent work is increasingly confluent with the aims of Koch network donors, calling on big businesses to rebuild "liberty without permission," through a program of corporate civil disobedience to the regulatory state.[89]

In addition to funding Murray's professional career, his campus tour was also largely underwritten by the AEI and other Koch-funded campus programs. At Middlebury, the school's campus chapter of the American Enterprise Institute Club funded the visit. The club's stated purpose is "to promote free market values and principles."[90] Murray's earlier visit to Indiana University was co-sponsored by the Koch-funded Tocqueville Program,[91] and AEI paid the speakers' fee (which, according to Murray's agent, runs between $20,000 and $30,000).[92]

Murray is often brought to campus as part of AEI student "executive councils," which have spread to more than 80 campuses since being launched in 2013 in an effort to make up "the core of AEI's outreach to undergraduates."[93]

THE MARKETPLACE OF IDEAS

In the months that followed the protested visits of Milo Yiannopoulos, Ben Shapiro, and Ann Coulter to the University of California,

Berkeley, the university's chancellor convened a Commission on Free Speech charged with investigating and debating how the institution responded to external speakers and the thorny issues they raised. After months of deliberation the commission reached a number of conclusions, making suggestions about how administration, faculty, and students could protect free speech rights while also "reducing the likelihood of disruption from provocative events ... [and] avoid[ing] harm to the community when such events occur."[94] The commission also concluded that the various controversial speaking engagements were manufactured by outside groups seeking to score political points by portraying college campuses as intolerant to conservatives:

> All the 2017 events that led to disruption were sponsored by very small groups of students working closely with outside organizations. Although those speakers had every right to speak and were entitled to protection, they did not need to be on campus to exercise the right of free speech. Indeed, at least some of the 2017 events at Berkeley can now be seen to be *part of a coordinated campaign* to organize appearances on American campuses likely to incite a violent reaction, in order *to advance a facile narrative that universities are not tolerant of conservative speech.*[95]

While the public outrage over those protesting Yiannopoulos, Shapiro, and Coulter was instantaneous, this deliberative fact-finding effort received little press attention. This disparity reveals a key fallacy in the campus free speech narrative. Speech does not take place in a free marketplace which evaluates ideas based solely on merit.

As with the strategy of weaponizing free speech to support tobacco, fossil fuel, and other corporate interests, campus free speech activists offer a similarly radical, hyper-individualist, and ideologically libertarian understanding of First Amendment protections. As legal scholar Mary Anne Franks argues, historically there have been three main legal arguments underpinning free speech in the United States: speech serves a critical function in a democracy; speech is critical to individual autonomy; and speech protections enrich the "marketplace of ideas." Starting in the 1960s, however, the right only worked to ensure that the marketplace metaphor displaces all other arguments for free speech, while insisting that the marketplace is understood in libertarian terms—as an unregulated space of individual liberty.[96]

A libertarian marketplace of ideas presumes that if "all ideas, even deeply offensive ideas, are allowed to freely circulate in the marketplace," then the "truth will ultimately prevail." Because this model assumes an overly idealized notion of free-market economics, it presumes that "competition, not regulation, is the best way to maximize both individual and general welfare," and accordingly assumes that "the gravest threat to freedom of speech is regulation, no matter how well intentioned."[97] This metaphor also ignores the fact that markets were never intended to arrive at truth, facts, or knowledge, but rather simply to register the "preferences of market participants."[98] After all, convincing a public to "prefer" climate denial does not make climate science any less true. Furthermore, all marketplaces (of ideas or otherwise) can be manipulated by grifters, monopolies, plutocrats, and malicious actors operating in bad faith.

Rather than driven by free inquiry and critical thought, an unregulated marketplace of ideas risks being flooded by claims pushed by corporate donors intent on manufacturing a response to those ideas, histories, facts, or opinions that challenge their interests.

Faculty, students, and speakers who benefit from the Koch-donor gravy train might find little incentive to concede to a well-formed counter-argument. No matter how soundly or how frequently an idea is discredited, nothing stops bad faith actors from simply repeating debunked ideas, finding new ways to amplify them, or dressing them up in new forms.[99] When that effort fails, paid proponents can prop up their position by making endless appeals for "equal time" in the name of free speech. An unregulated yet highly unequal market allows private donors to deploy what Charles Koch called "non-intellectual motivations" to fuel an endless war of ideas under the guise of an academic debate between two sides.[100]

As evidenced by the Koch network's student groups and paid provocateurs, the marketplace of ideas can also be easily manipulated by those who simply know how to engineer attention.

The pursuit of a libertarian marketplace of ideas is particularly troubling given the high levels of inequality that exist on campus. For example, traditional student groups seeking to bring a speaker to campus must pull together funding from departments, centers, administrative offices, endowed funds, or student government. The general understanding is that the invited speaker understands their role as contributing to disciplinary, scholarly, or broader social conversations, rather than merely scoring partisan political points. In contrast, the Koch donor network has created a machinery by which student groups—often comprised of a small handful of students—can access the financial resources necessary to bring highly controversial, big-name speakers to campus. Furthermore, these speakers are often well-trained (and legally supported) to engage in partisan bomb throwing.

The asymmetry continues. When Koch-funded student groups bring speakers to campus, one of the only available responses for outgunned students is protest. Doing so, however, not only produces fodder for the right-wing media ecosystem but also creates the raw materials used to lock in legislative and judicial victories.

The ability to turn a student protest at Middlebury College or Berkeley into a national story exists because the same plutocratic libertarians who fund both the student groups and the speakers also built a vast media outrage machine. These outlets reduce complex issues about campus free speech—such as those described by the Berkeley

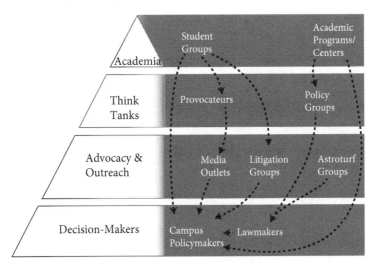

Figure 2   Koch-Diagram of Campus Free Speech Efforts

Commission—to a single talking point: outrage over college campuses curtailing conservative speech (Chapter 4). This media outrage then feeds into legal and legislative strategies that enable plutocratic libertarian donors to gain greater access to higher education (Chapters 5 and 6).

4

The Media Amplifiers[1]

Following the 2016 election, Harvard professors Yochai Benkler, Robert Faris, and Hal Roberts offered a thorough examination of the media environment that fueled Trump's unexpected victory. Their book *Network Propaganda* documents the existence of two very distinct media ecosystems. One—the mainstream media—centers around the *Washington Post*, *New York Times*, CNN, and *Politico* and includes newspapers, broadcast stations, magazines, websites, and other media sources that span the political spectrum. This ecosystem includes both "norm-constrained journalism" as well as many "diverse outlets for mobilizing activists, challenging agenda-setting, and questioning mainstream media narratives."[2] It also includes progressive and conservative activist outlets which, while disagreeing on many things, nonetheless cover similar content, events, and facts and remain in conversation with the journalistic sources at the center of their ecosystem.

Fox News and Breitbart, in contrast, serve as the central nodes in the right-wing media ecosystem, which operates largely independently of the mainstream media. Many media organizations within this ecosystem primarily distribute their material through social media, creating a powerful and insular feedback loop. In doing so, the right-wing media ecosystem "exhibits all the characteristics of an echo chamber that radicalizes its inhabitants, destabilizes their ability to tell truth from fiction, and undermines their confidence in institutions."[3]

This chapter demonstrates that the Koch donor network funds many of the major players within this right-wing media ecosystem, including those that have specialized in amplifying the campus free speech narrative.

The Koch network has shown a long-term interest in funding media. Many controversial campus speakers are right-wing media celebrities on platforms funded by the Koch donor network (Chapter 3). Other media personalities—including Rush Limbaugh, Glenn

Beck, Charles Krauthammer, John Stossel, and Ramesh Ponnuru—regularly attend the Koch donor summits.[4] And many top donors within the Koch network own or generously fund their own outlets, including Philip Anschutz (*Washington Examiner* and *The Weekly Standard*), Paul Singer (Washington Free Beacon), Dan and Farris Wilks (Daily Wire), Robert Mercer (Breitbart), and Foster Friess (The Daily Caller).[5] According to tax documents, in 2017 alone the Charles Koch Foundation (CKF) and the Charles Koch Institute (CKI) poured $2 million into conservative media platforms.[6] Outlets that received Koch funding—such as the American Spectator, Tucker Carlson's Daily Caller, and Glenn Beck's Mercury Radio Arts and The Blaze—produce highly partisan content, without disclosing their funders.[7]

The Koch network also invests heavily in developing a talent pipeline that feeds into this right-wing media ecosystem. For example, the Koch Internship Program and the Koch Associates Program exist to fund, train, and staff positions at various right-wing outlets including Real Clear, *Washington Examiner*, The College Fix, Ben Shapiro's Daily Wire, and the Daily Caller News Foundation, and cultivate a "shared focus on preserving free speech and improving a free press." These Koch internships also place students at the Leadership Institute and Young Americans for Liberty, which run aggressive campus media programs specializing in ginning up campus free speech controversies.[8]

Without the right-wing media ecosystem, most campus free speech controversies would likely remain local stories—the province of campus newspapers, regional news outlets, and professional publications like the *Chronicle of Higher Education* or *Inside Higher Ed.* However, Koch-funded media outlets such as Campus Reform and the College Fix generate content explicitly designed to advance a narrative about mass anti-conservative bias on college campuses. They run a steady stream of outrage stories focusing on protests over campus speakers, campus speech policies, safe spaces and trigger warnings, faculty and administrators shutting down student speech and, increasingly, institutional initiatives to increase campus diversity and inclusion (which they often refer to as "forced speech"). On one average day—January 22, 2020—Campus Reform and the College Fix ran headlines declaring: "U Kansas Professor Indicted for Working for Communist Party of China," "UA Promotes Program Only for 'Black, Hispanic, Native American and/or LGBTQ+ Students,'" "Study: Profs Donate to

Dems Over Republicans by 95:1 Ratio," "UW Lecturer Claims he was Demoted After Pointing out Male and Female Differences," "UConn Students Arrested for 'Ridiculing' Speech Won't Face Discipline … For Now," "The University of California's Diversity Screening Could Ruin the Quality of its Faculty," and "Yale Axes Problematic Art History Course Focused on Western Art, Student Claims."

Rather than engaging in good faith journalistic investigation into their subject matter, the paid agent-provocateurs behind these "stories"[9] churn out a daily stream of clickbait and culture war outrage designed to manufacture a narrative about college campuses as absurdly liberal and biased against conservative views. They attack faculty by circulating stories featuring decontextualized social media posts or other comments.[10] These stories often result in steady streams of hate mail, threats of violence, and sometimes the sanctioning of the faculty member.[11]

Other outlets within the right-wing media ecosystem often take these stories up, repeat them largely verbatim or make them increasingly diabolical and then republish them, "slowly but inexorably mutat[ing]" them "as in a game of telephone."[12] In effect, outlets like Campus Reform and the College Fix exist to mainline hyperbolic versions of otherwise minor campus stories straight into the heart of the right-wing media ecosystem.

This chapter demonstrates that this right-wing outrage machine is an important way in which the Koch donor network has manufactured the campus free speech crisis. These outlets weaponize a particular moralizing indignation over existing practices of academic inquiry and campus speech practices, demanding instead a radical libertarian free speech alternative. We first examine the platforms created by the Koch network to monitor higher education in particular, before turning to the broader right-wing media ecosystem that amplifies these "stories" to a wider audience.

CAMPUS REFORM (OPERATED BY THE LEADERSHIP INSTITUTE)

Campus Reform is one of the most inflammatory media outlets advancing the campus free speech narrative. Each of its "stories" includes a fundraising plea: "The radical left will stop at nothing to intimidate conservative students on college campuses," and the site claims to be "The #1 Source for College News." Campus Reform generates a steady stream of outrage stories about students protesting or disinviting speakers, campus speech codes and free speech zones, safe spaces and trigger warnings. It also posts numerous stories documenting the activities of Alliance Defend Freedom (ADF) and the Foundation for Individual Rights in Education (FIRE) in their free speech activism as well as reporting on free speech legislation making its way through state legislatures.

Founded in 2009, Campus Reform states its mission as "expos[ing] bias and abuse on the nation's college campuses" by reporting on "the conduct and misconduct of university administrators, faculty, and students."[13] Its goal is to "develop[ ] conservative students and young journalists into media and public policy professionals ... to launch their conservative media, communication, or public policy careers."[14] Campus Reform pays students between $50 to $100 to write stories about their campuses, with calls to action that include: "Get paid to hold your school accountable!" and "Be the eyes and ears on your campus. Launch your investigative journalism career!"[15] Campus Reform counts "victories" as those situations "in which a college changes a policy, fires someone, or otherwise responds to concerns raised by th[is] reporting."[16] Campus Reform solicits tips from "the Leadership Institute's network of nearly 1,600 conservative groups on college campuses,"[17] paying students $50 per tip.

Campus Reform also claims a number of alumni who have gone on to work at the Daily Caller, *Washington Examiner*, Daily Wire, *National Review*, Fox News, PragerU, and other mainstays in the libertarian donor-funded media ecosystem.[18] Campus Reform also serves as a "middleman" connecting Fox News with students who appear on the TV network's numerous segments demonizing higher education. For example, in March 2018, "Fox News ran at least 53 segments about controversies on college campuses, 40 of which were previously reported by Campus Reform. 15 of those 40 segments either cited Campus Reform explicitly, or contained an appearance from a Campus Reform correspondent."[19]

Campus Reform is a project of the Leadership Institute (LI), an organization created in 1979 by conservative activist Morton Blackwell. In its 2018 tax filings, the Leadership Institute reported a nearly $16

million operating budget. The LI uses these resources to provide training workshops and seminars to conservative student activists, offers
student groups funding to bring speakers and organizers to campus,
trains conservative candidates running for student government, and
helps establish conservative student newspapers.[20] The LI's National
Field Program boasts of supporting more than 1,700 college newspaper and student groups.[21] LI hosts international seminars to train
"freedom fighters" to "defeat the radical left."[22] The institute also offers
grants to students who want to bring "conservative or libertarian"
speakers to campus in order to "meet top leaders within the movement,
change policies, expose liberal bias, energize, educate and expand your
student group."[23] The LI takes pride in training journalists and conservative provocateurs to advance a right-wing agenda. Its alumni
include James O'Keefe, founder of the Koch-funded Project Veritas,
which uses falsely edited videos to attack ACORN, Planned Parent-
hood, and other organizations.[24] O'Keefe appears on LI fundraising
appeals, declaring that "The Left Wants to Ban All Conservatives."[25]
The Leadership Institute has also funded phony student groups to
bring O'Keefe to speak at college campuses,[26] and works closely with
other Koch network student groups. During the 2000s it "co-opted and
promoted" the then flailing YAF and helped revitalize it as a "brand
name for radical right-wing student activism."[27] LI also works with
Turning Point USA, which compiles its neo-McCarthyite "Professor
Watchlist" by drawing on articles published by Campus Reform, the
College Fix, David Horowitz's Freedom Center, and Project Veritas.[28]

Campus Reform clearly embodies the Powell and Koch view that
campuses are political battlefields. For example, former Campus
Reform editor-in-chief (and current host at Fox) Lawrence Jones
claims that "mob mentality" and "chaotic culture" on campus means
that "instead of battling it out with ideas, they resort to physical violence," and describes the Democratic Party as a "full-blown socialist
party that endorses Antifa, a domestic terrorist group."[29]

Much of the LI's funding comes from far-right donors, including
$2,588,106 from Koch family foundations, the Bradley Foundation,
DonorsTrust, and Donors Capital Fund.[30] The Koch Foundation and
Koch Institute routinely play a role in LI's "conservative intern work-
shops," and many staff members of the Charles Koch Foundation and
Koch Industries are guest speakers or volunteer faculty at the Insti-

tute, including Kevin Gentry (Koch Industries VP), Dave Dziok (Koch Industries), Reid Smith (CKI Foreign Policy Initiative manager), Catherine Rodriguez (CKI Talent Acquisition Business Partner), and Kasey Darling (CKI Partner Relations Specialist).[31]

THE COLLEGE FIX (OPERATED BY THE STUDENT
FREE PRESS ASSOCIATION)

The College Fix is another media platform created by right-wing activists to publish outrage stories about higher education. While claiming to be a source of "right-minded news and commentary," this outfit specializes in generating "provocative headlines [that] tend to be skeptical of higher education and frequently criticize the prevalence of liberalism on college campuses."[32] The College Fix claims to "help correct the bias that plagues our universities" by using "campus-focused journalism" to "bear witness to the ongoing scandal of political correctness and left-wing orthodoxy."[33] Like Campus Reform, the College Fix regularly runs stories documenting so-called free speech violations on campuses, and similarly employs a rhetoric of outrage and disbelief. The College Fix pays student "journalists" $50 per article.[34]

As with Campus Reform, many stories are horribly skewed or patently false. Furthermore, professors and students identified by the outlet have become routine targets of online harassment, often after exaggerated, rage-baiting headlines spread virally through conservative social media. Student Free Press Association's president John Miller boasted that "if you want to focus on political correctness on campus, it is the gift that just keeps on giving."[35]

Donors are invited to support its efforts to "[c]hallenge biased university administrators and academics," "expose campus radicalism," and "giv[e] alternative ideas and voices a chance to be heard."[36] And the College Fix explicitly states its aim as "creat[ing] a pipeline of talented and principled young people," noting that many of their student journalists also run campus chapters of Young Americans for Freedom.[37]

The College Fix is operated by the Student Free Press Association (SFPA), founded in 2010 by the *National Review*'s John Miller and the late Whitney Ball, the founder of DonorsTrust and Donors Capital Fund. SFPA was originally created as an "individual membership organization," comprised of "college-aged writers, bloggers, tweeters, podcasters, and viral video makers." SFPA claimed to "identify and support college students who seek to improve campus journalism, explore careers in the media, and commit themselves to the principles of a free society."[38] SFPA launched the College Fix in 2011 with an identical mission, minus any mention of the "individual membership organization."[39] This change occurred at the same time that wealthy outside donors replaced individual membership as the SFPA's primary funding source.

Between 2012 and 2019, SFPA received $1,802,653 from Koch family foundations, the Bradley Foundation, and DonorsTrust, and Donors Capital Fund.[40] The SFPA's board of directors features many donors with longstanding connections to the Koch network, including the president of Art Pope's charitable foundation and the son of Betsy and Dick DeVos.[41] The College Fix gave former Education Secretary Betsy DeVos effusively positive coverage without disclosing the conflict of interest.[42]

Stories published by Campus Reform and the College Fix regularly move from these campus-focused websites into the broader right-wing media ecosystem. For example, the College Fix boasts having had 6 million unique visitors in 2017–18, producing 2,000 original articles, that were cited more than 5,000 times. Their "reporting" often first circulates within a right-wing media ecosystem consisting of *National Review*, The Blaze, Breitbart, the Daily Caller, the Washington Free Beacon, Newsmax, WND, PJ Media, The Federalist, Fox News, and the Rush Limbaugh Show. After gaining momentum there, some stories even jump to the mainstream media, appearing in *The Wall Street Journal*, CBS, MSN, *The Washington Post*, and *The New York Times*, and even progressive media like *The Huffington Post* and *Slate*.[43]

We should not be surprised that the broader right-wing media ecosystem that widely circulates stories generated by Campus Reform and the College Fix is also heavily funded by the Koch donor network.

BREITBART NEWS

Breitbart News is a major outlet for the campus free speech narrative. It regularly republishes "stories" produced by Campus Reform, with headings such as "Students: American Exceptionalism 'Egotistical,' Repeal All Donald Trump's Policies," "Students Marching for

Gun Control Stumble When Asked to Define 'Assault Weapon,'" and "Students Hate Quotes from Trump's State of the Union, Until Realizing They Are Obama's."[44] It generates a nearly daily stream of stories about campus speech issues, including many featuring the activities of campus chapters of Turning Point USA and Young Americans for Freedom.[45]

The website also launched the careers of a number of provocative campus speakers, including Milo Yiannopoulos, Ben Shapiro, and others. Under Steve Bannon, Breitbart became a notoriously bigoted platform for the alt-right.[46] As Yiannopoulos and Shapiro traveled from campus to campus, Breitbart routinely published inflammatory articles about the ensuing protests, disinvitations, and controversies.

In 2011 Breitbart received at least $10 million in funding from hedge fund billionaire Robert Mercer.[47] Known for his extreme libertarian views, Mercer believes that an individual's wealth correlates with their value to society. As one colleague explained: "Bob believes that human beings have no inherent value other than how much money they make … If someone is on welfare they have negative value. If he earns a thousand times more than a schoolteacher, then he's a thousand times more valuable."[48] Robert and his daughter Rebekah not only funded Trump's presidential campaign but also the UK's pro-Brexit campaign and the data-mining company Cambridge Analytica, which engaged in voter manipulation during both elections.[49] Mercer has historically been an active member and large contributor at Koch's secretive donor seminars, donating at least $2.5 million to Koch's Freedom Partners Action Fund in 2014.[50]

THE DAILY CALLER

The Daily Caller was founded in 2010 when Tucker Carlson and Neil Patel received $3 million from Foster Friess, another central player within the Koch donor network.[51] The free speech advocacy group PEN America describes the Daily Caller as one of many conservative organizations—along with Fox News, Breitbart, The Blaze and others—that have engaged in a "widespread effort to fan the flames of outrage" about speech issues on campus.[52] The outlet has a long record of false and manufactured reporting, including releasing James O'Keefe's doctored videos and paying sex workers to lie about politicians.[53] The

Daily Caller's staff has not only embraced and fueled the alt-right, the site has also become a haven for white supremacists, including one of the organizers of the 2017 Charlottesville Unite the Right rally, Jason Kessler.[54] Earlier that year, the Daily Caller posted a video glibly glorifying cars running over protestors, which has since become a strategy of white supremacists, starting with the murder of Heather Heyer in Charlottesville.[55] After being pressured to resign from Breitbart News in 2017, Milo Yiannopoulos was briefly hired by the Daily Caller until the outlet was pressured to discontinue his column.[56]

The Daily Caller has proven highly profitable in large part due to its dubious funding arrangement. Most of its 50 reporters actually work for the Daily Caller News Foundation (DCNF), a non-profit tax-exempt entity. This 501(c)(3) generates most of the content published on the for-profit site.[57] As a result, tax-deductible donations to the DCNF—$3 million in 2015, for example—subsidize the for-profit business.[58] Conservative foundations have gone to great lengths to create a right-wing media "infrastructure."[59]

Between 2012 and 2019, the Daily Caller News Foundation received $3,739,693 from Koch family foundations, the Bradley Foundation, DonorsTrust, and Donors Capital Fund.[60] The Center for Media and Democracy (CMD) reports that the Trump campaign paid the DCNF $150,000 to use its email list during the 2016 presidential campaign.[61] In 2016, Koch donations and Trump's data purchase amounted to 97.5% of the DCNF's revenue.[62]

NATIONAL REVIEW

The *National Review* is a for-profit publication operated by the non-profit National Review Institute (NRI; see above). Since 2015, the *National Review* has advanced and normalized the campus free speech narrative, including publishing numerous stories about the horrors of safe spaces, microaggressions, institutional efforts to prioritize diversity and inclusion, and the perceived censorship of conservative voices on campus. In the past year alone, the *National Review* has published dozens of articles with titles such as "An Ominous New Rationale for Trampling on Academic Freedom," "Against Safe Spaces," and "Fix Free Speech or No Higher-Ed Act Reauthorization." In one 2019 fundraising request, titled "Help Us Fight Campus Craziness," *National Review* reporter Katherine Timpf writes:

> To me, it seems pretty obvious that socialism is terrible. After all, do you know what's *not* terrible? Freedom. But unfortunately, folks at colleges and universities all across the country seem to be favoring extreme government intervention—intervention that would come, of course, at the expense of *exactly* those freedoms that anyone with a brain knows we should cherish. So I'm asking you to do your part—by donating to National Review. Just how in the doggone heck are the two connected, you might ask? Well, National Review gives me a platform to expose and ridicule all of the craziness that goes on on campuses every day.[63]

The *National Review* also routinely reposts material about campus free speech generated by the American Enterprise Institute (Chapter 2) as well as editorials on free speech written by George Leef, director of editorial content at the Art Pope-funded James G. Martin Center for Academic Renewal.[64]

The NRI has hosted campus events on the issue of campus free speech. In April 2019, two writers for the *National Review*—David French and Alexandra DeSanctis (who previously wrote for the College Fix)—gave a talk at the University of Michigan entitled "Can Students be Civil and Still 'Own the Libs'?"[65]

Beginning in August 2016, NRI's campus programing included several events sponsored or hosted by the Charles Koch Institute, Young Americans for Liberty, American Enterprise Institute, Young Americans for Freedom, Heritage Foundation, and other groups within the Koch network. David French was the former president of the Foundation for Individual Rights in Education (FIRE) and serves as senior counsel for the Alliance Defending Freedom (ADF; Chapter 5). In 2010 he "head[ed] efforts to restore the marketplace of ideas to university campuses, concentrating his litigation on religious freedom issues."[66] In 2017, French was an outspoken supporter of ADF when the Southern Poverty Law Center labeled it a hate group.[67] He was also a senior counsel for the American Center for Law and Justice, an anti-LGBTQ+ litigation group founded by Pat Robertson that, alongside

ADF, has defended anti-sodomy laws in the United States and pushes for criminalizing homosexuality in foreign countries.[68]

The NRI has also been active in the creation of campus free speech legislation. As explored in Chapter 6, the outlet was a powerful platform for *National Review* contributing editor Stanley Kurtz's "Plan to Restore Free Speech on Campus," which became the platform to criss-cross the country and give the legislative testimony to advance the model legislation he produced with the Goldwater Institute.[69] The National Review Institute is a member of the State Policy Network and received $250,000 from the Bradley Foundation (2011–15) to fund a fellowship program, which trained journalists who would go on to work for other SPN-member organizations.[70] It received $3,027,079 from the Koch family foundations, the Bradley Foundation, DonorsTrust, and Donors Capital Fund between 1998 and 2019.[71] A comparison of 990s shows that these donations have increased dramatically during the past decade, including a $1.2 million increase between 2018 and 2019. The Koch donor network's fingerprints are all over NRI's governance, with Richard DeVos personally sitting on its board of trustees.[72] Between 2011 and 2015, the Bradley Foundation donated $250,000 to the National Review Institute to fund the Thomas L. Rhodes Journalism Fellowship.

REAL CLEAR POLITICS

Real Clear Politics—probably best known outside the right-wing media ecosystem for its poll aggregation—is published by David Des-Rosiers, former Executive VP of the Manhattan Institute and Senior Fellow at the Manhattan Institute's Center for the American University.[73] George Mason University law professor F.H. Buckley describes DesRosiers as "the spitting image of the late Andrew Breitbart, with the same ebullience, the same energy and the same network of friends and allies. He knows everyone who matters on the right."[74] Real Clear Politics routinely runs headlines such as "Death of Campus Free Speech," "Stop Soft Despotism Stifling Campus Free Speech," "Colleges' Central Mission Erodes—and Free Speech With It," and "Wokeness, Free Speech, and the Role of Education." The outlet's panel of "Campus Speech Experts" includes provocateurs like Charles Murray and

Heather MacDonald, officers from Students for Liberty and Young Americans for Liberty, as well as litigation groups that sue on behalf of students and speakers, including the Alliance Defending Freedom, Foundation for Individual Rights in Education, and Speech First (Chapter 5).[75] Between 2014 and 2019, the Real Clear Foundation, the non-profit that supports Real Clear Politics, received $6,376,000 from Koch family foundations, DonorsTrust, and Donors Capital Fund.[76]

WASHINGTON EXAMINER

The *Washington Examiner*, a conservative weekly paper and website owned by Koch network donor Philip Anschutz, is known for its arch-conservative editorial page. Anschutz made his intentions clear when he started the paper in 2005—he only wanted conservatives on the op-ed page.[77] When Anschutz's other Washington-based conservative publication—*The Weekly Standard*—closed in 2018, the reliably pro-Trump *Washington Examiner* absorbed the subscriber base.[78] The paper regularly publishes misleading pieces on climate change, and was responsible for the false story prior to the 2018 midterm elections about prayer rugs found on the border with Mexico.[79] The paper regularly runs headlines such as "College Editors Turn Journalism Into Cuddly Kumbaya," "200 Colleges Use 'Speech Bullies' to Prevent 'Hurt Feelings,'" as well as a piece by Heather MacDonald, a fellow at the Manhattan Institute, titled "The Outrage Mob Came for Me at Emory University. Here's How to Stop It."

The Anschutz Foundation's 990s show additional funding for organizations directly involved in the campus free speech narrative, including the Young America's Foundation. Anschutz has given more than $5 million to members affiliated with the State Policy Network, including American Enterprise Institute, the Manhattan Institute, and DonorsTrust. He has attended at least one Koch network donor summit, in 2010.[80] A highly diversified industrialist, Anschutz owns the lucrative music festival Coachella. He provided at least $170,000 to the anti-LGBTQ+ hate group Alliance Defending Freedom between 2011 and 2014, but cut ties after public pressure on his music festival forced his hand.[81]

CHARLES KOCH FOUNDATION DIRECT INVESTMENTS

The Charles Koch Foundation also directly funds a number of efforts to legitimize the manufactured notion of a campus free speech crisis. For example, Big Think is a TED Talk-like website and YouTube channel that produces video content of academics and public intellectuals offering particular takes on the big ideas of the day.[82] In addition to a failed "educational media venture" called Floating University[83] and its subscription-based self-help courses, Big Think specializes in science-themed clickbait. It also increasingly publishes material that feeds into the campus free speech crisis narrative. In addition to the "Civil Discourse" series sponsored by the Institute for Humane Studies, it also hosts a number of Jordan Peterson videos, including the site's second most popular video in 2018—"The Fatal Flaw Lurking in American Leftist Politics"—in which Peterson claims that the right has successfully drawn a distinction between itself and white nationalists but the left lacks any guiding principles and therefore remains unable to root out its own extremism (which he characterizes as the pathological triumvirate of inclusion, equity, and diversity).[84]

In 2018, Big Think began producing sponsored content for the Charles Koch Foundation.[85] The material includes videos of university professors discussing various issues concerning free speech, including Jonathan Haidt on the need to treat students as "anti-fragile." These videos are framed alongside an essay titled "Forced Examination: How the Free Speech of Others Benefits us All," which draws upon a Cato Institute study arguing that Americans feel unable to express their political ideas.

In addition to sponsoring content at Big Think, the Charles Koch Foundation also paid to normalize its campus free speech narrative within more traditional media outlets. In 2018, the foundation announced a partnership with *The Atlantic* on a project entitled "The Speech Wars."[86] In parallel to Koch's more alarmist free speech programming, the project was a year-long series of events "exploring questions of American free expression and public discourse."[87] The *Chronicle of Higher Education* also published a paid advertisement "How to Handle Controversial Speakers on Campus." Made to look like Chronicle-produced content, the small disclaimers at the bottom of the page clarified that "[t]his content was paid for and created by The Institute for Humane Studies."[88]

In her contribution to the edited book *Disinformation Age*, Nancy MacLean documents how the Koch network relies on spreading disinformation, especially when it regularly confronts the fact that its preferred policy outcomes remain highly unpopular, and therefore are unlikely to become law though "honest persuasion and organizing."[89] MacLean writes that "operations funded by Koch and his wealthy allies ... have relied on disinformation and manipulation to advance their agenda of radical transformation, leveraging the specter of a supposedly threatening 'liberal elite' and strategic racism ... to compensate for lack of persuasive evidence."[90]

Such disinformation, designed to achieve political goals, should not be mistaken for a good faith discussion of ideas. Instead, news outlets within the right-wing media ecosystem regularly assert that academic arguments they disagree with (on political grounds) are groundless, crazy, and unworthy of consideration. For example, they routinely refuse to treat academic critiques of systemic racism, white supremacy, patriarchy, whiteness, and intersectionality as robust theoretical and historical arguments, preferring instead to boil them down to examples of "playing the victim card." They routinely dismiss as outrageous the various student, faculty, staff, and administrative demands to balance campus speech rights against very real concerns about safety and inclusions. The Koch-funded outrage machine routinely presents caricatures of these complex debates, ignoring decades of actual scholarship, often done by LGBTQ+, female, and scholars of color. Instead, these outlets insist that they be taken seriously based on an absolutist notion of free speech, in which their baseless claims and mischaracterizations carry equal (or more!) weight as those of the academics they unfairly lampoon. The goal is to whip up outrage not engage in good faith debate on issues of social importance.

Furthermore, because the right-wing media ecosystem often targets scholars who are themselves LGBTQ+, female, and/or scholars of color, the smug notion that these academic arguments do not, on their face, merit actual engagement is itself a supremacist claim.[91]

When following the money it becomes evident that the disinformation and outrage over higher education manufactured within the Koch-funded right-wing media ecosystem is actually part of a broader

political strategy. Those in the middle third—including many journalists, faculty, administrators, and the broader public—often naively
respond to the maelstrom of right-wing outrage by calling for "more
free speech!" and "more civil debate!" This equally absolutist response,
however, misses the fact that the so-called campus free speech crisis
does not revolve around some principled disagreement between liberals and conservatives.

While good faith debates over speech can (and do) happen on
campus all the time, they rarely do so within the right-wing media
ecosystem, which instead refines outrage into a narrative about an out-
of-control campus free speech crisis. This supposed crisis, however, is
actually manufactured; initiated by Koch-funded student groups, exe-
cuted by Koch-funded provocateurs, and amplified by Koch-funded
media outlets.

This manufactured outrage produces more than shock value,
however. It becomes the raw material that is refined into social change,
used by legal groups to sue colleges (Chapter 5) and by think tanks and
policy groups to advance legislation that further exposes universities
to donor influence (Chapter 6).

5

The Lawyers

The Koch network's long-term strategy of social change is not simply concerned with changing short-term public opinion. Rather, it seeks durable policy change that can be locked in and reliably leveraged. It should not be surprising, therefore, that Koch network donors also fund an array of organizations that help student groups file free speech lawsuits against colleges and universities. As described in Chapter 2, Koch-funded student groups regularly engage in lawsuits over alleged free speech violations. They often pursue legal action in coordination with organizations that specialize in litigating campus free speech.

These non-profit litigation groups generally present themselves as non-partisan organizations created to defend students against out-of-control administrations hostile to conservative campus speech. In practice they pressure universities into enforced compliance with a highly partisan—and billionaire-funded—libertarian notion of free speech absolutism.

Often lost in the barrage of litigation are good-faith campus efforts to carefully deliberate over how academic institutions should engage in the difficult work of both protecting speech and ensuring that universities remain hospitable to those targeted by harassment and hate speech. This is a difficult tension to navigate, and one that most institutions spend considerable time and energy trying to negotiate within institutional governance committees.

Koch-funded non-profit legal organizations, however, litigate a one-size-fits-all free speech absolutist position making it difficult for institutions to tackle this deliberative work. Instead, partisan litigation outfits often short circuit institutional governance efforts by using their external legal firepower to impose a libertarian understanding of free speech.

As foreseen by Lewis Powell, the language of free speech has become a particularly powerful and well-crafted cudgel that allows corporate funders to win a war of position within higher education, ultimately seeking to exert greater donor control over what is taught and researched. The origins of this legal strategy date back many decades to the collaborations between the corporate, anti-New Deal lawyers working together with anti-civil rights lawyers.

THE LEGAL MOVEMENT AGAINST CIVIL RIGHTS

Organizations funded by the Koch network have not only helped advance pro-corporate policy change like tax reform and deregulation but have also worked to roll back progressive gains made by the civil rights movement. Lee Cokorinos's 2003 study examined the "concerted effort mounted by sophisticated private organizations" to wage political, intellectual, and legal attacks on civil rights. The main donors identified at the time, the Bradley, Olin, Scaife, and Smith Richardson foundations, supported aggressive litigation groups including the Center for Individual Rights, Institute for Justice, American Civil Rights Institute, Center for Equal Opportunity, the Federalist Society's Civil Rights Practice Group, Pacific Legal Foundation, Southeastern Legal Foundation, and Mountain States Legal Foundation. These groups, many of which receive considerable funding from the Koch donor network, engaged in protracted legal battles with public institutions, looking to "erode the legal abilities of these institutions to practice affirmative action and promote diversity as a matter of policy."[1]

They sought to systematically "[p]recipitate a series of crises" between policymakers on different levels of government, or between different branches of government, in an attempt to "overturn some of the fundamental decisions protecting civil rights."[2] They championed individual liberty as the pretense for reversing the gains won by decades of mass organizing, civil disobedience, and civil rights litigation. More broadly, in the interest of their corporate donors, these groups sought to "turn a wave of public sentiment" into opposition to government regulations as part of a broader effort to "fundamentally transform the American public sector by eliminating the regulatory infrastructure."[3]

Since 2003, various groups within the Koch network have participated in these legal battles seeking to roll back voting rights, dismantle affirmative action, and legalize discrimination. Kimberly Dennis, founding chair of DonorsTrust and board member of Donors Capital Fund, described how their "biggest victories lately have come in the legal arena," including Supreme Court cases they funded resulting in decisions on "voting rights," as well as "environmental regulation, education, and health care."[4] She notes that two of their most aggressive legal operations to roll back voting rights have been the Project on Fair Representation and the Center for Individual Rights (CIR). Tax documents reveal that both are supported almost entirely by DonorsTrust and Donors Capital Fund.

In 2013, the US Supreme Court's *Shelby County v. Holder* decision gutted the Voting Rights Act, allowing states to more easily disenfranchise voters. The case was brought by the Project on Fair Representation, a legal defense fund created to support litigation in state and federal courts that challenges "racial and ethnic classifications and preferences" in voting, education, federal contracts, and employment.[5] The project was founded and housed within DonorsTrust itself and led by American Enterprise Institute fellow Edward Blum.[6]

The Project on Fair Representation also brought *Fischer v. University of Texas* to the Supreme Court, which would have dismantled affirmative action in universities across the country. Following that case, Blum launched an offshoot group called Students for Fair Admissions to oppose racial classifications in admissions in order to "restore the original principles of our nation's civil rights movement."[7]

Using civil rights movement tactics backed by a gusher of corporate funding, Blum sought out plaintiffs in the *Shelby County* and *Fisher* cases and "persuaded them to file suit, matched them with lawyers, and secured funding to appeal the cases all the way to the high court."[8] The project has been funded by the Searle Freedom Trust and the Bradley Foundation, and Blum confirmed a recent $100,000 donation from the latter for the project after he "wrote them a pitch letter."[9] Just a year before the Shelby County case dismantled the Voting Rights Act, the Supreme Court declined to review *Nix v. Holder*, a similar case brought by the Center for Individual Rights (CIR).[10]

Looking at CIR demonstrates how Koch donors have been influential in creating a right-wing legal movement that drapes itself in the language of a new civil rights movement. This conservative legal movement is concerned with protecting persecuted conservatives and defending a radical libertarian notion of individual liberty and personal freedom from the supposed evils of state imposition (including state-mandated integration and equal access). This well-funded legal operation has taken particular aim at political, legal, and social victories that have resulted from decades of democratic struggle in the pursuit of racial justice and equality. Higher education, and free speech in particular, have proven a particularly fertile terrain for mounting this legal assault.

CIR was founded in 1989 by two law professors, Michael Greve and Jeremy Rabkin, at George Mason University. CIR's mission is to pursue an aggressive "defense of individual liberties against the increasingly aggressive and unchecked authority of federal and state governments."[11] According to documents released as part of the tobacco settlements during the 1990s, shortly after its founding CIR appealed to the tobacco industry for funding. In its introductory letter, CIR described its strategy as "mount[ing] legal challenges to [government] agency actions that constrict individual freedom or trammel upon protected economic rights" as well as protecting corporate free speech in "broadcasting, campaign finance, higher education, and advertising." Acknowledging that they also received funding from the petroleum industry (ARCO and Chevron), CIR made its funding appeal to tobacco based on the fact that it only pursues "cases that present novel constitutional issues in carefully selected areas of the law: primarily economic regulation and Freedom of Speech."[12]

In many ways CIR has engineered the conservative legal movement's strategy of weaponizing free speech to push back against demands for racial equality in higher education. CIR is highly aggressive in its practices, often seeking to set legal precedents as radically and quickly as possible, even asking lower courts to "rule against their own clients" so that the case can move "up to the Supreme Court as quickly as possible."[13] Civil rights activist and attorney Theodore Cross documented CIR's "Racial Goals" in higher education, exemplified by their ads placed in at least 15 campus newspapers urging white students to sue their school "even if they had no proof that they were being discriminated against."[14] Cross described CIR's use of "staged litigation, deceptive public statements, and incitements of racial fears" as the stated excuse for their larger goal of "ethnically reengineering" college admissions in a manner that would "remove most African Americans from our leading colleges." In this way, CIR's goals are "far less concerned with equal treatment of the races than with guarding the interests of segregationists and protecting the established economic and class advantages that enable whites to maintain their superior access to the leading colleges in the United States."[15]

In their 1996–97 Annual Report, CIR celebrated its ongoing and successful litigation, which included challenging the Voting Rights Act and the Violence Against Women Act, protecting the use of offensive speech in the workplace, suing colleges and universities to strike down affirmative action, ending race-based hiring preferences and gender-based wage increases, and defending harassment in the classroom in the name of free speech. The report opens with a quote from *Washington City Paper*:

> When the history of the anti-P.C. backlash is written, there will be chapters reserved for the *Wall Street Journal* editorial page, Rush Limbaugh, Charles Murray, and, no doubt, Washington, D.C.'s own Center for Individual Rights.[16]

In fact, CIR pioneered the strategy of targeting universities by deploying free speech arguments to push back on other popular student and faculty demands that universities take active measures to ensure equal access to marginalized populations. During the 1980s and 1990s scholarship within various academic fields (including feminism and critical race theory) combined with considerable student and faculty activism to push colleges and universities to develop codes regulating hate speech. They also pressed colleges and universities to promote campus diversity, admit a more diverse student population, and protect students from bigoted abuse on campus.[17] By the end of the 1980s, 60 percent of American institutions of higher education had created hate speech codes of some kind.[18]

During the same period, the right pushed back against these efforts, belittling them as "Political Correctness." Even though, in reality, the "successes achieved by communities of color, women, and other subordinated groups" remained "extremely modest," these marginalized groups nonetheless faced a massive and orchestrated backlash designed to preserve educational institutions as "run by and for white male elites."[19] This time, however, the backlash did not draw upon the "gutter hate speech" of previous generations but came wrapped in libertarian and neoliberal tropes of valuing "merit" over diversity and insisting upon the superiority of "great books" and "Western Civilization" over efforts to diversify the canon.[20]

Within this context, CIR capitalized on the "PC" backlash in higher education to carve out areas of legal specialization. At the time CIR was actively looking for a set of issues from which to launch its "broad critique of the administrative state, and [advance] a set of roughly libertarian principles." It dabbled in libel law but found this venue difficult terrain since prosecution of cases requires overcoming high standards of evidence.[21] However, the "arrival of the 'PC craze' solved this problem." On the one hand, suing colleges and universities over free speech, hiring practices, and affirmative action "provided a happy hunting ground ... allow[ing] CIR to adopt a posture of defending individuals against large, oppressive organizations." On the other hand, deploying the First Amendment constituted what CIR founder Michael Greve called "a big constitutional club."[22] Greve acknowledged in a letter to his Olin Foundation funders that this issue was strategically useful for conservative legal activists precisely because "the 'PC' movement is really the first issue that has split the left on campus. This opportunity should be exploited: the more of a wedge we can drive between heretofore closely aligned leftist constituencies, the better."[23]

In 1992, the CIR successfully won *R.A.V. v. City of St. Paul* in the US Supreme Court, striking down St. Paul's citywide ordinance against bias-motivated crimes as "aimed at the selective suppression of politically disfavored 'hate speech.'" In this case CIR represented a teen convicted of burning a cross on the lawn of his Black neighbors. The Supreme Court overturned his conviction on the grounds that the ordinance's definition of prohibited acts was unconstitutionally broad, and not sufficiently viewpoint neutral. CIR later claimed that this particular case has "led to the invalidation of dozens of college and university speech codes."[24]

While CIR would go on to specialize in anti-affirmative action lawsuits, it nonetheless pioneered the strategy of combining culture war outrage with free speech moralism. It created the space for the next generation of campus litigation groups to sue universities over free speech zones and speech codes, as well as student programs and campus orientations designed to advance inclusion and equity within the academy.

Subsequent Koch network organizations would also harness "political correctness," and more recently an outrage over "cancel culture"
and "critical race theory," to advance their similarly individualist and
absolutist notions of free speech. Well-funded external legal groups
routinely sue schools into submission, demanding that they adhere to
an understanding of free speech that does not account for an analysis of power differentials, institutional contexts, or the broader social
benefits that might come from also prioritizing equal access and the
development of thoughtful regulation.

FOUNDATION FOR INDIVIDUAL RIGHTS IN EDUCATION
(FIRE)

Like the founders of CIR, University of Pennsylvania professor Alan
Charles Kors also became engaged in campus free speech issues during
the 1990s culture wars. His entrée came while defending a student who
yelled to a group of Black sorority sisters socializing outside his dorm
window: "Shut up, you black water buffalo!" and "If you want to party,
there's a zoo a mile from here."[25] Rather than counselling the student
to apologize and participate in campus diversity programming, Kors
advised him to contest the charges against him. The student admitted
to saying everything other than the word "black." When Kors leaked
this edited version of the story, the narrative was amplified by right-
wing media, stirring up a national debate over whether "water buffalo"
and "zoo" are racialized words. The women ultimately dropped their
charges stating that, in addition to being victimized by racial slurs,
they were "further victimized by the media, and thereafter by the judicial process and agents of the university."[26]

In 1998, Kors published *The Shadow University: The Betrayal of
Liberty On America's Campuses*, with Boston lawyer Harvey Silverglate. The book traffics in standard 1990s culture war anecdotes about
"political correctness" run amok and considerable handwringing over
all the "-isms bandied about—'racism' and 'sexism,' to be sure, but also
'postmodernism' and 'multiculturalism.'"[27] The book also lays out a
blueprint for using the legal system to change university policy. In a
chapter titled "Sue the Bastards?," Kors suggests a strategy of intimidating university administrators into compliance with libertarian
speech ideals. Kors and Silverglate note that a student lawsuit triggers

the "extraordinary process of 'discovery,'" which becomes a "nightmare for administrators and their general counsel." During discovery, students and their lawyers can compel administrators to "answer questions under oath" and produce "[d]ocuments otherwise hidden securely in university files." Kors assured his readers that few campuses that "persecute their politically incorrect students and professors can withstand this searching, profoundly invasive inquiry." Even in cases "where the plaintiff eventually loses," universities are "notoriously hesitant to engage in protracted litigation," and will likely settle out of court. The book concluded with the warning that academia "will have to answer for its betrayal of the nation's and its own traditions."[28]

The following year, Kors presented a lecture, later published by the Institute for Humane Studies, calling on his peers to "fight" against "multiculturalists" on campus, whom he referred to as "barbarians in our midst," and threats to the survival of Western civilization. Because Marxism had collapsed "everywhere but at Western universities," he saw it as necessary to actively promote the "great defenders" of free markets like Mises, Hayek and Friedman, whom he worried were "unexplored, marginalized, or dismissed as absurd" within the academy.[29]

Following the success of *The Shadow University*, Kors and Silverglate established the Foundation for Individual Rights in Education (FIRE) in 1999. With seed funding from the Bradley Foundation, they brought their free speech "sue the bastards" strategy to colleges and universities.[30] FIRE's litigation track record is so impressive that today they often need only send a threatening legal letter to university administrators to secure capitulation and policy change. In 2009, FIRE's Adam Kissel—who later became a program officer at the Charles Koch Foundation—closed a typical threat letter to University of Chicago's president with: "FIRE hopes to resolve this matter amicably and swiftly, but we are prepared to use all of our resources to see this situation through to a just and moral conclusion."[31]

In the years since, FIRE has remained faithful to Kors' culture war agenda. Its current president, Greg Lukianoff, built a career with several campus culture war books published by Encounter Books (a publisher founded with seed money from the Bradley Foundation).[32] In 2015, Lukianoff and Jonathan Haidt published "The Coddling of the American Mind" in *The Atlantic*, and later a book of the same title.

The piece relies on a series of anecdotes to demonstrate that campus policies prioritize "emotional well-being" in a way that "presumes an extraordinary fragility of the collegiate psyche" and excessively "elevates the goal of protecting students from psychological harm." Without engaging with or even acknowledging the actual documented patterns and effects of sexism, racism, and homophobia, the authors dismiss "allegedly racist, sexist, classist, or otherwise discriminatory microaggressions" on campus as the "magnification" and "labeling" of a problem that is either not real or is highly overstated.[33]

It should be noted that FIRE claims to be non-partisan and has regularly advocated for progressive faculty members who have experienced wrongful retaliation at the hands of their institution, including recently Garrett Felber and Lora Burnett. They also agree with the American Civil Liberties Union (ACLU) in a number of policy areas. As pointed out by PEN America, FIRE presents itself as non-partisan, with a staff that holds "a range of political leanings."[34] Lukianoff himself, for example, is a former ACLU First Amendment lawyer and self-proclaimed liberal Democrat.[35] The PEN report, however, also acknowledges that because FIRE is the largest group to focus solely on campus speech issues it enjoys a high level of visibility in this arena and, because "the most vociferous defenders of campus free speech are conservative or libertarian, it is becoming increasingly common to see [FIRE's] efforts to defend free expression described as part of a right-leaning agenda."[36]

The association between FIRE and a right-leaning political agenda is more than a matter of perception, however. In addition to receiving considerable funding from the Koch donor network, FIRE also shares an anti-PC and free speech absolutist position similar to that of right-wing legal entities such as CIR. Jim Sleeper, a journalist and lecturer in political science at Yale, notes that FIRE remains closely connected to the Koch donor networks "by virtue of its funding, many of its personnel, and most importantly, its strategy and tactics."[37]

In terms of strategy, FIRE plays into the political rhetoric of campus political correctness run amok. In its original registration with Guide-Star the group quite candidly states that it seeks to challenge an "academy [that] has been taken over by ignorance of and hostility toward individual liberty, and a culture of censorship and coddling has sponsored the rise of 'safe spaces,' calls to police 'trigger warnings' and 'microaggressions,' and even violence in the face of unpopular opinions."[38] Its president, Lukianoff, has continued this narrative of coddled students, not only in his own publications but also in his approach to campus controversy. For example, at a 2015 free speech conference at Yale's William F. Buckley, Jr. Program, Lukianoff mentioned the campus firestorm around Yale lecturer Erika Christakis, who criticized an administrative email calling for racial awareness in relation to Halloween costumes, such as avoiding Native American headdresses.[39] In his presentation, Lukianoff quipped "you would have thought someone wiped out an entire Indian village."[40] When Yale students heard about this, they protested outside the conference, chanting "Genocide is not a joke."[41] Lukianoff took a video of a Black protestor yelling at Erika's husband, Nicholas Christakis, which was later posted on Tucker Carlson's Daily Caller website, along with a picture of the student's $700,000 family house and the headline "Meet the Privileged Yale Student Who Shrieked at Her Professor."[42]

As with most campus free speech controversies the context is actually much more nuanced than the "coddled student" narrative that launched FIRE and which Lukianoff perpetuated in his glib aside. Student protests over Christakis's email, and later Lukianoff's comments, actually took place within the "two-year student uprising" by students of color at Yale "to demand respect and equality".[43] Lukianoff and FIRE, however, repeatedly portrayed the issue simply through the lens of a single video of a single student yelling, and successfully crafted the false narrative that students were actively organizing to have Nicholas and Erika Christakis fired.[44] FIRE's coverage—as with most media representations of the event—simply conflated heated speech at one protest with a widely held student position, while also ignoring the context in which that protest took place. FIRE nonetheless patronizingly commented that while "Yale students have every right to express their anger and frustration with Yale faculty … FIRE is concerned by yet another unfortunate example of students who demand upsetting opinions be entirely eradicated from the university in the name of fostering 'safe spaces' where students are protected from hurt feelings."[45]

In addition to shared culture war rhetoric and commitments to an absolutist notion of free speech, FIRE's leadership and benefactors also enjoy considerable overlap with the Koch donor network. Kors spent more than a decade serving as a faculty member at the Institute for Humane Studies. Leonard Liggio, longtime IHS president, served on FIRE's advisory board. Kors was also involved in more overtly political activities, leading seminars and lecturing during at least ten "judicial junkets" held at George Mason University's Law and Economics Center, where corporate academics facilitate closed door classes on business-friendly interpretations of law for state and federal judges. Until 2011, Kors was also a senior fellow at the Goldwater Institute, which played a critical role in writing model free speech legislation that punished student protestors (discussed in the next chapter). Kors has also spent more than a decade on the advisory board of the James Martin Center for Academic Renewal (formerly the John Pope Center for Higher Education), a North Carolina think tank founded by Koch network donor Art Pope.[46]

Funding from Koch network donors to FIRE has surged as the free speech "crisis" has blossomed, totaling $13,676,511 from Koch family foundations, the Bradley Foundation, DonorsTrust, and Donors Capital Fund between 2000 and 2019.[47]

In 2005, FIRE began their "Spotlight" project, ranking campus speech policies with a red, yellow, or green light. Their first Spotlight report in 2006 gave 90 percent of schools yellow or red rankings.[48] By 2009, 95 percent of their growing list of schools were yellow or red Light.[49] One scholar who double-checked FIRE's work detailed how this ranking consistently exaggerated their claims, "failing to distinguish enforceable rules from exhortative statements, confusing examples with definitions, and taking statements out of context."[50] In 2014, FIRE launched its Stand Up For Speech Litigation Project, consisting of "targeted First Amendment lawsuits" against public universities to "eliminate unconstitutional speech codes."[51]

Koch-funded student groups often enlist FIRE's help in suing administrations over responses to their top-down activism or campus talks by speaker provocateurs. Since 2012, FIRE has intervened or sued on behalf of Young Americans for Liberty chapters at least 14 times, including at Modesto Junior College, the University of Hawaii at Hilo, and Los Angeles Pierce College, where students sued after campus officials prevented them from handing out pocket-sized copies of the Constitution outside of free speech zones. All but one campus settled out of court and paid $50,000, while Los Angeles's Pierce College paid $225,000.[52] In 2012, after the University of Cincinnati's speech policies were targeted by FIRE's Spotlight project, the school's YAL chapter sued to abolish the school's free speech zones with the help of FIRE and the 1851 Center for Constitutional Law. The YAL students sued after they were prevented from gathering signatures in support of a statewide "Right to Work" ballot initiative spearheaded by the Center.[53]

FIRE has defended Young Americans for Freedom at least seven times since 2012, including at DePaul University, where it threatened litigation over attempts to obstruct visits by Ben Shapiro and Milo Yiannopoulos.[54] At the height of Yiannopoulos's turbulent US tour in 2017, FIRE threatened action if administrators at the University of New Mexico refused to waive the extra security costs.[55] And FIRE has repeatedly intervened to pressure students and administrators into recognizing Turning Point USA chapters at Hagerstown Community College, Northwestern University, Santa Clara University, and the University of Scranton, even as Turning Point USA's racism and manipulation of student elections was becoming increasingly public.[56]

Much of FIRE's work rests on the absolutist assumption that any limits to campus speech—such as speech codes, harassment policies, and free speech zones—are violations of free speech. This position precludes an institution's legitimate authority to regulate speech that threatens its mission, which includes—according to Title IX—the legal requirement to ensure people of all backgrounds feel welcome and safe within the campus community. Even when a campus capitulates to its deregulatory litigation, FIRE often follows up with additional pressure to further undermine the non-punitive alternatives developed to address hate speech on campus.

For example, some campuses have developed bias-reporting programs to track incidents, determine whether they constitute actual crimes, and to identify and support victims. In a 2017 study of 471 schools in its Spotlight database, FIRE identified 181 campuses with bias-response programs. It went on to criticize these efforts as violating free speech.[57] For example, the University of Kentucky's bias-response team monitors "activity that intimidates, demeans, mocks, degrades, marginalizes, or threatens individuals or groups."[58] A university representative affirmed "[t]here is no penalty for exercising your free speech rights on our campus," but the university pledged to "provide support to those who feel targeted by hurtful speech" and to speak "in opposition when someone uses speech or words to hurt or harm, to demean or denigrate."[59] Even though FIRE acknowledges that this team plays no role in disciplinary decisions, they nonetheless described this policy in terms of an Orwellian "speech police" and "mini-surveillance state" that asks students to report "their neighbors, friends, and professors for any instances of biased speech and expression."[60]

In addition to attacking bias-reporting mechanisms, FIRE has also taken aim at first-year orientations and "mandatory diversity 'training' that aims to intimidate students into abandoning deeply held beliefs ... [about] race, sex, and sexuality in our society." It calls these programs "[i]deologically tilted speech codes that privilege one point of view over others."[61]

FIRE has successfully presented itself as non-partisan, pointing to a diverse board and a willingness to take up campus free speech issues on the left. However, its culture war origins, Koch funding, and its brand of free speech absolutism make it one of the most effective—and well-funded—legal non-profits pushing the campus free speech narrative. Law professor Mary Anne Franks notes that FIRE is "one of the loudest voices proclaiming a state of emergency for freedom of expression in higher education," despite the fact that its own evidence does not support these claims. She attributes this "stark discrepancy between the rhetoric and the reality" to the interests of the "individuals who constitute FIRE's leadership and provide its funding."[62]

Other spin-off litigation groups, however, are even more explicitly partisan and similarly enjoy deep ties to the Koch donor network.

SPEECH FIRST

Speech First is a legal organization with the stated mission of "protect[ing] students' free speech rights on campus" through "advocacy, litigation, and other means," and to "put colleges and universities on notice that shutting down unwanted speech will no longer be tolerated."[63] Created in February 2018, at a time when white nationalist groups like the American Identity Movement were ramping up recruitment efforts on campus and campus hate crimes were on the rise, Speech First specializes in challenging bias-response teams and campus hate speech policies.[64]

The organization's first lawsuit took aim at the University of Michigan's bias-response team, created to "report and respond to discrimination claims such as white-supremacist leafleting and racist graffiti."[65] The lawsuit claimed that the UM team created an environment in which students "could face severe punishment" for voicing "a controversial or unpopular opinion" or using "humor, parody, or satire when discussing sensitive topics."[66] The university responded that the suit was "a false caricature" of its policies and practices.[67] A month later, a US District Court judge dismissed the injunction, agreeing that "there is no credible fear of punishment" from the bias-response team, "thus there is no harm to students' rights if its actions are not enjoined."[68] Before the District Court could dismiss the lawsuit, however, the university was frightened into clarifying to students that campus policy does allow students to engage in hate speech. Resident life employees were instructed that if someone puts racist or hateful speech on their dorm room door, they cannot be asked to take it down.[69] And, after Speech First appealed, the university ultimately capitulated and completely disbanded the response teams.

Speech First has since sued other schools, including Iowa State University, over their bias-response programs, leading administrators to agree to its policy recommendations out of court.[70] In 2019, Speech First sued the University of Texas at Austin over its ban on verbal harassment, arguing that the school's definition of what counts as "'offensive,' 'biased,' 'uncivil,' or 'rude'" is overly broad.[71] The case was initially dismissed when a District Court judge found that the anonymous students Speech First represented could not prove that the non-disciplinary policy actually chilled speech.[72] This ruling was later reversed, and the parties reached a settlement with UT in which it agreed to disband its bias-reporting system. Speech First's lawsuit received numerous amicus briefs on behalf of organizations also funded by the Koch donor network, including Independent Women's Forum, Pacific Legal Foundation, Southeastern Legal Foundation, Goldwater Institute, Cato Institute, Foundation for Individual Rights in Education, and the Alliance Defending Freedom.[73]

Speech First presents itself as a "nationwide community of students, parents, faculty, alumni, and concerned citizens."[74] However, its funding and corporate board show its considerable integration within the Koch donor network. While the organization claims to be powered

by \$5 membership fees, journalists have noted that the group oper-
ates more like "a highly professional astroturfing campaign."[75] Speech
First works with the notorious right-wing public relations firm Creative Response Concepts, best known for their "Swift Boat Veterans"
attacks on John Kerry and for spreading misinformation about Dr.
Christine Blasey Ford's sexual assault allegations against Brett Kavana-
ugh.[76] We know very little about the dark money bankrolling Speech
First, but the group's president has admitted that student memberships
"make up a 'negligible part' of its funding, which mainly comes from
undisclosed backers."[77] The Judicial Education Project (JEP), a Koch
network legal reform group, has provided Speech First and Creative
Response Concepts with more than \$2 million.[78]

In addition to funding, there is also considerable overlap between
the leadership of Speech First and the Koch network. Speech First's
executive director, Nicole Neily, was previously employed at a number
of Koch network organizations, including as executive director of the
Independent Women's Forum, manager of external relations for the
Cato Institute, and president of the Franklin News Foundation (formerly Franklin Center for Government and Public Integrity), which
operates the Koch network's investigative journalism franchise.[79]
Neily spent several years working for corporate PR firms, including as vice-president of Dezenhall Resources. Dezenhall is known
for defending corporations from progressive groups, and its founder,
Eric Dezenhall, has written that "corporate surrender is growing more
common" in the face of activism, with corporations "going to extraordinary lengths to please attackers who do not want to be pleased."[80]

Speech First's founding treasurer, Kim Dennis, also chairs the Koch
network's anonymous DonorsTrust, and the first two lawyers on
Speech First's board, Jamil Jaffer and Adam White, are faculty at George
Mason University. Further additions to the board have included Goo-
gle's corporate counsel Kathryn Ciano Mauler, who received an IHS
fellowship while training at GMU law school. She went on to work at
the Institute for Justice and the Koch network's voter data firm, i360.[81]
If these board-level connections are not evidence enough, Speech First
also joined the State Policy Network.

Nearly all of Speech First's lawsuits have been filed in coordination
with the Alliance Defending Freedom, which uses free speech arguments to legalize discrimination in the name of religious freedom.

ALLIANCE DEFENDING FREEDOM (ADF)

Created in 1994, ADF is a Christian legal organization that uses the courts to defend the Christian faith from perceived political threats. Lawyers have a particular role, ADF argues, in protecting Christianity from secular efforts to pluralize American society. Since its founding, it has seen its mission as "keeping the doors open for the Gospel by advocating for religious liberty, the sanctity of human life, freedom of speech, and marriage and family."[82] The Southern Poverty Law Center designates ADF as a hate group for its efforts to recriminalize homosexuality and defend sterilizing transgendered people, its condemnation of homosexuality as hostile to Christianity and likening of it to pedophilia, and for advocating "religious liberty" legislation legalizing the denial of services to LGBTQ+ persons.[83]

As with Speech First, ADF has taken particular aim at campus speech codes and policies against harassment. For example, in its document laying out the rights of students regarding "religious and conservative expression," ADF emboldens students by assuring them that their expression cannot be prohibited for being "deemed to be racist, sexist, homophobic, hateful, harassing, offensive, intimidating, controversial, provocative, or indecent, or because they provoke a violent response from listeners." Students are warned that administrators "still try to regulate such expression through speech codes, speech zones, so-called 'non-discrimination' policies."[84]

ADF became involved in campus free speech issues in response to university policies preventing Christian student groups from denying membership to gay students or those who objected to signing a statement of faith.[85] ADF has been highly successful litigating campus free speech issues claiming, as of 2017, to have won "over 400 contested legal matters with private campuses or universities," and boasting a 90 percent success rate with their campus lawsuits.[86] ADF stresses that "it is not enough to just win cases; we must change the culture, and the strategy of Alliance Defending Freedom ensures lasting victory."[87]

To this end, ADF often works closely with other conservative and libertarian political organizations, such as the Leadership Institute (Chapter 4).[88] It also lists an array of Koch network organizations among its allies, including FIRE and the Young America's Foundation.[89] One of ADF's lawyers specializing in campus free speech, Casey

Mattox, left ADF to join the Charles Koch Institute as a senior fellow working on issues of free speech.[90] He is now the vice-president of legal and judicial strategy at Americans for Prosperity.

ADF received $345,850 from DonorsTrust and Donors Capital Fund between 2016 and 2019, and counts the Richard and Helen DeVos Foundation as a major contributor.[91] It also regularly works closely with student groups within the Koch network. For example, it has helped Turning Point USA chapters sue Grand Valley State University, Arkansas State University, and Macomb Community College.[92] At least twice, ADF has sued on behalf of Young Americans for Freedom over events featuring Ben Shapiro, first at California State University, Los Angeles, and then at the University of Minnesota.[93] It has also sued a number of colleges and universities on behalf of YAL, including the University of Massachusetts, Amherst, the University of Georgia, Kellogg Community College, and the University of California, Berkeley.[94] In one instance, a Leadership Institute staffer and the vice-president of a YAL chapter at a neighboring institution visited Kellogg Community College to hand out pocket-sized copies of the Constitution, without having received sponsorship from a recognized student group. They were arrested for trespassing, and ADF sued on their behalf.[95] It also sued the University of Minnesota over the decision to move Ben Shapiro's talk to a smaller venue and charge $15,000 for security. In 2020, the case was thrown out when a judge found that the university had acted "[c]onsistent with the law that governs 'limited public forums'" and imposed "reasonable restrictions in place to ensure the event was secure."[96]

LITIGATING CIVIL RIGHTS

Colleges and universities have long struggled to figure out how to properly balance free speech, academic freedom, campus safety, and ensuring that their institutions are hospitable to wide and diverse populations. The particularities of striking this balance vary from institution to institution. For example, a state university has different First Amendment obligations than a private or religious college. Likewise, institutions with long histories of segregation or regular incidents of racist and hateful speech might take extra actions to help vulnerable populations feel welcome on campus. Striking the proper balance, however, is difficult, and generally involves larger academic, ethical, and governance discussions, in many cases motivated by student and faculty concerns and activism.

In many instances civil rights, feminist, LGBTQ+, and other social movements of students, faculty, and the broader public have successfully demanded greater social inclusion in colleges and universities. However, outside groups like FIRE, Speech First, and ADF have pushed back against these efforts through their litigation of a particularly abstract and absolutist notion of free speech. As crusaders for free speech absolutism they regularly show considerably less interest in addressing the underlying concerns voiced by students from marginalized communities.

The resulting lawsuits often play into the narrative of the persecuted conservative student bullied by an oppressive administration or out-of-control, PC-obsessed faculty and students. These free speech litigators often show little interest in understanding or balancing the complex and often competing political, ethical, and social challenges raised by free speech controversies. And, through their legal action, they often undermine institutional efforts to address hate on campus. These groups instead privilege a highly individualized, absolutist, and universalized notion of free speech—one that just so happens to dovetail nicely with the preferred ideology of their wealthy libertarian donors and broader political networks.

Until 2015, the Koch network relied on student groups, provocateurs, media attention, and lawsuits to impose their radical libertarian vision on the academy. Beginning in 2016, however, just as the campus free speech "crisis" was heating up, the network's web of think tanks, astroturf political organizations, and legislators launched yet another front in their efforts to transform higher education. In the years since, a wave of campus free speech legislation has swept the United States. Riding on the manufactured "crisis" narrative, such laws have sought to criminalize student protesters while granting unfettered opportunities for external actors to influence campus debate and discussion.

6

Changing the Laws

By the mid-2010s libertarian student activists, campus provocateurs, the right-wing media ecosystem, and various non-profit legal organizations had put considerable pressure on colleges and universities, focusing on protecting conservative speech against the supposed censoring impulses of "politically correct" administrators and faculty. After manufacturing this controversy, the Koch network sought to lock in these gains through policy, launching a coordinated campaign to force state and federal legislation that would radically deregulate campus speech. As Lewis Powell had instilled in Charles Koch's generation, "[t]here should not be the slightest hesitation to press vigorously in all political arenas for support of the enterprise system. Nor should there be reluctance to penalize politically those who oppose it."[1] The campus free speech legislation advocated by the Koch network did exactly that, seeking to punish and criminalize students who protest campus speakers.

This legislative agenda was pushed using the same strategy previously pioneered by the tobacco industry. The Koch-funded Atlas Network (Chapter 8)—an organization created to "litter the world with free-market think-tanks"[2]—played an important role in the corporate defense of the tobacco industry. While Citizens for a Sound Economy (CSE) tackled the ground game, Atlas sought to "influence public health policies from multiple directions" by establishing "multiple think tanks, within a shared network, [to] generate a conversation among independent policy experts, which reflected its position in tobacco control debates."[3] This allowed pro-industry and anti-science "experts" to fill the public sphere from multiple locations, making minoritarian (yet well-financed) voices appear as if they enjoyed overwhelming public support.

Today, campus free speech bills arrive before state legislatures from multiple directions, again originating from three members of the Atlas

Network: The American Legislative Exchange Council, the Goldwater Institute, and the Foundation for Individual Rights in Education (FIRE).[4] Each organization has developed competing "model" bills, each presented to lawmakers as urgently needed solutions to the supposedly out-of-control campus free speech crisis. The existence of these multiple bills makes it possible to muddy the debate by focusing on the small differences between them thereby ignoring their numerous commonalities and more problematic provisions. It also helps manufacture a chorus of voices in support of the basic premise that universities must fundamentally deregulate speech, and do so along the lines of a radically libertarian vision. Because these bills were introduced at the height of the manufactured free speech crisis, educators, advocacy groups, and legislators suddenly found themselves involved in policy debates already pre-seeded with endless anecdotes about conservative persecution, de-platformed speakers, videos of angry protestors, and a slew of successful litigation.

All three model bills punish students who protest speakers, redefining student protest as unlawful. They empower speakers and student groups to sue universities and individual protestors, leveling harsh financial and academic penalties. They all seek to fundamentally undermine an academic institutions' ability to regulate external speakers. However, they do all these things in slightly different ways (see Table 1).

The core irony of this legislation is that a manufactured outrage over the left's supposed repressive censorship is being used to advance reactionary policy changes that do actually, and demonstrably, chill campus free speech and punish dissent. Even more insidiously, these bills contain less-advertised provisions that destabilize the campus speech landscape by preempting universities from speaking publicly, while also creating politically appointed bodies to police campus speech, and in some cases mandating student orientations that advance the Koch network's brand of free speech fundamentalism.

These bills play into the Koch network's broader political strategy of drastically deregulating access to higher education. They do so by constraining administrators, faculty, and students in their ability to use established institutional governance bodies to deliberate when, where, and how campus and off-campus groups can participate in campus discourse.

Table 1   Comparing Different Provisions Found in the Three Different Campus Free Speech Model Bills

Policy Area	Effect	FIRE	Goldwater	ALEC
Eroding the Public Forum Doctrine	Strip campuses of protected status as a "limited forum"	X	X	X
	Prevent campus from disinviting a speaker		X	
	Redefine "harassment"		X	X
Punishing Protest	Redefine constitutionally protected speech as unlawful	X	X	X
	Create harsh punishment for "interfering" with free expression	X	X	X
	Impose mandatory minimum punishment	X	X	
	Allow out-of-state individuals to sue state entities for damages in Federal court			X
Re-Education and Monitoring	Require new freshman orientation curriculum		X	X
	Require/create state bodies to monitor campus free speech		X	X
Policing University Actions	Require university neutrality on controversial issues		X	
	Identifies university action on controversial issues as unlawful political speech forced on students and faculty		X	
	Require campus policy change	.	X	
Eroding Civil Rights Protections	Allow student groups to discriminate			X

FIRE'S CAFE ACT: LAYING THE GROUNDWORK TO UNDERMINE THE PUBLIC FORUM DOCTRINE

FIRE was the first to develop model legislation, releasing its Campus Free Expression (CAFE) Act in September 2015.[5] This legislation was developed during a time when FIRE was working to pass campus free speech legislation in Virginia (HB 258) and Missouri (SB 93). The act is presented as merely the encapsulation of the actionable part of the 2014 "Chicago Statement," a fairly modest affirmation of the University of Chicago's history of supporting free expression and open inquiry, written and adopted by a faculty committee in 2014. The statement concludes by affirming the position that "members of the University community are free to criticize and contest the views expressed on campus ... [however] they may not obstruct or otherwise interfere with the freedom of others to express views they reject or even loathe."[6] The FIRE bill, however, goes quite a way further than the Chicago Statement. In addition to mandating legal penalties for those disrupting a speaker, the CAFE Act also uses the possible threat of a campus spectacle as the context in which to fundamentally reformulate how universities regulate speech.

FIRE's CAFE Act seeks to make it easier for students to challenge speech restrictions in court.[7] Much of the public debate has focused on free speech zones, an issue that a number of organizations in the middle third—including the American Civil Liberties Union—have come out against. However, all three pieces of model legislation put forward by FIRE, the Goldwater Institute, and ALEC use outcry over free speech zones as the pretext to fundamentally transform universities from semi-regulated "limited forums" into unregulated "public forums." According to the US Supreme Court's public forum doctrine, "traditional public forums" (such as public parks and sidewalks) are open for all free expression as protected under the First Amendment. On the other extreme, "non-public forums" (such as military bases, courtrooms, and jails) prioritize the smooth functioning of essential government operations over individual free speech rights. Given their unique mission, public universities are a hybrid. Traditionally universities have been considered "limited forums," which prioritize academic function over some speech (in classrooms, administrative buildings, libraries) but allow universities to create a "designated forum" on some parts of campus that serve as a traditional public forum.

An institution providing a limited forum "is not required to and does not allow persons to engage in every type of speech," but once the forum is created, speech can only be regulated in ways that are viewpoint neutral and "reasonable in light of the forum's purpose."[8] Content restrictions are subject to strict scrutiny and must be "narrowly drawn" for the sake of protecting a "compelling state interest."[9] As a limited forum, a university can prevent students from giving political speeches in a physics classroom—since the institution maintains an interest in ensuring that physics is taught in a physics classroom. Unfettered free speech could disrupt that outcome. Similarly, some schools have restricted political speeches and the handing out of literature to designated parts of campus. As designated forums, institutions can require that only recognized student groups that have applied for permission can leaflet outside the student union, a reasonable barrier that prevents everything from overcrowding to, say, neo-Nazis handing out flyers on campus. Schools might also designate certain spaces free speech zones in recognition that universities are often also residential institutions, and therefore need to balance the right of public speech with the preservation of safety and privacy in one's personal space.

FIRE's CAFE Act strips away much of the university's limited forum designation, requiring that all "publicly accessible outdoor areas" of campuses "shall be deemed traditional public forums." The bill specifies that "[a]ny person who wishes to engage in noncommercial expressive activity on campus shall be permitted to do so freely." This includes opening all of campus to the outside, Koch-funded student organizations.

The CAFE Act also provides retaliatory power for speakers on campus who find themselves being protested. The bill redefines the free speech of protesters as unlawful if it "materially and substantially disrupts another person's expressive activity," including "blocking or significantly hindering any person from attending, listening to, [or] viewing" an expressive act. Lawful dissent is therefore limited to "minor, brief, or fleeting nonviolent disruptions of events that are isolated and short in duration." The bill creates a "cause of action" that allows anyone who feels their "expressive rights were violated" to sue for damages. The bill also establishes a mandatory minimum fine of $500 and maximum possible fine of $100,000.[10]

While FIRE's model bill was not widely adopted by legislatures, it provided the foundation for subsequent bills launched by other organizations in the Koch network.

THE GOLDWATER BILL: PUNISHING CIVIL DISOBEDIENCE

In February 2017, Arizona's Goldwater Institute released its model bill at the peak of the escalating campus free speech crisis, just one day before Yiannopoulos's ill-fated appearance at the University of California, Berkeley. Goldwater is a key Koch network think tank that received $6,447,514 from the Koch family foundations, the Bradley Foundation, DonorsTrust, and Donors Capital Fund between 2001 and 2019.[11] Created in 1988 with the blessing of its namesake, conservative icon Barry Goldwater, it is a libertarian think tank with a strong research, advocacy, and litigation emphasis.[12] The group has championed pro-corporate legislation designed to promote school privatization and voucher programs, privatize state pensions, and attacks on unions. It has also advocated legislation opposing Medicaid expansion, the regulation of carbon dioxide, and bans on the sale of e-cigarettes to minors.[13]

Goldwater's "Campus Free Speech Act" declares public areas of campuses to be "traditional public forums, open on the same terms to any speaker," not unlike FIRE's bill. Yet the Goldwater bill includes an irreversible invitation clause, allowing all other campus facilities to be "open to any speaker whom students, student groups, or members of the faculty have invited."[14] Granting open access to campus for anyone invited, by any member of the campus community, drastically undermines an institution's ability to govern itself, eroding regulations of both limited and designated forums. This clause also builds in unequal advantages for student groups with access to a pipeline of external dark money, allowing them to bring Koch-funded speakers to campus without accountability to their institution.

The Goldwater bill also outlaws "protests or demonstrations that infringe upon the rights of others to engage in or listen to expressive activity." The bill outlines a "range of disciplinary sanctions" including suspension or expulsion for students who have "twice been found responsible for infringing the expressive rights of others." The cause of action provision allowing anyone whose "expressive rights are violated" to sue is nearly identical to the language in FIRE's bill, but increases the mandatory minimum from $500 to "$1,000 or actual damages, whichever is higher."

The bill originated in 2016, when the Goldwater Institute entered into a partnership with Stanley Kurtz for the purpose of developing a free speech bill.[15] Kurtz was a contributing editor at the *National Review*, where he published his 2015 "Plan to Restore Free Speech on Campus." This piece called for disciplinary measures against students who disrupt or attempt to disrupt speakers.[16] Kurtz argued that doing so was necessary to save pro-capitalist ideology on campus. He worried that "many faculty members have rejected classic liberal values," and that this "faction of students and allied faculty has succeeded in intimidating the larger number of students who continue to adhere to classic liberalism."[17]

By 2015 Kurtz had already established himself as a leading culture war crusader. After the terrorist attacks of September 11, 2001, he targeted federally funded Middle East studies programs, accusing numerous scholars of being guided by Edward Said and "post-colonial theory," and therefore holding an "anti-American bias."[18] He supported the Middle East Forum, an anti-Muslim group that published a watchlist of scholars deemed too critical of US foreign policy and therefore insufficiently pro-American.

The Goldwater Institute's campus free speech bill, written by Stanley Kurtz and Goldwater Senior Fellows James Manley and Jonathan Butcher, also includes several largely unadvertised provisions that have potentially drastic consequences for universities. In an increasingly hostile political climate, universities routinely hire lobbyists to represent their relevant interests at the state and federal levels, including on issues of state and federal funding, accreditation, civil rights protections, and campus conceal carry laws. However, several provisions in the Goldwater bill create broad preemptive restrictions, or prior restraint, on the otherwise lawful speech of universities to advocate for themselves. A university must "remain neutral, as an institution, on the public policy controversies of the day." The Goldwater bill forbids a university from "tak[ing] action, as an institution" on public policy controversies "in such a way as to require students or faculty to publicly express a given view of social policy." This bill could prevent institutions from adopting curricular priorities deemed too "political" (such as taking up issues of diversity?), or making public statements about contemporary events (such as Black Lives Matter protests), or signing on to boycotts or carbon disinvestment initiatives. Furthermore, given the Koch network's considerable legal and legislative operations, this provision makes universities even more constrained by right-wing legislatures and threatened by potential legal risk.

The Goldwater bill also creates a politically appointed Committee on Free Expression that monitors and reports on the enforcement of the bill, including documenting any "barriers to or disruptions of free expression" on campus and the "administrative handling and discipline relating to these disruptions or barriers." The committee also monitors the suppression of institutional speech by reporting on any "substantial difficulties, controversies, or successes in maintaining a posture of administrative and institutional neutrality with regard to political or social issues."

The bill also mandates that all "freshman orientation programs" include materials "describing to all students the policies and regulations regarding free expression consistent with this act," including the new limitation on protest and students' rights to invite any speaker and to sue the institution. Apparently, diversity trainings are coerced speech, but orientations that advance free speech absolutism are simply "liberty."

Immediately after the Goldwater Institute released its model bill, legislators in several states scrambled to file similar bills. In Tennessee alone, four bills were filed within eight days of Yiannopoulos's appearance at the University of California, Berkeley. One lawmaker called his Goldwater-inspired bill the "Milo bill." At the press conference, a supporter read a statement written by Yiannopoulos: "There was a time, not too long ago in fact, when the Milo bill was not necessary ... but that time has passed." The statement warned that "the culture war that has erupted on campuses will not be over. We are winning the war, and will continue to win as long as students, and now defenders of free speech within the government, stand up to ivory tower intellectuals and left-wing administrators intent on shutting up any speech they don't find convenient."[19]

Legislators advancing the Goldwater bill in Tennessee and other states were not incidental civil libertarians; many already worked within a highly coordinated network of corporate-friendly lawmakers. The third model bill, the American Legislative Exchange Council's FORUM Act, built on the work of the FIRE and Goldwater, creating a policy agenda that conjoined their model legislation with ALEC's vast on-the-ground and integrated network of policy advocacy.

THE FORUM ACT: ALEC AND THE STATE POLICY NETWORK

The sponsor of Tennessee's "Milo bill," like many other lawmakers who would eventually file campus free speech bills around the country, was a "public sector member" of the American Legislative Exchange Council, as were ten other legislators sponsoring campus free speech bills in Tennessee.[20] ALEC is a unique non-profit within Charles Koch's strategy of social transformation. It connects corporations, lobbyists, and think tanks ("private sector members") to draft pro-corporate legislation that is then handed over to a network of receptive state lawmakers ("public sector members") to implement across the country.[21]

ALEC was formed in 1973 by religious-right activist Paul Weyrich, who also founded the Heritage Foundation—one of Washington, D.C.'s most powerful far-right think tanks.[22] In 1987, with the help of millionaire Thomas Roe, ALEC launched a national network of think tanks to influence state policy and help develop model bills. Roe described the effort as creating "something like a Heritage Foundation in each of the states," telling one colleague, "[y]ou capture the Soviet Union—I'm going to capture the states."[23]

This network was formalized in 1992 under the umbrella State Policy Network (SPN). With at least one member in all 50 states, SPN describes its purpose as providing support to "state-focused, free market think tanks and their national think tank partners."[24] The non-profits behind the campus free speech movement have overwhelmingly been members of SPN, including Students for Liberty, Young America's Foundation, American Enterprise Institute, Manhattan Institute, Leadership Institute, The College Fix, National Review Institute, the Goldwater Institute, Speech First, and (formerly) the Foundation for Individual Rights in Education.[25] SPN received $51.67 million from Koch family foundations, the Bradley Foundation, DonorsTrust, and Donors Capital Fund between 2001 and 2019, while ALEC received $11.6 million between 1998 and 2019.[26]

Between 2016 and 2020, 99 campus free speech bills modeled on the ALEC/SPN legislation were filed in 38 US states. In at least 26 of those states, a total of 186 ALEC legislators sponsored 63 of the bills.[27] In addition to providing a vast pool of legislators to shepherd the passage, ALEC also added another voice to the Koch network's campus free speech narrative. Again, we see the trusted strategy of using a network of think tanks and advocacy organizations to influence policy simply by flooding the discourse with networked—yet seemingly independent and even competing—voices.

ALEC began ramping up its focus on campus free speech in 2016 when it launched the Center to Protect Free Speech.[28] The mission of the Center is to "promote policies that ensure the ability for all to speak freely," and to "educate legislators and concerned citizens" on free speech.[29] Their focus includes campus speech as well as commercial speech, which ALEC argues governments should not determine to be "deceptive or misleading." Nor should government "unduly compel [private businesses] to engage in speech contrary to their commercial interests."[30] In other words, ALEC claims that, rather than regulations requiring labeling or health warnings (in the public interest), the free market should be left to self-regulate such commercial speech.

In May 2017, the Center to Protect Free Speech introduced its own model campus free speech bill, the "Forming Open and Robust University Minds" (FORUM) Act.[31] This bill was first unveiled at the organization's Education and Workforce Development Taskforce subcommittee.[32] The Goldwater Institute is a member not only of ALEC but also of the Education and Workforce Taskforce, whose chair at the time was the Goldwater Institute's Jonathan Butcher, co-author of the Goldwater bill.[33]

The FORUM Act contains many of the key provisions of FIRE's CAFE Act and Goldwater's Campus Free Speech Act, including the requirement that outdoor areas of campuses "be deemed traditional public forums," and defining speech that "materially and substantially prohibit[s] the free expression rights of others on campus"—i.e. protest—as unlawful.

Materials released by ALEC in 2017 sought to aggressively distinguish the FORUM Act from the Goldwater bill. The founding director of the Center to Protect Free Speech, Shelby Emmett, claimed that ALEC's bill was preferable because it is "purely educational" and does "not include disciplinary measures."[34] In its FAQ about the model legislation ALEC warns supporters that other proposals "chill speech by requiring mandatory suspension or expulsion of students for 'interfering with' the free speech of others."[35]

The FORUM Act, however, still establishes a cause of action for speakers to sue the school or "any other persons responsible for the violation." Students targeted by these actions would be taken to court by those seeking "appropriate relief, including, but not limited to, injunctive relief, monetary damages, reasonable attorneys' fees, and court costs." While ALEC's initial bill did not originally mention mandatory minimum fines or academic sanctions, it was quietly updated in 2018 to include a fine of $5,000, making it even more punitive than the Goldwater bill.[36]

To ensure out-of-state individuals or groups can easily sue, the FORUM Act requires that a state "waives immunity under the Eleventh Amendment" and "consents to suit in a federal court for lawsuits arising out of this act." The Eleventh Amendment of the US Constitution prevents a state from being sued in federal court by the resident of a different state. This safeguard has proven a considerable barrier in the aggressive litigation strategy deployed by the Koch network's various legal organizations. In Montana, the Koch-funded astroturf group Americans for Prosperity told its members to lobby for Montana's version of the FORUM Act (HB 735) on the grounds that it provides "access to state courts. Although students can file a First Amendment lawsuit in federal court, federal courts take more time and are more costly for students and our institutions. State courts, especially with the issues simplified by this legislation, will process the claims more quickly and more cost-effectively."[37]

Also harkening back to the Goldwater bill, ALEC's model legislation requires that universities re-educate students through their "handbooks, on their websites, and through their orientation programs" on the newly constrained definition of free speech and their rights to sue. It also requires that universities specially monitor and report on "any barriers to or incidents of disruption of free expression occurring on campus," including "attempts to block or prohibit speakers and investigations into students or student organizations for their speech."

However, rather than a politically appointed free speech committee established by the Goldwater bill, the ALEC bill requires universities to report on themselves. Shelby Emmet routinely highlighted this distinction, including during an appearance alongside Turning Point USA's Marcus Fotenos. She contrasted ALEC's FORUM Act with the "big government" or "top-down approach" of the Goldwater bill.[38] These exaggerated disagreements over minor differences normalize both bills' common effects and gloss over their nearly identical founding premises.

They also direct attention away from the more objectionable provisions. The FORUM Act prevents public universities from denying student groups institutional recognition or funding because they discriminate. This policy has been a long-term preoccupation of Alliance Defending Freedom (Chapter 5), which defends student groups that seek to exclude LGBTQ+ and non-Christian students. In 2017, a Christian student group at the University of Iowa had its status revoked after denying a leadership position to an openly gay member. While the university affirmed the rights of students to practice religion, they could "not tolerate discrimination of any kind in accordance with federal and state law." With the help of the Beckett Fund for Religious Liberty, the students sued the school for discrimination, claiming the student was excluded not for his sexual orientation, but because he refused to "agree" with "biblically based views on sexual conduct."[39] ALEC's Shelby Emmett has described coordinating with the Alliance Defending Freedom while developing the FORUM Act.[40]

The FORUM model legislation, therefore, legalizes discrimination by protecting belief-based student organizations that require their members and leadership to "adhere to the organization's sincerely held beliefs" and "standards of conduct." It describes potential acts of discrimination as "the expression of the organization," namely the expression of religious belief, and suggests that such discrimination is protected by the First Amendment.

The legislation of an absolutist notion of campus speech—at the expense of campus efforts to regulate hate speech and maximize inclusion—is not the only place ALEC has enjoyed legislative victories. In fact, ALEC has a long track record of supporting the most racially harmful legislative victories in recent years, often in the name of individual liberties and free-market principles. According to research compiled by the Center for Media and Democracy, ALEC has advocated "tough on crime" legislation, including the "Mandatory Minimum Sentencing Act," the "Truth in Sentencing Act," and "Three-Strikes-You're-Out," as well as bills allowing juveniles to be tried as adults, and the "Prison Industries Act" (allowing inmates to be systematically subjected to forced labor).[41] Throughout the 1990s and as recently as 2011, ALEC's Public Safety and Elections Taskforce included representatives from the private prison industry.[42] To bolster the network's voter suppression efforts, members and allies of ALEC sponsored more than half of the 62 Voter ID bills introduced in 37 states between 2011 and 2012.[43] A decade later, following the election of President Biden, ALEC continues to work with other right-wing organizations to pass legislation designed to suppress the vote.[44]

In 2020, ALEC also unveiled state laws designed to impose draconian criminal penalties on activities that have become common protest strategies among climate, indigenous, and Black Lives Matter activists, such as blocking pipelines and highways.[45]

ALEC was also a major backer of "Stand Your Ground" gun laws, and faced corporate boycotts following the racist murder of Treyvon Martin, when their advocacy received heightened scrutiny. Within six months of the shooting, ALEC lost thirty-eight corporate and nonprofit members including Coca-Cola, Walmart, McDonald's, and Kraft Foods.[46] Shelby Emmett, then working at the National Center for Public Policy Research (NCPPR), scolded corporations that disavowed ALEC, warning protestors that "families might lose jobs" as a result of "this boycotting and protesting thing."[47] Emmett's additional efforts to dissuade Black Lives Matter demonstrations include articles in which she argued that Eric Garner was not killed by violent police, but rather by big government.[48] Emmett left NCPPR—a corporate-funded, Koch network think tank—to work for FIRE, before moving on to lead ALEC's Center to Protect Free Speech. She recently rose to become director of Free Expression Policy for Stand Together, the umbrella organization that now oversees the Koch donor seminars. In this capacity she develops "strategy and policy positions to protect Free Speech both legally and culturally."[49]

MANUFACTURING POPULAR SUPPORT
FOR CAMPUS FREE SPEECH LEGISLATION

According to the Koch network strategy for social change, think tanks and advocacy organizations produce policy proposals and find legislators to sponsor these bills. Once filed, astroturf groups perform the next stage by engaging in corporate-funded "activism" to pressure lawmakers, neutralize critics, and further manufacture the appearance of widespread public support.

The Koch network's prized front group remains Americans for Prosperity, whose charitable arm, the AFP Foundation, received $84.77

million from Koch family foundations, the Bradley Foundation, DonorsTrust, and Donors Capital Fund between 2004 and 2019.[50] The ground operation that pushed state legislatures to pass model campus free speech bills has been waged largely by AFP, its millennial-focused subsidiary Generation Opportunity (GenOpp), and the Koch network's women-focused front, Concerned Women for America (CWA).

In Florida, AFP worked with GenOpp to aggressively support SB 1234, including presenting legislative testimony and sending out mailers paid for by AFP.[51] In North Carolina, GenOpp claims to have "led a movement of student activists to lobby" for the passage of the bill (HB 527). Americans for Prosperity has also supported campus free speech bills in South Dakota (HB 1073), Wisconsin (AB 299), and Montana (HB 735).[52] In Ohio, AFP appeared before the Senate alongside the Alliance Defending Freedom and FIRE to advance that state's campus free speech bill.[53] In Iowa, two AFP lobbyists appeared at least five times before the House and Senate to support various campus free speech bills, then published a statement of celebration after the governor's signature of the bill.[54] Two additional lobbyists from Concerned Women for America, appeared with AFP to shepherd the bills through the legislature.[55] A statement from CWA clarified that their intention was to "[s]top universities from drowning out conservative, Judeo-Christian values!" They assured readers that college chapters of Young Women for America were "shining the light of freedom" on campuses where "radical groups use the threat of violence" to cancel events and create a climate that "will blossom in hideous ways if we do not fight back."[56]

In 2018, Senator Ty Masterson introduced a bill to prevent a "dangerous path of no free speech" in Kansas, citing a recent (ALEC) conference that he attended on the free speech crisis. At the hearing one student activist opposing the bill noted that it would "force a university to accommodate speakers whose research and opinions have been clearly debunked," including the Ku Klux Klan.[57] But Kansas senator, and ALEC member, Bud Estes argued that he did not see this as a potential problem, recalling that the KKK regularly appeared at his college when he was a student. Senator Oletha Faust-Goudeau, the first Black woman to serve in the Kansas Senate, said she originally anticipated supporting the legislation but changed her mind after the

KKK discussion because the "intent of their speech was murdering people."[58]

Free speech bills have been passed at the state level with the help of key Koch network legislators, think tanks, and astroturf political mobilization groups. There has also been considerable effort to push similar legislation at the federal level as well.

In February 2018, Utah Senator Orrin Hatch introduced the "Free Right to Expression in Education Act" (S 2394), which mirrored the Goldwater bill. It provided a cause of action for those claiming their "expressive activity rights" have been violated, granting damages "not less than $500 for an initial violation." In the lead up to the 2018 election cycle, Koch Industries was Senator Hatch's seventh largest campaign contributor.[59] In December 2018, Virginia's David Brat introduced the "Student Rights Act of 2018" into the US House of Representatives (HR 7229). The bill mirrors Hatch's bill but reintroduces the Goldwater provision preventing schools from imposing additional security fees on speakers. It also allowed interrupted speakers to sue for a mandatory minimum of "not less than $1,000." Between 2014 and 2018, Koch Industries was Representative Brat's seventh largest donor. FreedomWorks was his second largest.[60] FIRE applauded the punitive "cause of action" provision in Brat's bill, announcing it was "pleased" to see Congress taking action and offering assistance to "any member of Congress interested in tackling these issues."[61]

In 2019 President Trump signed an executive order threatening to end federal funding to schools if they did not "promote free inquiry."[62] In August 2020, Arkansas Senator Tom Cotton announced the "Campus Free Speech Restoration Act," which does away with "free speech zones and restrictive speech codes" as well as reporting systems, and establishes a review process within the Department of Education "to determine whether campus speech policies infringe on the First Amendment rights of individuals on campus, on penalty of losing federal funding."[63] Had it passed, free speech complaints would have been reviewed in a department overseen by Koch mega-donor Betsy DeVos. Both Tom Cotton and the bill's co-sponsor, Mitch McConnell, attended at least one Koch seminar in 2014. Captured in a leaked audio recording, McConnell spoke alongside Koch Industries officials on a panel about political spending as free speech, and Cotton beamed about the critical role that Americans for Prosperity played in turning Arkansas away from "a one-party Democratic state."[64] Another co-sponsor, Georgia Senator Kelly Loeffler, has demonstrated her principled commitment to free speech by admonishing WNBA players (including those on the Atlanta Dream, which she co-owns) for speaking out in support of Black Lives Matter, which she claims is a Marxist ploy that "seeks to destroy America."[65]

Meanwhile, groups like the American Association of University Professors (AAUP) have done good work unmasking the political motivations behind such free speech legislation.[66] The AAUP affirms the important role colleges and universities play in cultivating "debate, dissent, and the free exchange of ideas," and in supporting "freedom of expression on campus and the rights of faculty and students to invite speakers of their choosing."[67] However, they point out that campus free speech legislation "interferes with the institutional autonomy of colleges" and undermines the "role of faculty, administration, and governing boards in institutional decision-making and the role of students in the formulation and application of institutional policies affecting student affairs."

In other words, the AAUP acknowledges that university policies on campus speech should continue to be "adopted through normal channels of institutional governance" rather than imposed as one-size-fits-all policy from state or federal government.[68] Despite a "superficial similarity," the AAUP points out that campus free speech laws and the principle of academic freedom are "false friends" since academic freedom involves vetting and evaluating ideas within long-established professional norms.[69] This process is not the same as throwing open campus doors to anyone to say whatever they want, no matter how false, discredited, or antithetical to the academic mission.

Legislation such as the Goldwater Bill, however, is not interested in overseeing a fair and deliberative academic "process" but rather seeks to achieve specific "outcomes"—namely, to "bring about a new 'balance of forces' on college campuses," one that not incidentally favors their billionaire donors.[70] This motivation is especially prevalent given the harsh sanctions designed to punish student protestors, which not only chills campus speech but also usurps the ability of institutions—trustees, administration, staff, faculty, and students—to navigate these tricky waters themselves. Careful deliberation is required to find ways to "balance unobstructed dialogue with the need to make all constituencies on campus feel included."[71] Imposing legislation from above, the AAUP argues, short circuits the careful deliberation and thoughtful governance process through which such a balance might be attained.

In contrast to the practice of institutional shared governance, Koch network lawyers, non-profits, and right-wing legislators seek to impose campus policies from above, as student groups attack from below, and paid provocateurs and the right-wing media ecosystem bludgeon the academy on all fronts. This strategy leaves administrators pressed between several crises that seem impossible to resolve, balancing the demands for greater inclusion and equity with growing incidents of hate on campus. All this in the context of a well-funded onslaught of legal action, political interference, and corporate speech.

Amidst such a maelstrom, Koch-funded faculty have successfully pushed campuses to adopt free speech policies by promising to prophylactically ward off such unwanted turmoil.

7

The Academics

In his 1974 speech at the Institute for Humane Studies, Charles Koch laid out a plan for building "a well financed cadre of sound proponents of the free enterprise philosophy" with the radical intent of capturing the state. This strategy was grounded in making "highly leveraged" investments in higher education, where funding would have a considerable "multiplier effect."[1] After all, well-funded academic centers and faculty could influence students through curriculum and campus events, change campus policy, and produce the ideas and talent needed to support the rest of the integrated political operation.

Koch insider Kevin Gentry confirmed that four decades later this remains the network's guiding strategy, telling a room full of donors that: "the network is fully integrated." The faculty "recruit the most passionate students from these programs and graduate programs, so they're training the next generation of the freedom movement." Those who "aren't interested in becoming professors" can go on to "populate [our] think tanks, and grassroots [organizations]." In this political operation faculty play the role of sponsoring reading groups, mentoring student groups, and engaging students "outside the classroom and [in] more casual group settings" where they "help those students see the message to fight for freedom."[2]

He assured the donors that their funding was not only providing quality educational opportunities for students, but also "building state-based capabilities and election capabilities, and integrating this talent pipeline. So you can see how this is useful to each other over time." Gentry touted a network of nearly 5,000 scholars, each with access to an estimated 6,000 students each year, amounting to a captive audience in the tens of millions. Despite its size and organization, however, Gentry feared that "this capability pales in comparison to the opposition. Our network is still greatly outnumbered by professors and faculty who hold a collectivist worldview" and "those who do not want to see intellectual diversity in universities."[3]

Created explicitly to combat the collectivist "opposition" on campus, this versatile and well-funded group of ultra-free-market libertarians produce the raw material for the Koch network's larger political operation. The ideas they generate, and the talent they cultivate, fuel the larger strategy of social transformation. They are also well positioned to help provoke, and then capitalize on, the so-called free speech crisis.

THE MODEL: GEORGE MASON AND THE KOCH FOUNDATION

In 2006, 11 schools received Koch Foundation funding, and among them only George Mason University (GMU) received more than $100,000 annually. Since 2010, the number of Koch-funded schools has doubled approximately every two years.[4] In 2016, 259 universities received a combined total of more than $50 million from Koch foundations alone, with 59 campuses receiving more than $100,000.[5] In 2019 Koch foundations contributed a total of $123 million to academic institutions, up $23.9 million from the previous year; 32 academic institutions received more than a million dollars.[6]

The various Koch family foundations spend money to establish lecture series and reading groups, hire faculty, and set up stand-alone, campus-affiliated centers. The aim of preserving donor control of these academic enterprises goes back to the origins of the Koch network. For example, as George Pearson, longtime Director of Public Affairs at Koch Industries, described at a 1976 conference, donors should only consider giving grants that help harness "academia to advance the libertarian ideology." In traditional philanthropic giving, such as endowing professorships, donors retain "no control beyond the appointment of the chair's first occupant." Therefore, he suggested, libertarians should focus on creating entirely new centers and programs "associated with a university that can tap its resources and reputation but still be primarily answerable to the donor." This strategy allows donors to "influence the hiring decisions of the department" while also "leveraging ... state funds."

Pearson warned against programs that "announced their intentions publicly" since doing so risked triggering a "reaction from the established faculty." To "keep control without creating such opposition," they must "use ambiguous and misleading names, obscure the true agenda, and conceal the means of control."[7] Pearson cited the Institute for Humane Studies, overseen by Charles Koch himself, as the perfect example of donor-controlled giving. Between 1998 and 2019, IHS received $52,150,543 from Koch family foundations, the Bradley Foundation, DonorsTrust, and Donors Capital Fund.[8]

Koch officials also disclosed, at their 2014 donor summit, that they bankrolled 24 "university based research centers," a figure that had almost doubled in the past two years "due primarily to the partnership of this group."[9] Two years later, Charlie Ruger announced that they were funding 53 centers, anchored by 255 tenure track faculty. He made this announcement at the 2016 conference of the Association of Private Enterprise Education (APEE),[10] before a roomful of corporate-friendly academics. He clarified that Koch only funds about 40 percent of their total academic programs, with the rest coming from a "network of business leaders" who see "free enterprise as being in great peril" and are willing to put "their fortunes on the line to help that not happen."[11]

The precise donor influence over the funding of free enterprise academic centers remains surrounded by considerable secrecy. However, a growing body of scholarship, investigative reporting, and activist research by students, faculty, and community members has shed some light on the Koch network's higher education infrastructure. Of the $325.3 million in charitable donations made by the Charles Koch Foundation between 2008 and 2017, more than 70 percent ($233.5 million) went to colleges and universities.[12] Activism by students and faculty uncovered widespread evidence that Charles Koch and his operatives often exert undue influence over programs, including violations of donor policies, exerting donor oversight over hiring and firing, selecting department chairs, even approving fellowship recipients and dissertation topics, and influencing the creation of majors, minors, courses, and student groups.[13] Koch funding often comes with considerable strings attached, outlined in secretive contracts hidden behind non-disclosure clauses.

For example, student activists filed suit against George Mason University after years of rejected Freedom of Information Act requests. Despite winning in court, GMU's administrators eventually released several of the requested documents.[14] After years of denial, GMU's president finally admitted that these "problematic" agreements gave "donors some participation in faculty selection and evaluation," and "fall short of the standards of academic independence I expect any gift to meet."[15] Between 1998 and 2019, GMU received $246,955,443 from Koch family foundations, the Bradley Foundation, DonorsTrust, and Donors Capital Fund.[16]

In his study of these previously concealed contracts Douglas Beets discovered that they often include very specific conditions, ranging from a requirement to hire specific named individuals to requirements to abide by a very narrow ideological mission statement. Standard Koch Foundation contracts also include severance clauses which allow funding to be cut off with as little as 30 days notice. This stipulation reenforces donor leverage, requiring that recipients operate under the constant threat of defunding.[17] These tactics undermine faculty governance, academic freedom, and professional norms designed to protect scholarship and teaching from external interference.[18]

Even when intentionally hidden behind a veil of secrecy, evidence of Koch donor influence is prevalent not only at George Mason but across the academy. Below are just a few sketches of the most glaring examples of Koch-funded academic centers, programs, and faculty. Given the magnitude of overall funding, and the clear pattern that emerges from these examples, there is obviously more to be discovered.

THE PATTERN

George Mason University professor (and past APEE president) Peter Boettke recalled an analogy Richard Fink often used to get students "hyped up," likening their commitment to Austrian economics to that of the civil rights movement. "Before, we just wanted to be let on the bus and not raise a ruckus. Now we're gonna be like Malcolm X, Austrian and proud."[19] Inspired by Fink, Boettke would say, "[o]ur goal is not just to get a seat on the bus. Our goal is to take over the bus. Our goal is not just to sit in the back of the classroom and make a small point. Our goal is to be running the classroom."[20] Emboldened by their wealthy benefactors, Koch-funded academic centers have appeared on campuses across the country.

At Florida State University, for example, economics department chair (and past APEE president) Bruce Benson described Koch's multi-million-dollar donation to the department as "coming from a group of funding organizations with strong libertarian views" adding that these "organizations have an explicit agenda," meaning the department could no longer "hire anyone we want and fund any graduate student that we choose."[21] Between 2007 and 2019, FSU received $12,973,879 from Koch family foundations, DonorsTrust, and Donors Capital Fund.[22] A faculty investigation concluded that Benson ultimately forced the agreement on his department through "intimidation and administrative dictate," in violation of basic principles of faculty governance.[23] Benson also received a $105,000 bonus, negotiated through a Koch Foundation employee who was also his graduate student.[24]

At Auburn University in 2008, a Koch-funded center was created without faculty consent and hired a past APEE officer, Robert Lawson, without a search process.[25] A lawsuit later filed by the former chair of the economics department alleged the scheme consisted of "rigged hiring in exchange for money."[26] Auburn received $300,000 from Koch family foundations the same year.[27]

At Texas Tech University, the Koch-funded Free Market Institute (led by past APEE president Ben Powell) was established in the business college, after being rejected by three academic departments. Economics faculty described the proposed mandatory outside hire as not "satisfy[ing] the minimum criteria for a tenure position," having a "weak [curriculum] vita," and of a "libertarian Austrian bent" that "wasn't consistent with the culture in our department ... [of] mainstream economists."[28] Between 2013 and 2019, Texas Tech received $6,761,100 from Koch, Bradley, and DonorsTrust.[29]

At Troy University, professors leading the Center for Political Economy were caught bragging about how the Koch network's "big gift" allowed them to "hire a whole bunch of people all at once," "ram through" curricular changes, and "take over, for lack of a better term."[30] Troy received $1,363,000 from Koch and DonorsTrust between 2010 and 2019.[31]

Many of these Koch contracts were negotiated outside normal channels of faculty governance and oversight, and often only announced once the contract was finalized. For example, at Wake Forest a faculty committee created to investigate the then-proposed Eudaimonia Institute concluded that the Charles Koch Foundation engages in "unprecedented and well documented efforts to coopt higher education for ideological, political, and financial ends" and therefore any affiliation would "damage[ ] the integrity and sull[y] the academic reputation of the university."[32] The Institute was created nonetheless. Between 2009 and 2016 Wake Forest University received $3,129,510 from Koch and the Bradley Foundation.[33] Likewise, the George Mason University faculty senate rejected the Charles Koch Foundation's efforts to tie a $30 million gift to, among other things, the continuing appointment of the law school's dean.[34]

Faculty at Western Carolina University explicitly voted down the Koch-funded Center for the Study of Free Enterprise, only to have the board of trustees approve the donation.[35] It was later discovered that the center director (and former APEE president) Ed Lopez misinformed faculty and administrators, sharing only an edited "campus version" of his proposal. In the version actually submitted to the Koch Foundation, Lopez listed a number of "deliverables," including "developing a 'pipeline of students' exposed to free enterprise teaching and 'cultivating students' long-term interest and participation in the larger community of free enterprise scholars, implementers, activists and related professionals."[36] The campus version simply stated that the center would host conferences, seminars and workshops; the Koch version clarified that these events would feature speakers from Liberty Fund and the Institute for Humane Studies, and would help solidify a "regional cluster" of Koch-funded institutions.[37] Western Carolina University received $1,199,054 from the Koch Foundation between 2008 and 2019.[38]

With so many academic centers enjoying so much external funding, and acting autonomously from faculty governance and institutional constraint, it is not surprising that these libertarian beachheads have also played an important role in stoking the highly partisan campus free speech crisis. Manufacturing that crisis also serves to leverage and justify expanded donor-guided funding of academic programing. The all-too-common solution to a perceived persecution of conversative voices seems to be creating more libertarian centers, hiring more faculty, and attracting more money from conservative donors.

KOCH-FUNDED FREE SPEECH ACADEMICS

Koch funding comes with the clear expectation that faculty will not simply immerse themselves in their teaching and research but will also actively participate in the larger Koch political operation. It is quite common for faculty at Koch-funded academic programs to simultaneously hold positions in a revolving door of Koch network non-profits and State Policy Network-affiliated think tanks. The Koch Foundation's Charlie Ruger assured APEE attendees that Koch's funding is used to bring research "out of the academy." Ruger declared that "we want these great ideas of the APEE network to be applied ... across ... an integrated structure of production for culture change." The faculty receiving Koch funding are expected to engage with "different kinds of stakeholders in these social institutions," including "arranging state legislative testimony" thereby ensuring that "these kinds of ideas have a seat on the table in public policy." Ruger told prospective faculty members that "it's not just the money, we also bring a network with us," citing the Charles Koch Foundation's "constellation of network organizations that are focused on applying what comes out of universities to change the world." "[T]hat's sort of the core of the partnership," said Ruger. "Money plus the network."[39]

This combination of money and network has proven foundational in manufacturing the so-called campus free speech crisis. To understand the scale and ambition of this Koch-funded academic network, let's take a quick look at a few of those academic centers most directly engaged in free speech issues.

Institute for Humane Studies

The Institute for Humane Studies launched their Free Speech and Open Inquiry (FSOI) initiative in the late 2010s with funding from Koch seminar attendee (and hedge fund billionaire) Cliff Asness. The project provides grants to faculty "interested in fostering free speech and civil discourse" to fund research, events, and curricula "that explore how the classical liberal tradition of individual rights, free markets, and self-governance" contributes to free speech and open inquiry.[40]

In a leaked 2017 proposal to the Charles Koch Foundation, IHS stated that FSOI sought to "grow[ ] and leverage[e] our faculty network" to enact "change ... driven by faculty partners."[41] The proposal laid out the longstanding tenets of the Koch donor network: "Change the academy, and we change the world ... This is why we invest in growing the pool of academic talent capable of advancing classical liberal (CL) ideas." The proposal acknowledges that "our academic pipeline is too slow to realize the magnitude of change we seek," and could be expanded to include more "trusted faculty at PhD-granting institutions act[ing] as our agents," more graduate students, greater "leveraging [of] our current faculty network and collaborating with aligned non-alumni faculty," and expanded "partnerships with digital textbook publishers and open-source education platforms to become a leading source of CL ideas at the introductory level." The FSOI initiative was therefore pitched as an effort to "support" these attempts to bring about "campus-wide cultural change."[42]

The proposal described free speech as the key political lever that could be used to expand the Institute's goals of training, funding, advising, and placing graduate students and faculty with libertarian ideological commitments. The FSOI initiative laid out a plan to publish manuals on developing campus free speech policy, spearheaded by University of Wisconsin professor and IHS fellow Donald Downs, as well as to create Student Orientation Kits to deploy in first-year programs. The proposal claims that these investments make it possible to "blow past these near-term goals and have a 10X+ impact."[43]

After successfully securing the funding, IHS delivered on its promises, publishing *The Framework for Campus Crisis Management*[44] and *The Framework for Campus Free Speech Policy*[45] aimed at assisting faculty and administrators seeking to adopt campus free speech policies. These documents guide them toward policies that align with proposals developed by FIRE, ALEC, and the Goldwater Institute, affirming the position that there should be no "limits on speech," even when a "speaker lacks academic credibility, and/or purposefully breaks all codes of civil discourse."[46] They also recommend that academic institutions adopt "strong sanctions" against students who "abridge the legitimate speech rights of others."[47] Campus policies should protect the marketplace of ideas from the threat of disinvitations and disruptions, as well as "bias reporting systems," "safe spaces, trigger warnings, or free speech zones."[48] IHS also recommended developing policies to punish students who engage in activist strategies such as "occupy[ing] administrative offices" and "plac[ing] lists of demands upon administrators."[49] The documents also warn that faculty and administrators enacting campus free speech policies should avoid seeming "out of touch with concerns over social justice and inclusivity," and avoid "belittling 'trigger warnings' and 'safe spaces.'"[50] Instead, policy change should give the appearance of "emerg[ing] from within the university community, rather than being imposed by an external authority," or through "top-down and politically partisan" means.[51]

In their proposal, IHS planned to "demonstrate culture/institutional change on at least 200 campuses" by fall 2018 and to partner with "500 faculty and reach[ ] 20,000 faculty and administrators on this issue."[52] They pursued these goals by distributing their free speech framework documents to "more than 6,000 presidents, provosts, and deans" around the country, while warning that in a "post-Charlottesville era" campus leadership needs to be ready "when (not if) controversy comes knocking."[53]

Georgetown University

At an IHS free speech event, Georgetown professor John Hasnas explained how he successfully leveraged the threat of controversy to achieve favorable campus policy change. "The anecdotes [of campus disruption] are great," he explained. After each controversy, administrators declare "we don't want that here ... let's act prophylactically." IHS hailed Hasnas as a "terrific model" and "internal entrepreneur" for "working quietly" to first secure free speech commitments "on the administrative level,"[54] then working with faculty to make all campus policies "consistent with that commitment." Georgetown campus speech policy now reflects the network's model bills, including disciplinary measures for those "disrupting" free speech.[55]

Hasnas assured the IHS audience, "you don't need to mobilize the majority." Instead, "[y]ou only need to mobilize one or two faculty members, or one or two student groups, who are engaged enough to say 'let's make the change.'"[56] In contrast to the bottom-up mass movements for racial justice on campus, the Koch network can asymmetrically deploy their top-down political, legal, and intellectual apparatus to institutionalize policies preferred by a small group of donors.

Before pushing free speech policy changes as a faculty member at Georgetown, Hasnas served as assistant general counsel for Koch

Industries. After a stint at George Mason University, he was hired to found Georgetown's Institute for the Study of Markets and Ethics.[57] Since his arrival in 2005, Georgetown programs have received $3,502,500 from the Koch Foundation, DonorsTrust, and Donors Capital Fund. Georgetown has received $6,653,412 from the Koch Foundation, DonorsTrust, and Donors Capital Fund since 1998. However, after Hasnas' work changing speech policies, the donation from the Charles Koch Foundation spiked from $82,500 in 2017 to more than $1.2 million in 2018.[58]

University of Wisconsin–Madison

Donald Downs assumed faculty lead of IHS's FSOI initiative in 2017, the same year his Center for the Study of Liberal Democracy (CSLD) at the University of Wisconsin-Madison received a $1.1 million donation from the Koch Foundation.[59] Downs initially founded the center to address the "problem of intellectual diversity," namely the marginalization of "conservative political thought and libertarian thought."[60] The center, originally founded with $67,000 from the Bradley Foundation, offers students a $1,000 scholarship to complete a "Conservative Political Thought" course.[61] Between 1998 and 2019, the University of Wisconsin-Madison received $8.2 million from Koch and Bradley foundations.[62]

A decade before founding CSLD, Downs had already established himself as a free speech warrior against "political correctness." In 1996 he co-founded the Committee for Academic Freedom and Rights (CAFAR) in response to harassment by a "radical feminist" as part of an "ideology of multicultural diversity and sensitivity."[63] At the time CAFAR received $100,000 in seed funding from the Bradley Foundation and became an early inspiration for the creation of FIRE.[64] Downs sums up his free speech advocacy in his 2004 book, *Restoring Free Speech and Liberty on Campus*, in which he blames "postmodern" ideologies (such as those of Frantz Fanon, Paolo Freire, and Herbert Marcuse) and feminist and critical race legal theory as "tools for moral bullies to enforce an ideological orthodoxy that undermines the intellectual freedom and intellectual diversity that are the hallmarks of great universities."[65] Downs argued that this "victim ideology treats individuals as inherently incapable of handling the rigors of open discourse."[66]

Sarah Lawrence University

The leaked proposal for IHS's FSOI program bemoans the fact that media outlets regularly fail to cover "campus protests, heckler's vetoes, and dis-invitations." IHS blames this on a "dearth of empirical evidence" about various efforts to "shut down the free exchange of ideas." To "close this gap," IHS proposed supporting "empirical research" on free speech violations, based on a "pilot research project" completed in early 2017 by Sarah Lawrence University professor (and American Enterprise Institute scholar) Samuel Abrams.[67] The IHS proposal describes Abrams's research as focusing on "non-academic," "student-facing" leadership, diversity, and inclusion officers, who he claims are responsible for "policies and practices hostile to [free speech]." He suggests that staff members are "actively involved in student protests," possibly to "advance a particular ideological perspective." The FSOI funded Abrams's national survey, which led to a "series of op-eds in major national publications and higher education publications" covering the results.[68]

In an opinion piece published in *The New York Times*, Abrams described his survey of "roughly 900 'student-facing' administrators" as finding that "liberal staff members outnumber conservative counterparts by the astonishing ratio of 12-to-one."[69] He framed his findings with indignant anecdotes about "politically lopsided" programming at Sarah Lawrence. He lamented that events on "Black Lives Matter and justice for women" or "Understanding White Privilege" were being offered without "a meaningful ideological alternative."[70] Yet, when asked by student journalists, Abrams proved unable to give an example of what "alternatives" should be offered.[71] In response, Sarah Lawrence students protested by posting signs on his office door, which he described as vandalism and intimidation (not free speech).[72] Abrams did not disclose his affiliation or funding from IHS. It is likely that he was involved in the $103,500 that Sarah Lawrence received from the Koch Foundation between 2010 and 2018.[73]

Abrams also presented "an exclusive first look" at his survey findings at IHS donor events, presenting alongside Koch officials and

ALEC's Shelby Emmett at both ALEC and IHS events focused on discussing legislative responses to campus free speech issues.[74]

University of California, Los Angeles

In 2017, UCLA professor John Villasenor published a Koch-funded opinion poll that appeared to make an overwhelming case for the harsh campus free speech laws being filed in statehouses across the country. He reported that a "surprisingly large fraction of students" believe it acceptable to shut down expression they consider offensive, "including resorting to violence."[75] The Koch Foundation provided the funding to field the survey, and the data analyst at FIRE provided feedback.[76] The Koch Foundation released a statement amplifying his findings and claiming that Villasenor demonstrated a "pressing need for an open atmosphere of civil debate and early education about its merits."[77] These findings were widely criticized by polling experts who described the opt-in online panel, fielded a week after the Unite the Right rally, as "junk science."[78] This did not prevent the findings from being circulated widely within the right-wing media ecosystem. In 2020, Villasenor launched the multi-million-dollar Institute for Technology, Law, and Policy at UCLA with $4 million in funding from the Koch Foundation.[79]

Another UCLA school of law faculty member, and IHS faculty partner, Eugene Volokh runs the Banister First Amendment Law Clinic at UCLA, where students assist Volokh in filing amicus briefs "on behalf of non-profits and academics" in cases involving student speech.[80] Volokh has called for video-taping protestors and suing schools in order to inflict "libertarian-approved pain" on administrators.[81] In 2016, one attendee of an IHS event described how Volokh encouraged his listeners to "push the envelope in expressing controversial conservative and libertarian views" so as to "draw the ire of their university administrations and progressive students." Volokh instructed them to document the incidents for him to publicize on his blog, the Volokh Conspiracy.[82] Volokh presented this speech encouraging the provocation of free speech controversies seven times at IHS donor events between December 2015 and June 2017.[83]

The Koch and Bradley Foundations have joined with DonorsTrust and Donors Capital Fund to donate a total of $2.1 million to UCLA.[84]

Middlebury College

Middlebury College's political science professor Keegan Callanan is another recipient of IHS grants. [85] Callanan launched a campus initiative called the Alexander Hamilton Forum in 2018, which has become a hub for controversial programming. He told the *Washington Examiner* that he conceived of the program years earlier in talks with an unnamed foundation, but the program "didn't get off the ground" until after the Charles Murray fiasco. Once Middlebury gained national attention, "the idea emerged afresh," arguably under heightened threat of further free speech scrutiny.[86] The program's focus includes the "foundations and meaning of First Amendment freedoms," as well as a focus on relationships between "economic liberty" and "human flourishing."[87]

The forum's 2019 event with the far-right, anti-LGBTQ+ Polish politician Ryszard Legutko was canceled over planned protests. Callanan defended the right to hear "heterodox scholars" because "no questions are out of bounds."[88] However, when asked by the campus newspaper to disclose the source of the Alexander Hamilton Forum's funding, he refused.[89] Callanan also served as faculty advisor for Middlebury's Open Campus Initiative, which uses IHS funding to host events such as "Why Free Speech is the Only Safe Space for Minorities" and a campus return visit by Charles Murray in spring 2020, which was canceled due to COVID.[90]

Arizona State University and the University of Arizona

Two of Koch's academic centers in Arizona worked closely with the Koch network to pass Arizona's campus free speech legislation (HB 2615 and HB 2548 in 2016, and HB 2563 in 2018). Arizona State University's School for Civic and Economic Thought and Leadership ran free speech programming featuring authors of the Goldwater bill, Arizona Governor (and Koch seminar attendee) Doug Ducey, IHS faculty Eugene Volokh and Donald Downs, as well Black Lives Matter denialist Heather MacDonald.[91] ASU received $7,920,578 from Koch, Bradley, DonorsTrust, and Donors Capital Fund between 2009 and 2019.[92]

After the passage of Arizona's free speech bill, University of Arizona professor (and Koch center director) David Schmidtz joined the state's

Committee on Free Expression, created by the new law to monitor and report on state universities.[93] The committee revised 33 campus policies to conform to HB 2563, including adding academic sanctions and financial punishments. Arizona's 2018 Committee on Free Expression report applauded the training of 48 "First Amendment Monitors," the newly unveiled #Speakyourpeace pledge at the University of Arizona, and boasted that Arizona State University received FIRE's "coveted 'green light' rating."[94]

Schmidtz served in several positions at Koch network non-profits, including the Goldwater Institute, before founding UA's Center for the Philosophy of Freedom.[95] Since then, UA administrators have created a stand-alone Department of Political Economy and Moral Sciences to house his center and now offer a related major. UA received $3,588,094 from Koch, Bradley, DonorsTrust, and Donors Capital Fund between 2008 and 2019.[96]

ASU similarly created the School for Civic and Economic Thought and Leadership—a "pet project of Arizona conservatives"—this time by folding two Koch-funded stand-alone think tanks (the Center for the Study of Economic Liberty and the Center for Political Thought and Leadership) into one taxpayer-funded on-campus academic program.[97] This program creates its own curriculum based around Western civilization and the "Great Books." Since 2016, the legislature has spent $12 million to fund these "ideologically driven centers, which previously had been funded by the Charles Koch Foundation."[98] Arizona, in other words, has become the model not only for developing free speech legislation, but also for convincing the state to shoulder the operating costs of academic centers originally established as libertarian think tanks.

Clemson University

In 2014, hate incidents at Clemson University spiked, with online harassment, threats, and racist student activities, including gang-themed white fraternity parties.[99] C. Bradley Thompson, a faculty member at the Koch-funded Clemson Institute for the Study of Capitalism, chided anti-racist student protesters in a co-authored op-ed that mischaracterized their demands and called instead for greater free speech.[100] Koch network organizations and media, including FIRE, the Martin Center, and Campus Reform, cheered on the "heroic" professors standing up for free speech.[101] Clemson's chapters of Turning Point USA and Young Americans for Liberty distributed copies of the op-ed and eventually formed a free speech group explicitly designed to oppose the demands of anti-racist protestors.[102] This group invited Milo Yiannopoulos to campus in late 2016.[103]

Thompson told APEE's 2016 conference that his decision to oppose the "Clemson branch of Black Lives Matter" came after considering that "Leftists [on campus] certainly outweigh conservatives, libertarians, classical liberals, objectivists … Not 145 to one, but … more like 20 to one," calling that "fighting odds" that he would "take any day of the week in the battle of ideas."[104] The programming put on by Thompson's center includes $10,000 in student fellowships to participate in a Great Books curriculum and learn about "the moral foundations of capitalism."[105] Clemson University received $3,739,084 from Koch, Bradley, and DonorsTrust between 1999 and 2019.[106]

University of Maryland, College Park

In 2017 and 2018, racist incidents spiked at the University of Maryland, College Park, including the appearance of racist fliers, swastikas, nooses, and the murder of a Black student by a white supremacist on campus.[107] Faculty and students discussed ways to protect students from such hate. Acknowledging that hate symbols could not be banned because of First Amendment protections at state schools, the Campus Affairs Committee looked into a non-discrimination policy as one option to help protect students from harassment.[108] The Koch-funded Center for Enterprise and Markets swiftly held free speech events to counter these efforts. The center's director, Rajshree Agarwal, suggested that "words can have a lasting impression on you, and they can damage," but that is "only if you allow yourself to buy into that."[109] The University of Maryland, College Park received $2,388,427 from Koch, Bradley, and DonorsTrust between 2001 and 2019.[110]

Many of the faculty members listed above, as well as other Koch-funded faculty, are also members of the Academic Freedom Alliance (AFA) launched in March 2021.[111] The newly created AFA promises to provide legal support to its members—and approved nonmembers

upon request—when they feel their "academic freedom is threatened by institutions' or officials' violations of constitutional, statutory,
contractual, or school-based rights."[112] To fund this legal war chest—
dedicated to protecting a membership of primarily tenured faculty at
elite institutions—the AFA has collected millions of dollars "from a
primary conservative donor."[113] AFA was founded by Robert George of
the Princeton-based James Madison Program in American Ideals and
Institutions, which received $1.7 million from the Bradley Foundation
between 2001 and 2018.[114]

THE REPUBLIC OF SCIENCE

David Koch once described his philanthropic efforts this way: "[i]f
we're going to give a lot of money, we'll make darn sure they spend it in
a way that goes along with our intent. And if they make a wrong turn
and start doing things we don't agree with, we withdraw funding. We
do exert that kind of control."[115] The same leverage exists within Koch's
academic philanthropy, deployed with calculating efficiency to create
a network of academics willing and able to feed into the broader political and ideological apparatus. As with tobacco and climate denial,
the aim is not to push a single doctrinaire point but rather to seed
a debate where none previously existed. In effect, Koch investments
are not merely purchasing a particular piece of writing or buying a
specific class (although this sometimes happens). Rather, they are creating a whole academic ecosystem in which donor-preferred ideas can
thrive. This ecosystem includes its own journals, conferences, professional organizations, and academic centers.

Publicly, operatives within the Koch donor network justify their
academic philanthropy through the metaphor of expanding the marketplace of ideas. Privately, they fully acknowledge the relationship
between the funding of academic centers and the political outcomes
these investments will yield. For example, before introducing several
of the previously profiled professors at the 2016 APEE conference,
the Koch Foundation's Brennan Brown extolled each of them as an
"intellectual entrepreneur" who engages students in "meaningful conversations about a marketplace of ideas, a diversity of thought."[116]
Implicit in this claim, however, is the assumption that a marketplace
of ideas functions as an idealized libertarian free market—in which

individuals enjoy full liberty and autonomy (to say what they want), where money is speech, corporations are people, and all regulations are oppressive.

In a 2015 interview, Charles Koch laid out this particular understanding of the marketplace of ideas using Michael Polanyi's concept of the "Republic of Science," which draws a direct equivalence between the production of knowledge and the invisible hand of the market. Polanyi suggests that "self-coordinated initiatives" are the "most efficient" way to organize science, and as such, he envisions a capitalist utopia in which autonomous scientists produce knowledge, using funding from "private sources," to push knowledge forward.[117]

Asked whether he funds libertarian scholarship for his own benefit, Koch said no, contending instead that "[w]hat I want to see is the marketplace of ideas" where there is "no perfect balance, and how would you know what the perfect balance is? ... [L]et people figure this out on their own." When asked what guides his campus investments, Koch expressed a desire to see "every university apply a Republic of Science" and said "let us be open to all different ideas." However, he expressed fear that universities do not teach the full spectrum, "[a]nytime students shout down a speaker ... And 'safe zones' to express your opinion? That's the opposite of the Republic of Science."[118]

Lofty Republic of Science language aside, Koch's public claim that his massive private (and donor-directed) spending on academic centers is simply a selfless attempt to create a free marketplace of ideas is obviously misleading. First, he assumes that academic knowledge is merely a process by which people choose between competing partisan positions—that universities introduce students to "one side" and he therefore funds faculty to tell the "other sides." This claim assumes that academic ideas exist on "sides." This assumption only makes sense if one believes that Austrian economics is unduly marginalized within the academy, and that this marginalization stems from political malice rather than the ideas themselves being largely discredited.

Similarly, Koch presents academic knowledge as something one discovers individually, denying the social nature of knowledge production and cultivation.[119] He sees knowledge as coming from the individual freedom to choose—as if individual consumer preferences are the same as generating knowledge. He assumes that when private interests fund faculty, the "knowledge" such patronage produces is necessarily free from coercion, power, or hierarchy. Yet Koch himself boasts about directly overseeing how academics use his money. And, more importantly, as shown throughout this book, the public claim that Koch funding of academic centers follows from a selfless interest in the pursuit of a true marketplace of ideas is patently disproven by what plutocratic libertarians say in private. They explicitly and unapologetically describe the funding of centers, programs, and faculty positions as part of a partisan struggle, designed to bring about desired political outcomes.

After all, it's clear from the networks they affiliate with that Koch-funded academic programs are fully integrated within the Koch political infrastructure. For example, the Institute for Humane Studies and Mercatus Center at GMU, as well as the recently created Center for Growth and Opportunity at Utah State University, are all members of the State Policy Network. SPN's 2019 conference was even co-sponsored by Arizona State's Center for the Study of Economic Liberty.[120] Many of the aforementioned centers—at Clemson University, the University of Maryland, the University of Arizona, Arizona State University, and George Mason University—are also part of the Atlas Network, which, like the SPN, links together Koch-funded think tanks and political mobilization efforts, but does so internationally (Chapter 8). In fact, the Atlas Network brings together many of the groups most actively involved in manufacturing the campus free speech crisis, including Students for Liberty, Young Americans for Liberty, the National Review Institute, Speech First, the Goldwater Institute, ALEC, and SPN.[121]

Given this network, it is hardly surprising that those responsible for manufacturing the campus free speech crisis in the US are also exporting it abroad.

8

The Free Speech International

As demonstrated in previous chapters, the Koch donor network has established a vast political apparatus in the United States, successfully pursuing market fundamentalist policies within the academy, the media, state legislatures, federal government, and the courts. This political network has provoked campus controversies, then amplified them as evidence of a full-blown crisis. The strategy has proven highly effective in advancing the network's preferred political agendas, staking a partisan culture war, recruiting student talent, shaping conversations on campus, and legitimizing greater donor influence in higher education. Given this domestic success it is not entirely surprising that Atlas Network think tanks have helped export this strategy abroad.

The Atlas Economic Research Foundation (renamed the Atlas Network) was established by Hayek devotee Antony Fisher in 1981. Fisher had previously helped found the highly influential British free-market think tank, the Institute for Economic Affairs, before going on to establish several other libertarian think tanks in the US, Canada, and Australia, including the Adam Smith Institute, the Manhattan Institute, the Pacific Research Institute, the Center for Independent Studies, and the Fraser Institute.[1] Based on his growing expertise in creating such organizations, Fisher formed the Atlas Network to help grow libertarian think tanks around the world—the "'Johnny Appleseed' of antiregulation groups."[2] Today the Atlas Network partners with 502 think tanks in 99 countries.[3] Its work includes "giv[ing] grants for new think tanks, provid[ing] courses on political management and public relations, [and] sponsor[ing] networking events around the world."[4] It works closely with IHS, and received $5,312,627 from Koch, Bradley, DonorsTrust, and Donors Capital Fund between 2001 to 2019.[5]

The Atlas Network has not only exported Austrian-school economics abroad, but also played a key role—along with elements of the right-wing media ecosystem—in attempting to replicate campus free speech crises in Canada, the United Kingdom, and Australia. In all three countries, the free speech narrative draws heavily from examples in the United States, and receives greater attention than it otherwise deserves given the absence of tangible evidence of rampant speech violations in these countries. Because their education systems are federally funded, and therefore generally less dependent upon tuition and private philanthropy, Koch-network efforts to build donor-controlled academic programs and centers have proven far less successful than in the US. However, in all three countries, arguments about the need to completely deregulate campus speech have similarly proven highly compatible with the work of libertarian think tanks as well as white nationalist and alt-right political tendencies.

CANADA

The same week Milo Yiannopoulos spoke at University of California, Berkeley, and the Goldwater Institute released their model bill, a Quebecois student at Laval University walked into the Islamic Cultural Centre of Quebec City and opened fire, murdering six worshipers and injuring 19 others. An outspoken white nationalist, anti-feminist, and anti-Muslim internet agitator, the shooter was heavily influenced by United States and Canadian right-wing provocateurs.[6] Parallel with the rise of the violent right in the US, researchers found a "20 to 25 percent jump" in active right-wing extremist groups in Canada between 2015 and 2018, noting that "far-right causes and ideas [were] infiltrating mainstream politics."[7] A leaked report showed that Canada's intelligence agency had noted a "significant growth" in online right-wing and white supremacist groups.[8] Both sides of the US/Canada border saw a spike in campus fliers, rallies, and incidents of violence from far-right and alt-right extremist groups.[9] In response, many Canadian students and faculty pushed back against dangerous speech on campus. However, the manufacturing of a campus free speech narrative in Canada, aided by considerable strategic and financial support from Koch-funded think tanks and media outlets, has villainized these anti-racist student activists.

Rebel News

Rebel News Network is Canada's leading provocative alt-right media outlet, often referred to as "Breitbart North." Its founder, Ezra Levant, began his career as a campus provocateur in 1993 at the University of Alberta's law school, where he wrote editorials denouncing the university's decision to prioritize hiring female and First Nation professors. He quickly became an outspoken media personality within the right-wing Reform Party and known on campus for "trying to proselytize his fellow students to free-market principles."[10] By 1994, Levant earned the attention of the Charles Koch Foundation, which awarded him a fellowship to work at Citizens for a Sound Economy, established by Charles Koch and Richard Fink.[11] Upon returning to Canada, Levant worked at the Fraser Institute, a libertarian think tank launched by Antony Fisher, which received $2,036,500 from the Koch and Bradley foundations between 1998 and 2019.[12]

At the Fraser Institute, Levant created a youth movement that pushed anti-union laws as well as a pension privatization scheme modeled by Chile's free-market fascist dictator. In describing his anti-pension campaign, which channeled youth outrage at paying taxes to cover older workers, Levant wrote that it was framed to look "an awful lot like the civil rights movement," but "not about race or gender," it was "about economics."[13] The Fraser Institute's founding director, Michael Walker, regaled attendees of the 2016 Association of Private Enterprise Education (APEE) conference with the success Levant had using a "student-focused picture of government activity" as benefiting pensioners at the expense of young taxpayers. The campaign was designed to trigger "emotional outbursts" in students while simultaneously "inform[ing] their outrage." As Walker tells it, "[t]hose students rose up, and they joined us" from "campuses all across the country."[14]

Since then, Levant has leveraged a similar outrage strategy to manufacture Canada's so-called free speech crisis. Rebel News's Campus Unmasked initiative publishes examples of what it calls "poisonous left-wing ideology" based in "lies, censorship and, at its most extreme, violence," as exemplified in "anti-Semitic groups like Students for Justice in Palestine," Antifa, and "leftwing professors."[15] Rebel News reporters are themselves frequently provocateurs who specialize in triggering outrage. Lauren Southern started her career at Rebel, attending protests with provocative signs suggesting that women and ethnic minorities were "faking bigotry and [sexual] assault" for their own gain, and was quickly radicalized within alt-right and white

identitarian circles.[16] Other Rebel reporters are regular campus provocateurs, including the neo-Nazi Faith Goldy, the violent anti-Islamic
founder of the English Defence League Tommy Robinson, and Proud
Boy founder Gavin McInnes. This overlap between the media organization and alt-right provocateurs became so troublesome that Rebel's
co-founder resigned after Goldy's favorable coverage of white supremacists at the Charlottesville Unite the Right rally.[17] Over the years,
Levant has run afoul of Canada's hate speech laws, which forbid speech
that "willfully promotes" or "incites hatred against any identifiable
group" in a way that may lead to a "breach of peace."[18]

Justice Centre for Constitutional Freedom

The Justice Centre for Constitutional Freedom (JCCF), an Atlas
Network member, has been particularly active in replicating campus
free speech gimmicks from the United States—including publishing a
report similar to FIRE's green, yellow, and red-light ratings for campus
speech policies. Since 2011 JCCF has published the "Campus Freedom
Index," a report that assigns Canadian universities a letter grade, A
through F, for their policies and practices and those of their student
unions.[19] A university gets an A score if it "permits controversial and
offensive expression" by "rejecting demands to cancel" speakers, ensuring events are not "obstructed or interrupted," "disciplining those who
engage in disruptive behaviour" and "publicly speaking out against
censorship perpetrated by the student union."[20] The JCCF gives grants
to student groups to help them bring speakers to campus, hosts free
speech events, and collaborates with Students for Liberty.[21]

In 2015 JCCF admitted to receiving an annual grant from the Atlas
Network, which called into question whether it had violated its charity
status according to Canadian law.[22] The organization's founder, John
Carpay, was subject to further scrutiny after remarks he made at a
conference organized by Rebel News where he claimed "the slogans
of 'diversity,' 'equity,' 'tolerance' and 'inclusion'" undermine "our free
society," and that campus activists hide a "hostility to individual freedoms" behind symbols, "whether it's the swastika for Nazi Germany or
whether it's a rainbow flag."[23] Carpay previously directed another Atlas
Network member organization, the Canadian Taxpayers Association
(CTA).[24] CTA's youth-focused group "Generation Screwed" claims to

have dozens of national chapters that organize campus events.[25] In 2017 the group co-organized "Toronto Action Forum: Free Speech and Fiscal Responsibility," which featured Ezra Levant, Jordan Peterson, and a number of speakers from the Fraser Institute and other Atlas-aligned think tanks.[26]

Jordan Peterson

Peterson rose to prominence as an outspoken critic of transgender rights, claiming that requirements to recognize someone's preferred gender pronouns constitute "compelled speech" and an "assault on biology."[27] Peterson is a psychology professor at the University of Toronto who has promoted his convoluted ideas about personality, belief, and conflict to garner a cult-like following. He corrects critics who refer to him as conservative or alt-right, claiming instead to be a "classical British liberal."[28] In 2016, Canada's parliament passed Bill C-16 which expands anti-discrimination protections to include "gender identity or expression." That September, Peterson released a frantic and scattered video response, entitled "Professor Against Political Correctness," where he warned Canadians against the "dangerous and ideologically motivated" law as part of a larger totalitarian trend. He acknowledged that his grave concern about "what's happening in the universities" was largely drawn from examples from the United States, conceding "[i]t's not so bad in Canada."[29]

Peterson invokes the "free market society" as sufficient to provide for the needs of "free individuals," compares the C-16 bill's egalitarian aspirations to the "economically suicidal" and "murderous" Soviet authoritarianism, and rails against Marxist professors, calling them Nazis. He notes that his "classically liberal" colleagues are also "scared," "nervous," and "profoundly" upset by the bill.[30] The following month, Peterson spoke at a free speech rally where he shrieked at journalists and told Rebel News's Lauren Southern "there are ugly things brewing."[31] When he was denied a grant from Canada's Social Sciences and Humanities Research Council, Rebel News took up his cause, raising more than $150,000, and by the summer of 2017, Peterson was making more than $50,000 a month by streaming his class lectures and receiving crowdfunded donations.[32]

Peterson's libertarian, "anti-PC" efforts quickly spun beyond his control. His August 2017 event titled "The Stifling of Free Speech on University Campuses" originally featured Rebel News's Faith Goldy. After Goldy drew intense criticism for her favorable coverage of white nationalists, Peterson abruptly rescheduled the event and dropped Goldy from the lineup, saying she had become "too hot of a property." One attendee called Peterson's decision a "performative contradiction" from someone who claims "to believe in freedom of speech." Andrew Anglin, the neo-Nazi blogger from the Daily Stormer, stated that he had supported Peterson up to that point, but was disappointed by his failure to uphold free speech.[33]

A few months later, a graduate student at Wilfrid Laurier University, Lindsay Shepherd, showed a video of Peterson in her first-year class. Introducing a discussion on grammar, she played a clip of Peterson denouncing gender neutral pronouns as "constructions of people who have a political ideology that I don't believe in and I also regard as dangerous." One student complained that the video was not relevant to class. Shepherd became a celebrity of the free speech cause after releasing a secret recording of a meeting in which concerned university faculty and administrators warned that she had created a toxic classroom environment.[34]

In 2018, Lindsay Shepherd founded a student group called the Laurier Society for Open Inquiry, which hosted the "Unpopular Opinion Speaker Series," beginning with Faith Goldy. The talk, entitled "Ethnocide: Multiculturalism and European Canadian Identity," triggered a large demonstration and was eventually shut down after protestors pulled a fire alarm. Shepherd's second event featured an anti-indigenous speaker who asked, "Does University Indigenization Threaten Open Inquiry?"[35]

In recent years, campus free speech groups have sprung up across Canada, championing Peterson, Shepherd, and other extreme speakers. Students advocating free speech principles have repeatedly found themselves unable to prevent their groups from becoming platforms for white nationalist, neo-Nazi, and anti-immigrant speakers.[36] As universities struggle to balance free speech, equal access, and safety, groups like the Justice Centre for Constitutional Freedom pressure campuses to adopt an absolutist notion of free speech. The Centre changed its Campus Freedom Index to include "efforts by universities to promote ideological advocacy under the guise of Equity, Diversity and Inclusion," such as "mandatory trainings (for students, faculty and staff) on 'anti-oppression' and 'unconscious bias' strategies," as indications of free speech violations. The expanded research for the Index was compiled by their new Campus Free Speech Fellow, Lindsay Shepherd.[37]

Doug Ford, Ontario's far-right Progressive Conservative Party premier, ran for election on a platform tying university funding to free speech protections.[38] The same day Ford released his policy, he hosted Jordan Peterson and a free speech student group at his house.[39] Ezra Levant also noted his "great working relationship" with Ford's office. Ford refused to disavow Faith Goldy after photos of Ford with Goldy were widely celebrated by white nationalists as an endorsement.[40] In January 2019, Ford held a secretive meeting with Jordan Peterson to discuss free speech after Peterson had called on Ford to abolish the Ontario Human Rights Commission.[41] By the end of the year, Ford's government announced that all Ontario universities had adopted the mandatory free speech policies, noting that only one out of 40,000 campus events had been canceled—a room reservation made by the Canadian Nationalist Party, a neo-Nazi group.[42]

Within this milieu, Atlas Network members have actively protected hate speech in the name of free speech. The Canadian Constitution Foundation (CCF) has launched numerous lawsuits similar to those won by its US counterparts, including FIRE, Alliance Defending Freedom, and the Center for Individual Rights. It seeks to protect individuals' rights to express hateful opinions and prosecutes those engaged in enforcing "compelled speech" (a dog whistle for various campus diversity and inclusion efforts).[43] The CCF's personnel has included the Fraser Institute's Michael Walker. It has also launched the Runnymede Society, a "national student membership organization" for law students, aimed at reshaping Canada's legal and judicial systems. Modeled on the Koch-funded Federalist Society, the Runnymede Society seeks to ensure that "free speech and intellectual diversity remain an active part of Canadian law school life."[44] Their events have featured controversial US figures and triggered protests. The 2018 Runnymede Society National Conference was devoted to "Attacks of the Rule of Law from Within," which, according to the call for papers, includes "[e]xcesses of the 'cultural appropriation' criticisms," and the threat that "[i]dentity politics" pose to "freedoms of expression, association, and religion."[45] The Runnymede Society's $250,000 annual budget is overseen by the Canadian Constitution Foundation, and includes a $10,000 grant from the Atlas Network.[46]

UNITED KINGDOM

Free speech discussions in the United Kingdom largely focus on "no-platforming" campus speakers. Most student unions abide by the National Union of Students' No Platform policy. This policy, created in the 1970s following the rise of several far-right groups, prohibits individuals or groups with known racist or fascist views from speaking at union events and prevents student union officers from sharing a public platform with those individuals or groups.[47] The policy lists only six groups for de-platforming, including the anti-Islamic English Defense League, the jihadist group Al-Muhajiroun, the far-right fascist British National Party, and the neo-Nazi group National Action.[48]

Spiked Online

Spiked Online—a website that generally rails "against the welfare state, against regulation, the Occupy movement, anti-capitalists, Jeremy Corbyn, George Soros, #MeToo, 'black privilege' and Black Lives Matter'"—has taken up the issue of campus free speech in the United Kingdom, condemning no-platforming policies, safe spaces, trigger warnings, and university sanctions against hate speech.[49] Spiked unveiled its Down with Campus Censorship campaign in 2014, and released its first Free Speech University Rankings the following year.[50] Explicitly mimicking rankings published by FIRE, Spiked ranks universities and student unions using a red, yellow, or green scale.[51] In 2016, it organized "The New Intolerance on Campus" conference, highlighting its campus campaign.[52]

Within the first year of its free speech programming, Spiked's US fundraising arm, Spiked US Inc—received $280,000 from the Charles Koch Foundation.[53] The managing editor told *The Guardian* that the money was used to "produce public debates in the US about free speech, as part of its charitable activities," and to fund campus debates called the "Unsafe Space Tour" as well as "four live events, the first of which is titled 'Should we be free to hate?'"[54] At least one tour event was sponsored by the local Young Americans for Liberty chapter. The Institute for Humane Studies' video arm, Learn Liberty, developed video content drawn from the tour.[55] While not publicly disclosing the Koch funding to its readers, Spiked did acknowledge that its university rankings received sponsorship from Policy Exchange, a right-wing British think tank.[56] In 2016 Spiked criticized Dakota Access Pipeline protestors, and frequently publishes climate denialism, without disclosing its Charles Koch Foundation funding.

Policy Exchange

Policy Exchange's close ties to the Tory Party have allowed it to play an important role in promoting the UK free speech narrative. The think tank has been listed as an Atlas Network partner,[57] and watchdog groups have raised concerns about its "highly opaque" funding.[58] In fact, the other four UK organizations to receive Transparify's label of "highly opaque"—the Institute of Economic Affairs, Civitas, Centre for Policy Studies, and the Adam Smith Institute—are also all members of the Atlas Network.[59] One investigation found that Policy Exchange received funding from several of the UK's leading energy firms while simultaneously publishing reports accusing climate activist groups of being "extremists," and recommending laws that "place restrictions on planned protest and deal more effectively with mass law breaking tactics" in order to preserve the "rule of law."[60]

Free Speech Union

Two years after Spiked launched its university rankings, the Higher Education Minister Jo Johnson established the national Office for Students (OfS), which went on the offensive against no-platform policies, threatening to "fine or suspend institutions" that no-platformed speakers. Johnson claimed that in "universities in America and, worryingly, in the UK, we have seen examples of groups seeking to stifle those who do not agree with them."[61] This campus free speech narrative was largely manufactured by a number of Koch-funded and Atlas Network think tanks. The Koch-funded Legatum Institute released its 2019 "Prosperity Index" report, which claimed to measure a "decline" in free speech.[62] Legatum received $77,000 from the Koch Foundation in 2018, and another $77,000 in 2019.[63] Citing Spiked's claim that 90% of universities censor speech, the Adam Smith Institute (an Atlas Network think tank founded by Antony Fisher) released a report warning that "[i]deological homogeneity within the academy" was undermining free speech within academia.[64] The Institute has received money from Koch network donors such as $1.2 million from the John Templeton Foundation and $11,000 in 2019 from DonorsTrust.[65]

Citing Spiked's university rankings, the United Kingdom's Joint Committee on Human Rights launched an investigation into student speech rights. However, despite the "repeated and high-profile claims that freedom of speech in universities is under attack," the committee found no evidence of "wholesale censorship of debate in universities," concluding that "press accounts of widespread suppression of free speech are clearly out of kilter with reality."[66] A 2018 BBC study similarly found that in actuality—across eight years and 120 universities—reporters could only identify nine instances of universities canceling speakers due to a formal complaint, or 0.0094 cases per school per year.[67]

However, after the Tories' 2019 electoral victory, Policy Exchange issued a brief encouraging the party to make good on its election promises to double down on campus free speech. The think tank proposed legislation that would protect campus speech that was "unwelcome, disagreeable, and even deeply offensive" and allow legal action against those responsible for disrupting speakers.[68] Policy Exchange also targeted the autonomy of students' unions, recommending that the government's newly created OfS be allowed to "investigate allegations of academic freedom or free speech violations and lead on the imposition of sanctions where appropriate." Its 2019 report called for the adoption of the Chicago Principles, and a 2020 publication took aim at protecting the academic freedom of right-wing faculty.[69] The free speech legislation looked likely to pass in 2019, until Education Minister Jo Johnson's abrupt resignation.

Among the actions that led to Johnson's removal was the appointment of Toby Young to the OfS board of directors. Shortly after his appointment, Young's academic credentials were found to have been misrepresented by the Department of Education.[70] His public writing and social media posts then surfaced, containing several misogynistic, homophobic, and eugenicist statements. In Young's defense, Jo

Johnson decried the "one-sided caricature from his armchair critics."[71] Young resigned one day before it was reported that he had attended a secretive eugenics conference the previous year alongside neo-Nazis.[72] Not long after, Jo Johnson was removed from his position overseeing universities. An investigation later found political meddling by Johnson and other ministers and exposed "serious shortcomings in fairness and transparency" in Young's appointment process.[73]

Embittered and emboldened, Toby Young formed the Free Speech Union in 2020 on the belief that "free speech is currently under assault across the Anglosphere," particularly in "schools, universities, the arts, the entertainment industry and the media." The organization seeks to help "mobilise an army of supporters" for those who are no-platformed, attacked, or fired for their opinions.[74]

Young told one interviewer that the Free Speech Union planned to encourage students to "set up free speech societies," and would offer advice on how to "stop their guest speakers from being no-platformed" and how to deal with student unions and university authorities. He specifically took aim at what he called the "problem posed by the Equality Act 2010" which allowed "diversity-crats" at universities to "prevent the 'harassment' of minorities," and "ensure minorities aren't 'discriminated' against by their peers." At the end of 2020, the Free Speech Union listed nearly twenty lawyers on its Legal Advisory Council who were "setting up a fully-underwritten insurance scheme" to give paying members "access to specialist lawyers" and "completely cover any costs associated with legal action." This council includes two US employees of the Foundation for Individual Rights in Education, numerous Spiked personnel, and the Director General of the Institute of Economic Affairs.[75]

Recent reporting has revealed that the campus free speech groups set up by Young—called Free Speech Champions—are anything but places of free expression. Rather, they remain largely beholden to the preferred ideology of the Free Speech Union. A number of students resigned to protest the expectation that participants uphold a right-wing political perspective. Students were discouraged from speaking about racism, sexism, transphobia, and Islamophobia on the grounds that these analytical concepts shut down free speech, and the Union strongly insisted that "words opposing racial, sexual and gender equality should be protected."[76]

In December 2020, Toby Young claimed credit for the passage of Cambridge University's new free speech policy, suggesting that a significant portion of voting members in Cambridge's governing body were aligned with his Free Speech Union. Immediately afterward, Young called on Cambridge to revive an invitation to Jordan Peterson for a fellowship that the private university had withdrawn the previous year.[77] He bragged that the "coalition of journalists, politicians, and intellectuals" that supported Brexit is also "very supportive of free speech," adding that "[i]t feels to me as if this could be the next big issue for this coalition to get behind, now that Brexit's happened."[78] Young is also a vocal supporter of COVID disinformation and a proponent of scientific racism.[79]

Turning Point UK

By 2019, Turning Point USA had launched its British affiliate, to a mixture of fanfare among supporters and brutal online parody among skeptics.[80] The supporters of Turning Point UK (TPUK) also included a number of wealthy Brexiteers and Tory backers, including John Mappin, a pro-Trump hotelier. When asked about the funding of TPUK, Mappin replied: "the whole idea is to stay anonymous … That's how they do it in the United States. It actually doesn't matter who funds it because it's about the ideas."[81] This dark-money operation has gained limited traction in the United Kingdom, as evidenced by a website that still promises to list its campus chapters shortly.[82] Despite limited campus presence, TPUK still advances free speech narratives through its website "Education Watch"—modeled on the TPUSA's Professor Watchlist—which publishes photos and videos of professors expressing "political bias."[83] A spokesperson for TPUK rejected the accusation that this constitutes a McCarthyite effort to silence faculty, insisting that the external pressure encourages professors to tell "both sides." When asked about what "both sides" might entail, he gave the example of British colonialism: students might feel uncomfortable voicing support for colonialism and "[o]f course there were atrocities committed, of course there were terrible things done in the name of the British Empire, but we don't think it's completely straightforward."[84]

As in the United States, the UK campus free speech crisis has been manufactured by libertarian think tanks and right-wing media groups, creating a largely false "culture war" narrative that serves both libertarian and alt-right political objectives. TPUK exemplifies the cynical politics behind these efforts, given that none of the Facebook ads announcing its launch were targeted at the United Kingdom, but rather at Ohio, California, and Texas—describing supposed free speech outrages in the United Kingdom for the purpose of enraging an American audience.[85]

AUSTRALIA

The campus free speech narrative has also arrived in Australia, again largely disseminated by Atlas Network think tanks and adjacent right-wing media outlets. As in the United States, Canada, and the United Kingdom, there remains little evidence that a free speech crisis actually exists. However, the narrative that it does has been used to push back against anti-hate speech legislation.

Institute of Public Affairs

The Institute of Public Affairs (IPA) is a leading corporate-funded free-market think tank in Australia, and a member of the Atlas Network.[86] IPA receives much of its funding from mining magnate Gina Rinehart as well as various major mining, tobacco, telecom, oil and gas, and logging companies. It is not surprising, therefore, that the IPA has also become a major purveyor of climate disinformation.[87] In 2015 IPA was named a finalist for the Atlas Network's Templeton Freedom Award for its work on repealing Australia's carbon tax.[88]

The institute also replicates campus free speech crisis language, modeled on the United States. Between 2016 and 2018, IPA published an annual Free Speech on Campus Audit ranking universities on the now familiar red, amber, green scale.[89] IPA research fellow Matthew Lesh summed up his findings, warning that "universities are becoming closed intellectual shops" where those "who express a contrarian view are far too often treated like heretics."[90] Lesh called for the Australian government to legislate "US-style free speech on campus" if universities were unwilling to make such reforms themselves.[91]

Centre for Independent Studies

The IPA is not alone in importing the specter of a free speech crisis to Australia. The Centre for Independent Studies (CIS) is a "classical liberal" think tank founded in 1976 by Antony Fisher. CIS, a long-time member of the Atlas Network, claims inspiration from Rothbard, Hayek, and Friedman, and credits Hayek's essay "The Intellectuals and Socialism"—which charges young libertarians to become "second-hand dealers" in ideas—as its main source of inspiration.[92]

In November 2018, CIS senior fellow Jeremy Sammut released a policy paper declaring an Australian free speech crisis, making the now standard arguments: accusing "contemporary identity politics" of encouraging "political censorship" by de-platforming "racist, patriarchal or homo- or trans-phobic" speakers. Sammut called on lawmakers to adopt a "compulsory university freedom charter" that would require universities to adopt policies consistent with the University of Chicago Statement. The "freedom charter" would include a system of "financial sanctions" for universities that did not impose "disciplinary" measures on disruptive students.[93] Sammut's evidence for the crisis mainly cites controversies from North America and features long passages from IPA's free speech audits. The motivating anecdote, however, was a protest triggered at Sydney University by the appearance of the known campus provocateur Bettina Arndt. Arndt's speaking career is based on her assertions that sexual assault on campus is an overblown "fake rape crisis," and that #MeToo is a "crusade by feminists to crush male sexuality." The CIS misleadingly reported that protestors "sought to enforce their previously issued demand [that] the university deny Arndt" a platform on campus.[94] To the contrary, an inquiry by the university ultimately dismissed allegations that the protestors intended to de-platform or shut down the event.[95] CIS received $50,000 from the Bradley Foundation in the early 2000s.[96]

Policy Inquiry

Nevertheless, Minister for Education Dan Tehan cited the Arndt incident and reports by IPA and CIS as the catalysts behind the decision to create a commission to review free speech on Australian campuses, led by former High Court Chief Justice Robert French.[97] When the French

Report was published in March 2019, IPA celebrated their role in having "instigated" the inquiry and, in a piece titled "Looming Crisis of Free Speech," boasted that their "list of relevant campus incidents" was quoted "in toto."[98] IPA's remarks constitute a shocking display of dishonesty since the French Report actually finds no evidence that a free speech crisis exists. Naming IPA and CIS explicitly, the report states that the review was commissioned because of a "public airing of concerns" as well as "recent events in the United States" such as Milo Yiannopoulos's visit to University of California, Berkeley. However, "[f]rom the available evidence … claims of a freedom of speech crisis on Australian campuses are not substantiated."[99] The commission noted that nearly identical findings were reported in the United Kingdom parliamentary inquiry, which concluded that allegations of a crisis were "out of kilter with reality." The report concurred with officials from Australia's top eight universities who testified that the crisis narratives "most often draw upon events and trends in the United States to argue that the same trends are occurring in Australia," while recycling "some half a dozen incidents over four years … That does not amount to a systemic problem."[100]

The fight over free speech in Australia, however, is one front in an ongoing libertarian crusade against the country's federal civil rights protections. In particular, IPA and CIS have pushed back against the country's hate speech law, Section 18C, that was spurred by a government inquiry into racist violence.[101] In the run-up to the Turnbull government's 2016 efforts to reform 18C, the Institute for Public Affairs published "The Case for the Repeal of Section 18C" arguing that the law "must be repealed" in full and specifically rejecting other amendments as "compromises" and "inadequate."[102] The report's lead author argued that natural rights do not need governmental protection, and that civil rights—including protections from hate speech—originate from over-reaching UN treaties, and are akin to Soviet-style state control: "[c]oncepts like hate speech, racial vilification, and group defamation were conceived in significantly different political environments to our own."[103]

Neither the lack of evidence nor the staggering growth of violent far-right movements have stalled efforts to manufacture a campus free speech crisis abroad. The American-made free speech narrative—developed over decades with millions of dollars invested by the Koch donor network—has been successfully exported, such that the campus outrage machine has become more networked and increasingly transnational. Provocateurs such as Milo Yiannopoulos and Lauren Southern have taken their show overseas after their brands have become too toxic locally. American anti-Islamic groups, like the Bradley Foundation-funded Middle East Forum, helped fund Rebel News in Canada and supported a rally organized by the anti-Islam activist Tommy Robinson in London.[104] (The rally turned violent and included protesters giving the Nazi salute.)[105] Koch-funded think tanks and student groups have also undermined socialist governments in Latin America. In Brazil, for example, the Atlas Network helped oust the Workers' Party from office in 2016, with nearly 30 Brazilian Atlas think tanks working closely with members of Students for Liberty.[106] Atlas think tanks in Venezuela were also active in undermining the government of Hugo Chávez.[107]

As Nancy MacLean points out, organized by the Atlas Network, "the Koch-backed corporate-anchored libertarian cause is [now] transnational."[108] As in the United States, one major strategy deployed by the plutocratic libertarian class remains the spread of disinformation, originating from different directions, and propagated by a series of networked groups that, working together, give the appearance of widespread grassroots support. The absence of any real evidence demonstrating widespread campus free speech violation has not prevented this outrage machine from manufacturing and reproducing culture war tropes about "cancel culture," "social justice warriors," "snowflakes," "leftist professors," "trigger warnings," and "safe-spaces." This network has concocted a portrait of left-leaning academics and students as fascist enemies who pose an existential threat to individual liberty, economic prosperity, and Western Civilization itself.

One the one hand, this transnational barrage of disinformation serves plutocratic donors well. It becomes a cudgel with which to attack those scholars, students, and members of the public who challenge their particular brand of radical libertarianism. It paints these critics as fascists and communist zealots. Doing so, however, requires manufacturing a moral outrage that these perceived enemies are supposedly responsible for. After all, accusing someone of critiquing a pro-corporate economic and philosophical tradition—or merely demanding racial and economic justice—is not rhetorically sufficient to gain political traction. Instead, the false charge of violating free speech—and therefore reason, democracy, and decency itself—has become an international strategy used to bully those who challenge libertarian economic policies and the plutocrats who bankroll them.

While this strategy has been successful at building cultural support for otherwise unpopular libertarian economic policies, it has also created space for white nationalists, alt-right activists, misogynists, and others who also rally behind the banner of "free speech." It empowers those who demand the individual—and unregulated—right to engage in anti-social and supremacist speech and behavior. Scholars and activists wishing to understand the twin rise of global neoliberalism and the nationalist right would be well-served by starting with an understanding of the role the plutocratic libertarian class has played in fomenting a culture war on, and off, campus.

Conclusion: Refusing the Plutocratic Free Speech Narrative

This book has demonstrated that the so-called campus free speech crisis has been largely manufactured by plutocratic libertarian donors, operatives, and academics who operate within the context of the broader Koch political network. The hyperbolic narrative of an out-of-control campus "cancel culture" that maliciously targets conservatives, tramples on individual liberty, and routinely uses violence to prevent open dialogue is simply overstated. This is not to say that controversies over free speech on campus do not take place. After all, how to best protect free speech on campus—especially if one also values academic freedom and equal access—is always a difficult intellectual, ethical, legal, and political question. These are serious questions and therefore demand attention and careful deliberation.

However, the prevalence of a hyperbolic free speech narrative that portends the doom of Western society is far from an innocent error. Rather, it is a narrative manufactured within a robust political infrastructure. And, unfortunately, many faculty, administrators, students, journalists, and members of the broader public have fallen for it. If the Koch network's goal is to manufacture social change, then the creation of largely integrated academic centers, student groups, media outlets, litigation outfits, and political groups has proven incredibly successful at advancing the narrative that "free speech" and "cancel culture" are the biggest threats facing higher education today.

How might we push back more successfully against the campus free speech narrative? How can we challenge this manufactured "common sense"? We suggest three broad strategies. First, do not engage the campus free speech narrative; instead follow the money. Second, insist upon a distinction between free speech and academic freedom. And, finally, draw out the similarities between the manufacturing of the campus free speech crisis and other examples of the plutocratic libertarian class weaponizing free speech to make equally disingenuous, yet politically expedient, arguments.

REJECT THE NARRATIVE, FOLLOW THE MONEY

A good example of accepting the Koch-manufactured campus free speech narrative at face value can be found in a September 2019 article from *Inside Higher Ed*, titled "Free Speech Laws Mushroom in Wake of Campus Protests." This piece examines the various free speech bills then making their way through legislatures in Wisconsin, Texas, Alabama, and elsewhere. The story begins with the now common anecdote of Charles Murray's 2017 visit to Middlebury College. It then provides a quote from FIRE's legislative director describing their work with college administrators to "craft language for colleges that uses a lighter touch" than the legislation designed to punish student protestors. The author then quotes Chris Kapenga, the sponsor of Wisconsin's highly punitive bill. We learn that this bill builds on the template created by the Goldwater Institute, which was written following student protests at Middlebury and Berkeley. The story goes on to quote the American Council of Trustees and Alumni vice-president, who affirms the council's preference that schools adopt free speech policies without legislative mandates. The article nears conclusion by referencing the director of education policy at the American Enterprise Institute, who chides university administrators for not doing enough to protect free speech.[1]

The story never mentions, however, that the careers of Murray and Yiannopoulos, as well as the student groups that brought them to the Middlebury and Berkeley campuses, were funded by the Koch donor network. Nor does it mention the connections between the Koch network and FIRE, or that Representative Kapenga is also a member of the American Legislative Exchange Council.[2] The story does not mention that the Goldwater Institute, ACTA, and AEI are not only funded by the Koch donor network but are also members of the State Policy Network, which coordinates political strategy between various Koch-funded entities. In fact, only *one* source mentioned in the entire story is *not* affiliated with the Koch network—a concluding aside about the importance of free speech among student athletes. Given the article's overall sourcing and framing, a better headline would be: "A Mushrooming Political Operation, Funded by Wealthy Libertarians, Makes Free Speech Laws Appear Needed in the Wake of Campus Protests, Which Were Themselves Bankrolled by These Same Donors."

While an admittedly clunky title, this nonetheless more accurately represents the reality of the so-called free speech crisis.

As with the *Inside Higher Ed* piece, most discussions of the so-called campus free speech crisis follow a similar script. They start by recounting one of a very small handful of high-profile student protests or altercations. These anecdotes are then presented as evidence that a crisis actually exists. The narratives then pivot to discussing how students, faculty, administrators, and legislators should address this supposedly pressing issue, concentrating on discussing who does (and does not) have speech rights on campus, bemoaning student protesters and liberal professors as having gone too far, asserting the persecution of conservative students, and concluding with ideas about how "both sides" might be fairly heard. We hear about the need for greater civility, and for "good speech" (rather than rowdy protests) to be the antidote to "bad speech." These stories often also repeat the trope of conservative students as a persecuted minority, boldly standing up against an army of coddled snowflakes and out-of-control liberal professors.

One implication of *Free Speech and Koch Money* is that rather than taking these stories at their face value we should instead pay close attention to the gross asymmetry in funding and political organizing that allows this political narrative to thrive. Rather than talking about whether Milo Yiannopoulos, Ben Shapiro, Charles Murray, or other right-wing political pundits, operatives, and provocateurs should be allowed on campus, we should instead be discussing how they are groomed within a political network, with careers funded by a wealthy plutocratic libertarian class, and how these same donors also fund the student groups that bring these speakers to campus, as well as the legal groups that threaten litigation against universities that deny them access. We should also point out the media ecosystem that amplifies outrage when these speakers are protested, as well as the academic centers, think tanks, and astroturf political organizations that normalize the story of persecuted conservative students.

We have demonstrated how the political infrastructure that manufactures this narrative is not ad hoc or fleeting but rather one part of a broader and multifaceted strategy originally created to fundamentally transform society in the ways desired by its plutocratic libertarian funders. As seen in the *Inside Higher Ed* piece, the narrative that conservative students need special protections becomes normalized precisely because Koch-funded think tanks and non-profits flood the discourse with culture war outrage, which is then leveraged by a number of different actors for political purposes.

Those who want to push back against the role that plutocratic libertarians play in higher education, and in society more generally, can start by following the money, rather than simply adopting the framework manufactured by the Koch network itself.

ACADEMIC FREEDOM, NOT CAMPUS FREE SPEECH

Contrary to what the libertarian right claims, colleges and universities are not institutions created to uphold an absolutist notion of free speech. As discussed in Chapter 6, public forum doctrine shows that campuses were never intended to be open forums where everyone can say whatever they want. Rather, universities are created to regulate speech and to do so in two crucial ways. First, free inquiry requires equal participation in the production and vetting of knowledge. Free discussion is only possible among participants who are not excluded or dehumanized based on their race, gender, or orientation. Universities are therefore professionally, pedagogically, and legally required to promote both free inquiry *and* equal access.[3] As such, colleges and universities regularly find themselves developing speech policies as well as inclusion and diversity initiatives that attempt to navigate this complicated tension.

The Koch-funded political operatives, in contrast, pressure universities into embracing only the most "abstract and rather limited conception of the individual outside of a specific social or political context."[4] This radical libertarian approach to free speech simply ignores the very real histories of power, hierarchy, and marginalization as well as structures of racism, sexism, and class. Furthermore, when universities are pressured into abandoning campus policies designed to promote equal access—often policies developed through normal governance procedures—this opens the door for the loudest, brashest, whitest, wealthiest, and most provocative voices on campus to remain disproportionately empowered. Whether under threat of lawsuit or because of recently passed free speech legislation, students who have spent years struggling for racial justice on campus are expected to quietly listen to Charles Murray—engaging his claims as if they merit engagement. They are also expected to refrain from forcefully demanding that their own claims be given at least as much weight. The next Milo Yiannopoulos is allowed to spew racist and transphobic rants, while trans students and students of color are expected to engage in a civil debate to justify their own humanity. These asymmetries only become even more exacerbated when some students on campus have access to vast resources enabling them to bring controversial speakers to campus, and access to lawyers who threaten schools into submission on their behalf.

Creating campus policies that genuinely allow for a free exchange of ideas requires the hard and delicate work of regulating speech in ways that attempt to address these underlying inequalities and asymmetries in access. The thoughtful and careful regulation of speech, in other words, is a necessary tool for muddling our way through the complicated processes of creating institutions where all students can enjoy equal access to the social, political, and intellectual life of the campus. Only then is it possible to have a free exchange of ideas.

Universities also regulate speech through their essential work of evaluating arguments and distinguishing good ones from bad ones. Arguments falsified by science, the historical record, or academic debate are no longer entertained. Colleges and universities, after all, are not the same as public forums—they are not intended to be Speakers' Corner at London's Hyde Park where everybody can stand on their soapbox and say whatever they want. As critic Stanley Fish writes: "[f]reedom of speech is not an academic value; freedom of inquiry is, and freedom of inquiry requires the silencing of voices."[5] In other words, the academic enterprise itself is guided not by an absolutist version of free speech but rather by the principles of rigorous and consequential debate. Colleges and universities—in contrast to, say, newspaper editorial pages, late-night comedy shows, talk radio, or internet conspiracy websites—exist to vet ideas, evidence, and arguments. The protections of academic freedom are designed to empower faculty and students to make controversial claims and push the boundaries of knowledge.

The protection of academic freedom, however, is predicated on the demonstration of expertise and participation in a community of inquiry. This is why universities routinely refuse to platform all kinds of speech. Historians, for example, do not invite Holocaust deniers to campus. Biologists do not teach creationism as a valid argument within a discipline founded on the scientific method. Climate scientists do not platform climate change deniers at their conferences. Public health experts reject out-of-hand those who deny a causal relationship between smoking and cancer. Sociologists do not indulge eugenicist theories about natural differences between people with different skin colors. Feminist and queer theorists do not find it necessary within their discipline to continually defend the established finding that gender is socially constructed. These arguments have been settled through the process of peer review and rigorous academic inquiry. Scholars debate, criticize, and review each other's work until something like an agreed-upon field emerges. Once settled, these debates become the foundations for additional investigation. Anyone who desires to disprove these otherwise settled arguments must subject their counter-propositions to the rigors of academic scrutiny. The principle of academic inquiry, in other words, holds that "speech regulation is the university's very business."[6]

However, when the Koch donor network reimagines colleges and universities through the metaphor of a radically unregulated libertarian marketplace of ideas, it seeks to supplant rigorous evidence and peer review with the absolutist notion that all claims deserve equal attention. Milo Yiannopoulos and Ben Shapiro attack feminism and so-called cultural Marxism, yet never demonstrate any evidence that they even understand the basic terms of these academic debates. In fact, claims that they deserve to speak on campus at all only make sense if one assumes that "both sides"—the trained feminist theorist and the misogynist provocateur—deserve equal attention. When libertarians and conservatives denounce universities as biased and hostile, they are often actually insisting on being taught what they want to hear rather than being taught the actual academic discussion taking place in the disciplinary field. Within the right's free-speech-as-both-sides framework, teaching an actual academic debate becomes misinterpreted as merely expressing political bias.

Joan Scott makes this argument when she notes that "the Right's reference to free speech sweeps away the guarantees of academic freedom," claiming instead that "the thoughtful, critical articulation of ideas, the demonstration of proof based on rigorous examination of evidence, the distinction between true and false, between careful and sloppy work, [and] the exercise of reasoned judgment"—namely, the judgment of whether certain ideas meet scholarly standards—is interpreted as censorship.[7] As such, "Their free speech means the right to one's opinion, however unfounded, however ungrounded, and it extends to every venue, every institution."[8]

This political weaponization of free speech within higher education is especially problematic given that the Koch network platforms an armada of speakers professionally groomed to roll back the current state of academic debates, especially on issues pertaining to race, class, and gender. This barrage takes specific aim at those academic arguments that challenge the ideological underpinnings of their preferred worldview, often an ultra-free-market interpretation of classical liberalism.

This should not necessarily come as a surprise, given that many academic fields have already raised serious challenges to this libertarian intellectual project. Decades of humanities and social science scholarship, for example, have powerfully demonstrated that enlightenment notions of individual freedom emerge from asymmetrical racialized, gendered, and class relations. Rather than engaging these arguments, however, the Koch donor network has simply dismissed them as "cultural Marxism" and "critical race theory," and opt instead for creating a parallel academy where ideas that were soundly rejected in actual academic fields are revived and widely circulated within privately funded academic centers, institutes, journals, and professional associations. Freed from the need to subject these ideas to rigorous debate, these particularly radical interpretations of classical liberalism circulate within a closed and highly subsidized marketplace. The Koch-funded academy, in other words, uses donor money to side-step the norms of academic rigor. Or, as Ulrich Baer describes it, these:

> well-funded efforts exist to impose conservative political viewpoints on the curriculum at various universities. These efforts are made in the name of fighting political correctness, liberal groupthink, and the alleged ideological corruption of the hallowed realms of teaching and research. But they blatantly undermine the principle of academic freedom, which aims at establishing the truth and not a particular ideological outcome, and which protects the authority of experts from political pressure.[9]

As such, Koch's largess and influence in the academic process actually reveals the fundamental fallacy of the libertarian notion that a free marketplace of ideas will weed out weak ideas. After all, the Koch donor network finds it necessary to provide external subsidies and orchestrate interventionist protections to ensure that its preferred ideas remain solvent in the face of otherwise overwhelming competition. (Not unlike its claim to oppose "crony capitalism" while still receiving over a half a billion dollars in federal, state, and local subsidies).[10]

Students, faculty, and institutions facing the maelstrom of a manufactured free speech crisis will inevitably be told that more speech, not regulation, is the best response to problematic speech. This argument, however, not only ignores the asymmetrical access to the proverbial marketplace but also demands that students and scholars participate in the endless labor of engaging otherwise discredited ideas simply because a donor can pay for a thousand soapboxes. For the Koch network, however, this is exactly the point: replacing community-regulated academic speech with donor-bankrolled speech. Doing so means that academics, and the broader public, become increasingly compelled to treat the manufactured positions as worthy of engagement.

CONTEXT, CONTEXT, CONTEXT

As demonstrated in this book, the campus free speech crisis exists as part of a broader political strategy, one that involves creating well-funded and integrated networks of coordinated and interlocking organizations. This strategy works when these interlocking parts appear to act independently of one another. Situating the manufacture of the campus free speech crisis within the broader political strategy clearly illustrates the cynical and anti-democratic nature of this strategy.

Theda Skocpol and Alexander Hertel-Fernandez demonstrate that the broader Koch-funded political network has made the Republican Party, and therefore American politics, more extreme and polarized. The Koch network has pushed the party to adopt radical policies endorsed by donors but not by the general public, resulting in laws that are more partisan, polarizing, and unequal.[11] Rather than making policy based on majority opinion, policy expertise, and scientific research, the Koch network pushes Republican lawmakers to become increasingly deferential to corporate donors and their preferred economic interests and ideological positions.

This corporate-funded political strategy, and corresponding infrastructure, makes deliberate use of weaponized free speech. For decades the Koch network of academics, think tanks, media outfits, legal organizations, and political mobilization operations have manufactured structural changes by polluting the discursive space with misleading or outright false—but nonetheless politically expedient— claims and assertions. With their well-funded alternatives, they have challenged policies that otherwise enjoy broad public support, and often scientifically agreed-upon consensus. Two other manufactured crises—the uproar over cap-and-trade legislation and the more recent anti-COVID lockdown protests—share many similarities with the campus free speech movement.

In recent years Koch-funded think tanks have become the vanguard of climate denial.[12] In fact, by the late 2000s the Koch network had become the primary backer of climate denial, having established a veritable "cottage industry" designed to "highlight all the points of uncertainty in the scientific debate."[13] After Obama's 2008 election, cap-and-trade legislation was fairly popular and seemed likely to pass. However, Koch-funded operatives set out to defeat the Waxman-Markey bill by establishing what they called an "echo chamber."[14] Koch lobbyists commissioned think tanks to write reports that grossly inflated the economic costs of the legislation. Koch Industries then paid the National Association of Manufacturers to "sponsor" this report, along with the Institute for Energy Research (personally founded by Charles Koch) and the American Energy Alliance, another Koch-funded think tank. In coordinated fashion, Americans For Prosperity harnessed the energy of the Tea Party, supplying material and strategic support to turn an otherwise disorganized group of activists into a well-resourced weapon, capable of channeling ire not only on the Affordable Care Act but also on the much more arcane cap-and-trade bill. To the unwitting legislators, journalists, and general public the opposition to cap-and-trade looked widespread and a mile deep. In reality, however, the coordinated manufacture and then weaponization of think-tank reports "had the effect of making the message from

Koch Industries' lobbying shop seem louder, and far more popular, than it really was."[15]

The same strategy was on display in 2020 during the Koch-funded protests against coronavirus lockdowns, which similarly included creating an echo chamber of opposition. On April 15, 2020, thousands of demonstrators arrived in Lansing, Michigan to protest the stay-at-home orders put in place by the Democratic governor. These seemingly grassroots protests were actually organized by the Michigan Freedom Fund, established in 2012 to support ALEC's anti-union legislation. Funded by Betsy DeVos, Michigan Freedom Fund works closely with the Koch-funded astroturf organization Americans for Prosperity.[16] Protestors berated public health officials, claiming that the stay-at-home orders and mandatory mask wearing violated individual liberty and represented a totalitarian governmental over-reach. Two weeks later, unmasked protestors with guns—some carrying "a Confederate flag and a noose"—pushed their way into the capital building and shouted down the legislature in session, which ultimately voted against extending Governor Whitmer's emergency declaration.[17]

In addition to the DeVos-funded Michigan Freedom Fund, another central organization behind the anti-lockdown protests—the Robert Mercer-funded Convention of States—began "leveraging its sweeping national network and digital arsenal to help stitch together scattered demonstrations across the country, making opposition to stay-at-home orders appear more widespread than is suggested by polling."[18] The Convention of States is funded by DonorsTrust, and its president, Mark Meckler, co-founded the Tea Party Patriots. Eric O'Keefe, the board president of the Convention of States' parent organization, is also a longtime Koch operative (dating back to David Koch's 1980 vice-presidential run on the libertarian ticket). Another founding board member is vice-chair of the Texas Public Policy Foundation, a State Policy Network member.[19] The group America's Frontline Doctors—which made headlines when it was revealed that one doctor had made wacky claims about alien DNA and demon sperm—held close ties to Tea Party Patriots. Following the 2020 presidential election and leading up to the far-right insurrection of January 6, 2021, Koch network organizations were also behind the #StopTheSteal protests.[20]

Paying careful attention to the similarities between the so-called campus free speech crisis and the similarly manufactured outrage over cap-and-trade and COVID lockdowns clearly demonstrates how this strategy works. First, these three cases all reframe sincere and reasonable institutional and governmental responses to complex social issues as hyperbolically coercive suppressions of individual liberty and free speech. They fetishize an anti-social notion of personal liberty and demonize efforts to develop democratic and collaborative ways of addressing systemic harm. Climate denialists, anti-lockdown protesters, and campus free speech activists consider good faith efforts to develop public policy (what they call "collectivism") to be dangerous governmental over-reach and, therefore, an existential threat to individual freedom. Furthermore, all three groups benefit from an outsized right-wing media ecosystem that uncritically reports on and circulates their efforts. This ecosystem traffics in outrage and disbelief, framing those who argue for university, state, or federal policies to address complex social issues as despotic, unhinged, and threatening.

Finally, all three cases appear as spontaneous expressions of grassroots opposition. However, like the Tea Party,[21] they are not organic and only enjoy an outsized impact because they are incorporated into an existing well-oiled and well-funded infrastructure constructed for the purpose of preserving the political, economic, and ideological interests of the plutocratic libertarian class.

Backed by the same funders, sharing overlapping boards, proselytizing the same anti-government ideology, and benefiting from the same right-wing media megaphone, these groups specialize in skewing public discussion in ways that perpetuate the myth that only individual market choices can solve social ills, and only collectivists and governments stand in the way. The ultimate goal, however, is not only to defeat particular policies—such as cap-and-trade, lockdown orders, or campus hate speech policies—but to use these confrontations to advance a radically anti-social ideology that seeks to fundamentally discredit otherwise popular governmental policies and institutions. After all, if people fundamentally trust the Intergovernmental Panel on Climate Change, the Centers for Disease Control, the World Health Organization, or the education provided by state universities then it becomes harder to justify replacing these organizations with market alternatives. If government interventions are proven necessary to address the threats of climate change and a global pandemic then this poses an existential threat to the radical libertarian agenda propagated by the Koch network.

Drawing out the similarities across these three cases also demonstrates the important role that the weaponization of free speech plays in the larger political strategy. As with the campus free speech movement, the effort to legitimize a radical libertarian ideology by disguising corporate interests as widely held grassroots concerns requires first claiming that the alternative vision is unfairly victimized. For example, in a 2019 op-ed, the Charles G. Koch Professor of Economics at Troy University, Daniel Sutter, claimed that the usage of the term "climate change denier" poses a "threat [to] liberal democracy." Democracy, he argued, is based on "accept[ing] the legitimacy of each other's beliefs" and "using words, ideas, and arguments to advance our favored positions and accept compromises when necessary." However, Sutter contends that when someone is labeled a "climate change denier" the conversation is shut down, making it impossible to hold a reasonable discussion about climate policy. Labeling someone a climate denier, Sutter concludes, ensures that "many Americans are not allowed to advocate for their favored policies through the political process."[22]

The issue, however, is not whether one should be "allowed" to advocate climate denial. The right to say stupid, dangerous, and scientifically false things is a protected right. However, Sutter is actually complaining because his preferred "belief" is not being taken seriously because it lacks scientific merit. Yet, in line with the Koch network's broader political strategy, Sutter asserts that his "favored position"— one manufactured within think tanks and non-profits funded by fossil fuel companies—should garner equal attention and legitimacy as that of climate scientists who have subjected their work to rigorous peer review and academic scrutiny. As with climate denial, all kinds of libertarian fantasies are cooked up within well-funded academic centers and think tanks. And when they are revealed as false or otherwise unworthy of attention their supporters cry "Foul!" (or, more accurately, "Free speech!").

ASKING DIFFERENT QUESTIONS

Rejecting the campus free speech narrative, making a distinction between free speech and academic freedom, and situating the campus free speech narrative within a broader political strategy makes it possible to understand just how much is at stake. It also reveals that pushing back requires changing the framework within which we address these issues. While free speech controversies are not new to college campuses, they do not have to be discussed using the framework manufactured by the Koch network. Rather than tolerating overblown claims about the decline of free inquiry, we should instead be asking: "How can we better balance free speech, academic freedom, and equal access?" What kind of thoughtful examinations, vigorous contestations, democratic deliberations, and institutional governance can make campus more inclusive, democratic, equitable, and just? Rather than engaging in hyperbolic handwringing, we should instead commit ourselves to ensuring that college campuses live up to their potential to be spaces for institutional inquiry, soul-searching, and social good. Rather than allowing them to be hijacked by externally funded political operations with clear partisan objectives, we should appreciate that complex issues cannot be reduced to a simple insistence that speech is always free and absolute.

This book demonstrates that contestations over free speech always exist within social, institutional, and political contexts. When a free speech crisis erupts on a campus, we recommend that students, faculty, administrators, journalists, and the broader public not fall into the well-honed narrative crafted by the Koch network. Likewise, we recommend avoiding arguments about who does (and does not) have the right to speak on campus and whether student protestors are overreacting. Rather we should ask what made that moment possible, and who stands to benefit. We should follow the money.

After all, without proper context, the seemingly simple question "Did students go too far in protesting Charles Murray?" is a loaded question. It's an entirely different question, however, to ask: "Did students go too far in protesting Charles Murray, given the fraught racial unrest already existing on Middlebury campus; given that Murray was brought to campus by the Koch-funded American Enterprise Institute, which also funded his entire career, which included writing academically discredited and racist books; and given that Murray received a warm institutional welcome, including from the college president introducing his talk?" That is an entirely different question, and one that more accurately accounts for the inequalities that exist around speech on college campuses, and in society more generally. Also, by acknowledging the true complexity, it becomes evident that reasonable people can arrive at different conclusions to these difficult questions.

What are some practical steps to push back against the manufactured culture war narrative? First, we suggest that students and faculty research and expose the dark-money-funded academic centers, programs, and institutes on their campuses. Appendix 2 lists a number of useful research tools and resources. Students, faculty, administrators, and the general public should also encourage their schools to adopt policies that require greater donor transparency. And if provocative speakers are brought to campus, consider planning a strategic response (see Appendix 2 for recommendations). We also suggest aggressively pushing back against campus free speech legislation being introduced at the state level.

The Koch network is a formidable political adversary. Fortunately, their strategy works best when it remains hidden, thereby increasing their ability to manufacture an exaggerated position that is perceived as enjoying widespread, organic, and popular support. Therefore, drawing greater attention to the Koch network's political machinery, and the echo chambers it creates (and depends upon), helps increase the costs for these organizations and decreases the likelihood that they will be successful.

There are also many important lessons to be learned from understanding and exposing the broader plutocratic libertarian strategy. As far back as the 1970s, Charles Koch recognized that investing in the university—more so than in lobbying, the media, political parties, or the courts—provided the greatest return on investment. As such, the Koch network has always understood universities to be a strategic terrain worth fighting for. Those of us fighting instead for greater civil rights, environmental justice, consumer protection, and an equitable economy should take this insight seriously. We should commit ourselves to preserving the university as a potential source of greater social equality. While we lack the hundreds of millions of dollars to create our own centers, programs, journals, professional organizations, and student groups, we can still use the positions we do hold to prevent the plutocratic donors from remaking our universities in the image of their corporatist fantasy. The examples of climate denial and anti-lockdown protest demonstrate that the myth of autonomous individuals pursuing their self-interest within a radically unregulated marketplace cannot provide complex answers to critical social problems—especially when this proverbial free marketplace includes paid propagators of disinformation who demand equal time and attention. As such, part of our project is to weed out those ideas that lack merit, even if they are bankrolled by millions of dollars. We are not required to buy the junk plutocratic libertarians are selling.

There are some indications that the Koch-funded strategy is weakening under increased public scrutiny. For example, in March 2021 a leaked phone call revealed the unsurprising fact that the Koch-funded political operation is leading the coordinated opposition to the massive election reform package. HR1 promises more transparency, greater voter access, and democratic inclusion in the electoral process. As if scripted, it turns out that a Mercatus-trained researcher was involved in conducting the research to craft a response to this bill for Heritage Action. This research, however, demonstrated that when HR1 was plainly framed as a measure to "sto[p] billionaires from buying elections" it was a "winning message" across the political spectrum. In the leaked recording, Kyle McKenzie reported that they had tried to craft responses to this highly effective framing, even testing the message that HR1 was "the left's attempt to use cancel culture to cancel conservatives." That culture war messaging failed to garner much traction. Therefore, to counter the bill, the Koch operatives concluded that they were better off going around the court of public opinion and lobbying Congress directly, since "winning over public support for this is actually incredibly difficult."[23]

When the culture war veneer wears thin it becomes possible to see the bigger play: an anti-democratic power grab organized by a brilliantly conceptualized, deeply integrated, and well-funded partisan operation, bankrolled by a plutocratic libertarian class. Understanding that makes visible everything at stake. The campus free speech issue is not simply about who does, and doesn't, have the right to speak on campus. Rather, it is fundamentally about the kind of a society, and university, we want.

Appendix 1: Koch Network Payments to Organizations Mentioned in the Text

Non-profit organizations in the United States are not legally obligated to disclose where they receive funding from. However, non-profits that make donations must disclose the recipient and the amounts in their 990 tax documents. For example, while we cannot look at Students for Liberty's 990s to find a list of their donors, we can find SFL listed as a recipient of donations in the Charles Koch Foundation's tax filings.

This appendix focuses on three of the largest funders within the Koch donor network: the Koch family foundations (Charles Koch Foundation, Charles Koch Institute, and Claude R. Lambe Foundation), the Bradley Foundation (including the Bradley Impact Fund), and the twin donor-advised funds used by the Koch network, DonorsTrust and Donors Capital Fund (DT/DCF).

Please note that, except on rare occasions, we do not claim that these donations were solicited or explicitly used to fund work around campus free speech. Furthermore, because contracts and memorandums of understanding (MOUs) tend to be confidential, we cannot demonstrate that particular donations to a non-profit or university were earmarked to fund, for example, the writing of a specific report, creating certain programing, filing specific legislation or lawsuits, or setting up particular academic centers. In fact, many 990s list these donations as going towards operating expenses, which either obscures the true motivation behind the donation or demonstrates that these organizations are funded because they generally contribute to the Koch donor network's long-term political interests, which often includes advancing the campus free speech narrative.

This information was compiled from 990s using the Corporate Genome Project, a tool developed by Ralph Wilson to identify the structure and function of entities within the Koch network, including the flow of money, people, and policy. Updated figures can be found at corporategenomeproject.org.

Because a considerable lag exists in the public disclosure of tax information, as of spring 2021 the most recent tax data available is from 2019. Furthermore, this list of donors is by no means exhaustive. There are countless other well-connected and wealthy libertarian institutions who regularly contribute to the Koch political network, including the Dick and Betsy DeVos Foundation, Thomas W. Smith Foundation, and the Cliff Asness Foundation. Corporations and wealthy individuals can also donate independently of their foundations. As such, the funding numbers listed here should be considered extremely conservative.

Organization	Koch	Bradley	DT/DCF	Total	Time	Ch
Adam Smith Institute	$0	$0	$11,000*	$11,000	2019	8
Alliance Defending Freedom	$0	$0	$345,850	$345,850	2004–2018	5
American Enterprise Institute	$2,413,621	$12,202,921	$29,493,730	$44,110,272	1998–2019	3
American Legislative Exchange Council	$3,992,831	$4,182,500	$3,460,821	$11,636,152	1998–2019	6
Americans for Prosperity	$52,831,790	$2,587,500	$29,352,752	$84,772,042	2004–2019	6
Arizona State University	$7,790,078	$50,000	$80,500	$7,920,578	2009–2019	7
Association of Private Enterprise Education	$390,500	$0	$0	$390,500	2006–2018	7
Atlas Network	$689,637	$357,000	$4,265,990	$5,312,627	2001–2019	8
Auburn University	$300,000	$0	$350	$300,350	2002–2008	7
Centre for Independent Studies	$0	$50,000	$0	$50,000	2000–2002	8
Clemson University	$3,462,084	$270,000	$7,000	$3,739,084	1999–2019	7
Daily Caller	$3,109,693	$500,000	$130,000	$3,739,693	2012–2019	4

Organization	Koch	Bradley	DT/DCF	Total	Time	Ch
Florida State University	$11,497,957	$0	$1,475,922	$12,973,879	2007–2019	7
Foundation for Individual Rights in Education	$5,747,561	$1,995,000	$5,933,950	$13,676,511	2000–2019	5
Fraser Institute	$1,996,500	$30,000	$10,000	$2,036,500	1998–2019	8
George Mason University	$187,208,553	$3,414,000	$56,332,890	$246,955,443	1998–2019	7
Georgetown University	$3,581,500	$1,958,912	$1,113,000	$6,653,412	1998–2019	7
Goldwater Institute for Public Policy	$317,000	$1,251,000	$4,879,514	$6,447,514	2001–2019	6
Institute for Humane Studies	$44,665,986	$700,000	$6,784,557	$52,150,543	1998–2019	7
Leadership Institute	$233,077	$730,500	$1,624,529	$2,588,106	2001–2019	4
Legatum Institute Foundation	$154,000	$0	$0	$154,000	2018–2019	8
Manhattan Institute for Policy Research	$3,117,717	$9,095,000	$2,833,885	$15,046,602	1998–2019	3
National Review Institute	$42,815	$1,038,000	$1,946,264	$3,027,079	1998–2019	4
RealClear Foundation	$141,000	$110,000	$6,125,000	$6,376,000	2014–2019	4
Sarah Lawrence College	$103,500	$0	$0	$103,500	2010–2018	7
Spiked U.S.	$280,000	$0	$0	$280,000	2016–2018	8
State Policy Network	$129,901	$1,811,500	$49,730,504	$51,671,905	2001–2019	6
Student Free Press Association	$181,800	$115,000	$1,505,853	$1,802,653	2011–2019	4
Students for Liberty	$850,114	$10,000	$2,577,099	$3,437,213	2009–2019	2
Texas Tech University	$6,586,100	$75,000	$100,000	$6,761,100	2013–2019	7
Troy University	$1,303,000	$0	$60,000	$1,363,000	2010–2019	7
Turning Point USA	$0	$583,750	$1,716,650	$2,300,400	2014–2019	2
University of Arizona	$2,684,095	$365,000	$538,999	$3,588,094	2008–2019	7

Organization	Koch	Bradley	DT/DCF	Total	Time	Ch
University of California, Los Angeles	$376,310	$1,359,883	$399,610	$2,135,803	1998–2019	7
University of Maryland, College Park	$2,153,927	$175,000	$59,500	$2,388,427	2001–2019	7
University of Wisconsin-Madison	$3,692,860	$4,520,870	$0	$8,213,730	1998–2019	7
Wake Forest University	$2,994,510	$135,000	$0	$3,129,510	2009–2016	7
Western Carolina University	$1,199,054	$0	$0	$1,199,054	2009–2019	7
Young America's Foundation	$37,300	$1,294,750	$1,693,607	$3,025,657	1998–2019	2
Young Americans for Liberty	$3,473,803	$0	$2,446,220	$5,920,023	2012–2019	2

* This amount includes two payments from DonorsTrust to the Atlas Foundation in 2019. One $10,000 payment to Atlas is described as "for the Adam Smith Institute Hayek Project." A note on the $1,000 payment reads "for the John Blundell Studentships/Adam Smith Institute project."

Appendix 2: Resources for Activists

This appendix provides resources for those seeking to push back against the Koch network on campus, including research tools and recommendations around organizing and protest.

HOW TO EXPOSE THE MONEY BEHIND THE CAMPUS FREE SPEECH CRISIS

Understanding the organizations at the heart of the Koch donor network's broader integrated political strategy, and how they intersect with your campus, requires research. As a starting bibliography, we recommend:

Mayer, Jane (2010) "Covert Operations: The Billionaire Brothers Who Are Waging War Against Obama." *The New Yorker*, August 23.

Mayer, Jane (2017) *Dark Money: The Hidden History of the Billionaires Behind the Rise of the Radical Right.* Anchor Books.

Mims, Steve (2016) *Starving the Beast* (documentary). Railyard Films.

Vogel, Pam (2017) "The Conservative Dark-Money Groups Infiltrating Campus Politics," *Media Matters for America*. At https://www.mediamatters.org/james-okeefe/conservative-dark-money-groups-infiltrating-campus-politics (last accessed May 2021).

Wilson, Ralph (2018) "Donor Intent of the Koch Network: Leveraging Universities for Self-Interested Policy Change," *UnKoch My Campus*, December. At https://tinyurl.com/y3zugtdb (last accessed August 2020).

Wilson, Ralph (2018) "Exposing the Association of Private Enterprise Education (APEE)," *UnKoch My Campus*, December. At https://tinyurl.com/yxok78fe (last accessed December 2020)

Activist groups and media organizations have also complied a number of online tools to help uncover and better understand the Koch donor network.

Charles Koch University Funding Database (Polluterwatch/ Greenpeace)

This database compiles information from tax forms (990s) to document how much money Koch family foundations have given to individual colleges and universities. Check out how much Koch money is on your campus!

https://polluterwatch.org/charles-koch-university-funding-database

SourceWatch (Center for Media and Democracy)

This wiki provides detailed content pages on major players, organizations, and individuals within the Koch world. They also provide extensive research on ALEC and the State Policy Network (SPN).

https://www.sourcewatch.org

DeSmog Blog

This website tracks how energy companies have funded climate denial, and offers a comprehensive database of individuals and organizations within the Koch donor network.

https://www.desmogblog.com; https://www.desmog.co.uk

KochDocs

This website curates books, videos, and a number of primary sources from Charles Koch and various Koch funded organizations, including speeches, tax forms, annual reports, correspondence, and other documents. This website is ideal for incorporating into student- or faculty-organized research seminars.

https://kochdocs.org

Corporate Genome Project

This is the author's database of the Koch network's highly integrated political machine.

https://www.corporategenomeproject.org/

WHEN AND HOW TO PROTEST A SPEAKER

Should you seek to exercise your right to protest or demonstrate during a speaker's event on campus, consider the following:

- *Define your goal:* Do you just want to disrupt the speaker so their rhetoric cannot be heard or do you want to provide a counter-narrative? What do you want attendees to take away from your demonstration? This question will help you decide which tactics are best to pursue.
- *Understand the risks:* Be sure you are informed of your state's latest protest laws and your campus policies related to student conduct to help you understand the risks involved with various forms of demonstration and the necessary safety measures, as well as to inform alternatives for those who cannot engage in certain levels of risk.
- *Be mindful of who is taking the risk:* One's identity often informs the risks related to policing and punishment. Can white students and allies take on higher risk roles? How will you be mindful of the roles of undocumented students, students on scholarships, and students with disabilities play in the action?
- *Prepare for retaliation:* Have plans in place for a variety of interventions, including by the police, Immigration and Customs Enforcement, armed militias and counter-protestors, and the staff of your institution. Know ahead of time whether demonstrators intend to obey orders or risk arrest/detention. Have a system in place to provide support to students who may be detained or arrested. Be equipped to advocate for students who are transgender. Make sure you have access to legal counsel.

ALTERNATIVES TO DISRUPTIVE DEMONSTRATIONS

- *Fill event seats:* Organize your peers and allies to attend the event, fill the seats, and then turn your backs on the speaker once the event begins. This strategy allows students to demonstrate while minimizing the risk of being accused of infringing upon another's speech, and it takes seats away from others.
- *Host an alternative event or teach-in:* Host a teach-in outside of the event as a counter-protest. You can approach attendees as

they enter the event and ask them to attend your event instead. This alternative event could be many things—a facilitated conversation, a planning meeting, an educational event, a pizza party, whatever. It doesn't have to be perfect, it just has to exist.

- *Projection:* Using a cordless projector, project something on the wall behind the speaker as they begin to speak. You may get removed eventually, but it will get your message across without disrupting the speaker with noise. You can also use this tactic outside of the event by projecting onto the entrance to the building.
- *Flyering:* Hand out flyers with counterpoints to the speaker's standard tropes, as well as research that highlights their past actions and funding sources to inform attendees and the general public.
- *Staggered demonstration:* Make a significant number of signs that are small enough to carry into an event without drawing attention. One by one, have students holding a sign move to the front of the room and stand in front of the speaker. Once the first student gets removed or is asked to leave, allow the speaker to start speaking again and then have a second student go to the front... so on and so on.
- *Q&A Filibuster:* Show up and sit dispersed throughout the audience. During the Q&A session, ask pointed questions. Everyone participating should be equipped with the list of questions and be on the same page about which questions are a priority. The first person who gets called on needs to ask question #1, and so on. You can also use this time to make a speech/comment. This could serve as a filibuster, and it might allow students to make their voices heard.

CONSIDERATIONS FOR ALL DEMONSTRATIONS

- *Know the facts.* Completing the research suggested above will help make sure you're able to confidently defend your decision to demonstrate.
- *Have your talking points prepared and practiced.* What are the top three most important points you want to raise? Use those points to inform your flyers, chants, signs, etc. Oftentimes these

speakers have a whole host of problematic viewpoints and awful histories; it is important that you don't confuse your audience by trying to describe this all at once.

- *Have an op-ed ready.* Because the media may not cover the event, or may not cover your action well, you should have a statement ready to go out to campus and local media as soon as the event is over.
- *Always have a debrief session.* This work is heavy, and it often requires students subjecting themselves to listening to people who don't believe in their humanity, right to exist, or right to make their own decisions. You will become burned out if you mobilize around these events and don't make time to build community and support for one another afterward. After events like this, make time to share food with each other, spend some time creating art (outside if possible), grab a drink with each other, go dancing, etc. This is a critically important but often overlooked best practice.

IMPACTFUL CONSIDERATIONS FOR FACULTY AND COMMUNITY SUPPORTERS

- *Avoid respectability politics:* After risk and safety considerations are measured, faculty and community supporters should not make a habit of advising students against disruptive demonstrations and tactics. It is critical that allies do not apply pressure on young people, especially Black activists and non-Black activists of color, to abide by "respectability politics."
- *Center solidarity praxis:* If the goal is to use a demonstration that disrupts the speaker's message through noise, community members should play a vocal role in such actions. This preparation helps get the job done without putting students or faculty in jeopardy of expulsion, firing, or other punitive measures. This means that it is critical for students to build relationships with allies outside of campus, and for the community to accept the critical role they can play in facilitating change on campus.

This appendix was assembled with contributions from Samantha Parsons, former organizing director at UnKoch My Campus.

Notes

INTRODUCTION

1. An excellent overview of the context behind the Middlebury and Evergreen protests can be found in Moskowitz, P.E. (2019) *The Case Against Free Speech: The First Amendment, Fascism, and the Future of Dissent.* New York: Bold Type Books, Chapters 3 and 4.
2. Pew (2017) "Sharp Partisan Division in Views of National Institutions," Pew Research Center. At www.pewresearch.org/politics/2017/07/10/sharp-partisan-divisions-in-views-of-national-institutions (last accessed November 2020).
3. Kreighbaum, Andrew (2019) "Trump Signs Broad Executive Order," *Inside Higher Ed*, March 22.
4. Chemerinsky, Erwin and Howard Gillman (2017) *Free Speech on Campus.* New Haven: Yale University Press; Ben-Porath, Sigal R. (2017) *Free Speech on Campus.* Philadelphia: University of Pennsylvania Press; Palfrey, John (2017) *Safe Spaces, Brave Spaces: Diversity and Free Expression in Education.* Cambridge, MA: MIT Press; Roth, Michael S. (2019) *Safe Enough Spaces: A Pragmatist's Approach to Inclusion, Free Speech, and Political Correctness on College Campuses.* New Haven: Yale University Press.
5. Lukianoff, Greg and Jonathan Haidt (2018) *The Coddling of the American Mind: How Good Intentions and Bad Ideas Are Setting Up a Generation for Failure.* New York: Penguin Books.
6. Beauchamp, Zack (2018) "Data Shows a Surprising Campus Free Speech Problem: Left-Wingers Being Fired for Their Opinions," *Vox*, August 3.
7. Baer, Ulrich (2019) *What Snowflakes Get Right: Free Speech, Truth, and Equality on Campus.* Oxford: Oxford University Press, 26.
8. Sachs, Jefrey Adam (2018) "There Is No Campus Free Speech Crisis: A Close Look at the Evidence," *Niskanen Center*, April 27; PEN America (2019) *Chasm in the Classroom: Campus Free Speech in a Divided America*, April 2.
9. Rockenbach, Alyssa N. et al. (2020) "Professors Change Few Minds on Politics—But Conservative Ones May Have More Influence," Monkey Cage, *The Washington Post*, March 2.
10. Hanlon, Aaron R. (2018) "Political Correctness Has Run Amok—on the Right," *The Chronicle of Higher Education*, January 7; Kamola, Isaac (2019) "Dear Administrators: To Protect Your Faculty from Right-Wing Attacks, Follow the Money," *Journal of Academic Freedom*, 10, 1–22;

Quintana, Chris (2018) "The Real Free-Speech Crisis Is Professors Being Disciplined for Liberal Views, a Scholar Finds," *The Chronicle of Higher Education*, April 30.

11. Moskowitz, *The Case Against Free Speech*, 1.

12. Skocpol, Theda and Alexander Hertel-Fernandez (2016) "The Koch Network and Republican Party Extremism," *Perspective on Politics* 14 (3): 681–99; Mayer, Jane (2016) *Dark Money: The Hidden History of the Billionaires Behind the Rise of the Radical Right*. New York: Doubleday; Mayer, Jane (2016) "How Right-Wing Billionaires Infiltrated Higher Education," *The Chronicle of Higher Education*, February 12; MacLean, Nancy (2017) *Democracy in Chains: The Deep History of the Radical Right's Stealth Plan for America*. New York: Viking; Hertel-Fernandez, Alexander (2019) *State Capture: How Conservative Activists, Big Business, and Wealthy Donors Reshaped the American States—and the Nation*. New York: Oxford University Press; Leonard, Christopher (2020) *Kochland: The Secret History of Koch Industries and Corporate Power in America*. New York: Simon & Schuster; MacLean, Nancy (2020) "The Koch Network's Long Game and Its Implications for Progressive Organizing," in *Labor in the Time of Trump*, Kerrissey, Jasmine et al. (eds.). Ithaca: Cornell University, 19–33. See also the sources listed in Appendix 2.

1 THE DONOR STRATEGY

1. Forbes (2020) "#15 Charles Koch," December 21. At www.forbes.com/profile/charles-koch/?sh=952be2a57d70 (last accessed December 2020).

2. Oster, Patrick and Tom Metcalf (2019) "David Koch, Billionaire Industrialist Who Funded Conservatives, Dies at 79," *Financial Post*, August 23.

3. Confessore, Nicholas (2015) "Koch Brothers' Budget of $889 Million for 2016 Is on Par With Both Parties' Spending," *The New York Times*, January 26.

4. We understand that libertarians would probably bristle at being called plutocrats. After all, libertarianism espouses a notion of individual freedom antithetical to centralized authority. However, the vast political machinery purchased and assembled by the Koch donor network works incredibly hard to undo democratic institutions and economic safeguards with the aim of greater corporate control over political and economic decision-making. We use the term "plutocratic libertarians" to name those engaged in the political project of ensuring that wealthy individuals and corporations have greater control over the political process, which includes control over speech on campus. Nancy MacLean, Jane Mayer, and others have documented how this network operates in secret, lacks a popular base of support, and seeks to constrain democracy in order to pass an otherwise unpopular political and economic agenda.

5. MacLean, Nancy (2017) *Democracy in Chains: The Deep History of the Radical Right's Stealth Plan for America.* New York: Viking, 10; Hertel-Fernandez, Alexander (2019) *State Capture: How Conservative Activists, Big Business, and Wealthy Donors Reshaped the American States—and the Nation.* New York: Oxford University Press, 166; Skocpol, Theda and Alexander Hertel-Fernandez (2016) "The Koch Network and Republican Party Extremism," *Perspective on Politics* 14 (3): 682.

6. Koch, Charles G. (1974) "Anti-Capitalism and Business," Menlo Park, CA: Institute for Humane Studies, Inc., 4–7. Archived at KochDocs.org; MacLean, *Democracy in Chains*; Wilson, Ralph (2018) "Violations of Academic Freedom, Faculty Governance, and Academic Integrity: An Analysis of the Charles Koch Foundation," *UnKoch My Campus*, December. At https://tinyurl.com/y6fcx9c2 (last accessed November 2020).

7. Polluterwatch (n.d.) "Charles Koch University Funding Database," Greenpeace. At https://polluterwatch.org/charles-koch-university-funding-database (last accessed December 2020).

8. UnKoch My Campus (2021) "Increased Funding, Increased Influence: Koch University Funding Update," May. Report available at http://www.unkochmycampus.org/funding-report (last accessed May 2021).

9. Beets, S. Douglas (2019) "The Charles Koch Foundation and Contracted Universities: Evidence from Disclosed Agreements," *Journal of Academic Ethics* 17 (3): 219–43.

10. Schulman, Daniel (2014) *Sons of Wichita: How the Koch Brothers Became America's Most Powerful and Private Dynasty.* New York: Grand Central Publishing, 108. Schulman, Daniel (2014) "The Making of the Kochtopus," *The Nation*, November 3.

11. For a discussion of this tendency, and its limitations, see: Hertel-Fernandez, *State Capture*, 161. It was common to refer to Charles and David Koch as the Koch Brothers. However, Charles was always the main driver behind the political operation, and, with the passing of David Koch in August 2019, it makes most sense to focus on Charles Koch.

12. For example, the businesses empire of David and Charles Koch probably yielded $840 million to $1.4 billion in annual savings from the Trump tax cuts alone. Kitson, Kayla (2018) "The Koch Brothers' Best Investment," *The American Prospect*, June 28.

13. Skocpol and Hertel-Fernandez, "The Koch Network and Republican Party Extremism," 685.

14. Kroll, Andy (2013) "The Dark-Money ATM of the Conservative Movement," *Mother Jones*, February 5; SourceWatch (2020) "DonorTrust," Center for Media and Democracy. At www.sourcewatch.org/index.php/DonorsTrust (last accessed December 2020).

15. Mayer, Jane (2016) *Dark Money: The Hidden History of the Billionaires Behind the Rise of the Radical Right.* New York: Doubleday, 13–18.

16. Leonard, Christopher (2019) *Kochland: The Secret History of Koch Industries and Corporate Power in America.* New York: Simon & Schuster.

17. SourceWatch (2020) "Lynde and Harry Bradley Foundation," Center for Media and Democracy. At www.sourcewatch.org/index.php/Lynde_ and_Harry_Bradley_Foundation (last accessed December 2020); Peoples, Steve (2016) "Billionaire's Aide Says No Plan to Help Trump," *Associated Press*, July 30.
18. Mayer, *Dark Money*, 232–9.
19. Campbell, Colin and Will Doran (2020) "Conservative Political Donor Art Pope Will Join UNC Board of Governors," *The News and Observer*, June 25.
20. Smith, Adam (1999 [1776]) *Wealth of Nations Books I–III*, ed. Andrew Skinner, New York: Penguin, 109.
21. MacLean, *Democracy in Chains*, Chapter 1.
22. Ibid., 24–5.
23. Ibid. Friedman explicitly references Virginia's efforts as a positive example of a market-friendly response to segregation: Friedman, Milton (1962) *Capitalism and Freedom*. Chicago: University of Chicago Press, 117–18.
24. Hall, Timothy L. (2001) *Supreme Court Justices: A Biographical Dictionary*. New York: Facts on File, 393.
25. Powell, Lewis F. Jr. (1970) "The Attack on American Institutions, Address at the Southern Industrial Relations Conference," July 15. Powell Papers. Washington and Lee University School of Law Scholarly Commons. Archived at https://scholarlycommons.law.wlu.edu/cgi/viewcontent.cgi?article=1008&context=powellspeeches (last accessed December 2020).
26. Powell, Lewis (1971) "Confidential Memorandum: Attack on American Free Enterprise System." Archived at https://archive.org/details/Powell Memorandum-AttackOnAmericanFreeEnterpriseSystem (last accessed June 2020).
27. Powell, "Confidential Memorandum."
28. For more on the Powell Memo and higher education see: Ferguson, Roderick A. (2017) *We Demand: The University and Student Protest*. Oakland, CA: University of California Press, 35–53.
29. Schulman, *Sons of Wichita*, 35–9; Leonard, *Kochland*, 42. It is also worth noting that Fred Koch later anchored his fortune by building one of the most important oil refineries in Nazi Germany, a deal negotiated by Nazi agent William Rhodes Davis and approved by Hitler himself. Archival documents show that Fred Koch's adoration of the anti-communist Nazi regime lasted until late in World War II. Mayer, *Dark Money*, 27–32.
30. Koch, Fred (1960) *A Business Man Looks at Communism*. Wichita, KS: F.C. Koch.
31. Schulman, *Sons of Wichita*, 40; Mayer, *Dark Money*, 38–9.
32. Schulman, *Sons of Wichita*, 49–55.
33. The Austrian school of economics includes a heterodox collection of economists and social theorists. When using the term "Austrian eco-

nomics" we are actually referring to the particular subset of American Austrians, largely networked through George Mason University, who have benefited from considerable Koch largess. For an intellectual history of the Austrian School see: Wasserman, Janek (2019) *The Marginal Revolutionaries: How Austrian Economists Fought the War of Ideas*. New Haven: Yale University Press; Slobodian, Quinn (2018) *Globalists: The End of Empire and the Birth of Neoliberalism*. Cambridge, MA: Harvard University Press.

34. Schulman, *Sons of Wichita*, 93.

35. For example, Mises argues that "modern civilization" was created by "the white peoples in the last two hundred years," and that its preservation requires implementing the lessons of economic science—namely, that human beings should be free to comport themselves according to individual reason. He contends that all races have the same capacity for logic and reason, but that "up to now certain races have contributed nothing or very little to the development of civilization and can, in this sense, be called inferior." Mises, Ludwig von (2008) *Human Action: A Treatise on Economics*. Auburn, AL: Ludwig von Mises Institute, 10 and 90. For an extended critique of the racialized assumptions built into classical liberalism, see: Mills, Charles W. (2014) *The Racial Contract*. Ithaca, NY: Cornell University Press.

36. Slobodian, Quinn (2019) "Anti-'68ers and the Racist-Libertarian Alliance: How a Schism Among Austrian School Neoliberals Helped Spawn the Alt Right," *Cultural Politics*, 15(3), 379–82.

37. Hayek, F.A. (1994) *The Road to Serfdom*. Chicago: University of Chicago Press.

38. Wasserman, *The Marginal Revolutionaries*, 186–7.

39. Hayek, F.A. (1960) "The Intellectuals and Socialism," in *The Intellectuals: A Controversial Portrait*, ed. George B. de Huszar, Glencoe, IL: The Free Press, 371–84.

40. Jones, Daniel Stedman (2012) *Masters of the Universe: Hayek, Friedman and the Birth of Neoliberal Politics*. Princeton: Princeton University Press, 26.

41. Ibid., 91; Nik-Khah, Edward (2014) "Neoliberal Pharmaceutical Science and the Chicago School of Economics," *Social Studies of Science*, 44 (4), 489–517.

42. Koch, "Anti-Capitalism and Business."

43. Ibid., 10.

44. Coppin, Clayton A. (2003) *Stealth: The History of Charles Koch's Political Activities*. Excerpts from an unpublished manuscript commissioned by Bill Koch and written by Coppin, a George Mason University historian and chronicler of Koch Industries. Archived at https://ia600705. us.archive.org/3/items/Stealth2003Excerpt/Stealth%202003%20Excerpt. pdf (last accessed July 2020). See also: Mayer, Jane (2016) "The Secrets

of Charles Koch's Political Ascent," *Politico*, January 18; Mayer, *Dark Money*, 53.

45. Mayer, *Dark Money*, 54.

46. Ibid. Others have written about the anti-democratic nature of the political proposals advanced by Austrian economists, including strategies to put "democracy in chains" or "encase" laissez-faire capitalism with laws, thereby subverting political remedies to the harm caused by unregulated markets. See: MacLean, *Democracy in Chains*; Slobodian, *Globalists*.

47. Coppin, *Stealth*, 54–65.

48. Ibid.

49. Ibid., 69.

50. Fink, Richard H. (1996) "From Ideas to Action: The Role of Universities, Think Tanks, and Activist Groups," *Philanthropy* X (1), Winter, 11.

51. Ibid.

52. Ibid.

53. Skocpol, Theda and Vanessa Williamson (2016) *The Tea Party and the Remaking of Republican Conservatism*. Oxford: Oxford University Press; Fang, Lee (2012) *The Machine: A Field Guide to the Resurgent Right*. New York: The New Press; Nesbit, Jeff (2016) *Poison Tea: How Big Oil and Big Tobacco Invented the Tea Party and Captured the GOP*. New York: Thomas Dunne Books.

54. There are a number of helpful resources for understanding this national political operation, including: Skocpol and Hertel-Fernandez, "The Koch Network and Republican Party Extremism"; Hertel-Fernandez, *State Capture*; Mayer, Jane (2013) "Is IKEA the New Model for the Conservative Movement?" *The New Yorker*, November 15; SourceWatch (2020) "Koch Brothers," The Center for Media and Democracy. At www.sourcewatch.org/index.php/Koch_Brothers (last accessed December 2020).

55. *Larus Brother Company v. Federal Communications Commission*, 447 F. 2d 876 (United States Court of Appeals, Fourth Circuit 1971).

56. Fallin, Amanda, Rachel Grana, and Stanton A. Glantz (2014) "'To Quarterback Behind the Scenes, Third-Party Efforts': The Tobacco Industry and the Tea Party," *Tobacco Control* 23: 322–31.

57. Unknown (1994) "Tobacco Strategy," Philip Morris Records, Master Settlement Agreement, March. Archived at www.industrydocuments.ucsf.edu/docs/qkfw0114 (last accessed December 2020).

58. Smith, Julia, Sheryl Thompson, and Kelley Lee (2017) "The Atlas Network: A 'Strategic Ally' of the Tobacco Industry," *The International Journal of Health Planning and Management* 32 (4): 433.

59. MacLean, Nancy (2021) "'Since We Are Greatly Outnumbered': Why and How the Koch Network Uses Disinformation to Thwart Democracy," in *The Disinformation Age: Politics, Technology, and Disruptive Communication in the United States*, ed. W. Lance Bennet and Steven Livingston, Cambridge: Cambridge University Press, 127.

60. Ellison, Keith (2020) "AG Ellison Press Conference: Suing ExxonMobil, Koch Industries & American Petroleum Institute," YouTube, June 24. At www.youtube.com/watch?t=161&v=9c84tVd26nE&feature=youtu.be (Remarks at 2:41) (last accessed May 2021).

61. Keith Ellison (2020) "AG Ellison Sues ExxonMobil, Koch Industries & American Petroleum Institute for Deceiving, Defrauding Minnesotans about Climate Change," Office of the Attorney General, Saint Paul, MN. At www.ag.state.mn.us/Office/Communications/2020/06/24_ExxonKochAPI.asp (last accessed December 2020).

62. Ibid.

63. Greenpeace (n.d.) "Koch Industries: Secretly Funding the Climate Denial Machine." At www.greenpeace.org/usa/global-warming/climate-deniers/koch-industries (last accessed November 2020). Also: Brulle, Robert J. (2014) "Institutionalizing Delay: Foundation Funding and the Creation of US Climate Change Counter-Movement Organizations," *Climatic Change* 122 (4), 681–94.

64. Hohmann, James (2015) "The 16 Elected Officials Who Scored Invites to the Koch Brothers' Donor Retreat," *The Washington Post*, August 1; Ahern, Mary Ann (2017) "Illinois Gov. Bruce Rauner Attends Koch Brothers Donor Summit in California," *NBC Chicago*, January 29.

65. See Appendix 1. These groups are not major players in the campus free speech issue so do not appear on the table. However, these numbers were calculated using the same method.

66. SourceWatch (2019) "Janus vs. AFSCME, U.S. Supreme Court Case," Center for Media and Democracy. At www.sourcewatch.org/index.php/Janus_vs._AFSCME,_U.S._Supreme_Court_Case (last accessed December 2020).

67. Bottari, Mary (2019) "New Koch-Funded Toolkit Has Strategies to Bankrupt Unions," *Truthout*, January 24. At https://truthout.org/articles/alecs-union-busting-toolkit-intended-to-bankrupt-unions-not-protect-workers (last accessed June 2020).

68. Mercer is a member of the Koch donor network, having funded the State Policy Network, and a whole host of Koch-backed think tanks, activist organizations, and media groups. His daughter, Rebekah Mercer, is highly active in plutocratic libertarian circles and sits on the board of the Koch-funded Young America's Foundation. See: SourceWatch (2018) "Robert Mercer," Center for Media and Democracy. At https://www.sourcewatch.org/index.php/Robert_Mercer (last accessed May 2021); Mayer, Jane (2017) "The Reclusive Hedge-Fund Tycoon Behind the Trump Presidency," *The New Yorker*, March 27.

69. Zernike, Kate (2010) "Secretive Republican Donors Are Planning Ahead," *The New York Times*, October 19.

70. Fang, Lee (2011) "Koch Industries Promises To Double Money Raised This Weekend, 40% Of Donors Will Be New," *Think Progress*, January 27.

71. Schouten, Fredreka (2015) "Charles Koch: We Like 5 GOP Candidates in Primaries," *USA Today*, April 21.
72. Schouten, Fredreka (2020) "Koch Network Plans its Biggest Election-Year Effort in 2020," CNN, January 16.
73. Lee, Michelle Ye Hee (2018) "Court Ruling: Koch-backed Charity Must Reveal Donors," *The Mercury News*, September 11.
74. Kotch, Alex (2020) "Koch Funds Groups Supporting Lawsuit Against Donor Transparency," *PR Watch*, Center for Media and Democracy, January 10.
75. Mayer, Jane (2016) "New Koch," *The New Yorker*, January 18.

2 THE STUDENT GROUPS

1. Coppin, Clayton A. (2003) *Stealth: The History of Charles Koch's Political Activities*. For information on this text, see Chapter 1, fn. 44.
2. Fink, Richard (1996) "From Ideas to Action: The Role of Universities, Think Tanks, and Activist Groups," *Philanthropy* 10 (1): 10–11 & 34–5. See Chapter 1.
3. Leaked Alderson Reporting Company transcript of Koch donor summit seminar: Stowers, Ryan, Brian Hooks, Adam Millsap, Diana Thomas, and Jim Otteson (2014) "Leverage Science and the Universities," Freedom Partners, June 15. Archived at https://ia601203.us.archive.org/9/items/FreedomPartnersLeveragingScienceAndUniversities/Freedom%20Partners%20Leveraging%20Science%20and%20Universities.pdf (last accessed July 2020).
4. Students for Liberty (n.d.) "About Us." At https://studentsforliberty.org/north-america/about-us (last accessed December 2020).
5. Ibid.
6. Students for Liberty (n.d.) "Learn About Liberty." At www.learnliberty.org/sfl-academy (last accessed December 2019).
7. Laer, Wolf von (2018) "Free Speech & The Competition of Ideas," DonorsTrust, April 2. At www.donorstrust.org/strategic-giving/free-speech-competition-of-ideas (last accessed November 2020). In this piece von Laer credits SFL working with other Koch-funded groups on campus free speech issues, including Foundation for Individual Rights in Education (FIRE; see Chapter 5), Cato Institute's Free Speech and Technology team, Institute for Humane Studies (Chapter 7), Young Americans for Liberty (Chapter 2), and Speech First (Chapter 5).
8. HeadCount (n.d.) "Interview: Alexander McCorbin of Students for Liberty." At www.headcount.org/politics-and-elections/interview-alexander-mccobin-of-students-for-liberty (last accessed November 2020).
9. Students for Liberty (n.d.) "Meet Our Team." At https://studentsforliberty.org/north-america/team (last accessed December 2020).

10. Hicks, Ty (2014) "The Pyramid of Social Change," *Students for Liberty blog*. Archived at https://web.archive.org/web/20140625132652/https://studentsforliberty.org/blog/2014/06/19/the-pyramid-of-social-change (last accessed November 2020).

11. McCobin, Alexander (2015) *The Students for Liberty Leadership Handbook*, 2015 Edition. Students for Liberty, Washington, D.C. Archived at https://ia601408.us.archive.org/8/items/the-students-for-liberty-leadership-handbook/The-Students-for-Liberty-Leadership-Handbook.pdf#page=64.

12. Students for Liberty (2010) "Students for Liberty Defeats Bigotry at CPAC," YouTube, February 21.

13. Students for Liberty (n.d.) "Group Network Activism Kits." At https://studentsforliberty.org/north-america/group-network-kits (last accessed December 2020).

14. Lucas, Monica (2015) "New Strike Teams Focus on Encouraging Student Activism," *Students for Liberty Quarterly*, Fall, 4. At https://studentsforliberty.org/wp-content/uploads/2019/09/SFL-Quarterly-Final-reduced.pdf (last accessed December 2020).

15. Students for Liberty (2015) "Share Your Constitution Day Activism to Win $1,000." At https://archive.studentsforliberty.org/2015/09/18/share-your-constitution-day-activism-to-win-1000 (last accessed December 2020).

16. Students for Liberty (n.d.) "Tonight's All-SLF Webinar: When to Sue Your University." At https://archive.studentsforliberty.org/2015/09/15/tonights-all-sfl-webinar-when-to-sue-your-university (last accessed December 2020).

17. See Appendix 1.

18. Wasserman, Janek (2019) *The Marginal Revolutionaries: How Austrian Economists Fought the War of Ideas*. New Haven: Yale University Press, 278–89; Lewis, Matt (2017) "The Insidious Libertarian-to-Alt-Right Pipeline," *The Daily Beast*, August 23.

19. Slobodian, Quinn (2019) "Anti-'68ers and the Racist-Libertarian Alliance: How a Schism Among Austrian School Neoliberals Helped Spawn the Alt Right," *Cultural Politics* 15 (3): 380.

20. Daniel Schulman (2014) "Late Libertarian Icon Murray Rothbard on Charles Koch: He 'Considers Himself Above the Law,'" *Mother Jones*, June 5.

21. Quoted in Schulman, Daniel (2014) *Sons of Wichita: How the Koch Brothers Became America's Most Powerful and Private Dynasty*. New York: Grand Central Publishing, 116.

22. Rockwell, Jr., Llewelyn H. (2016) "The Case for Paleo-libertarianism," *Liberty Magazine*, January, 34–8.

23. Slobodian, "Anti-'68ers and the Racist-Libertarian Alliance," 381.

24. Rothbard, Murray (1992) "Right-Wing Populism: A Strategy for the Paleo Movement," *Rothbard-Rockwell Report*, January 5.

25. Cobb, Joe (1985) "Interview with Ron Paul," *Reason Magazine*, July 1985.
26. Kirchick, James (2008) "Angry White Man," *The New Republic*, January 8; Ames, Mark (2015) "For the Record, Here's the Ron Paul Newsletter on 1992's L.A. Riots and Advice on Killing Black 'Animals,'" *Pando*, May 2.
27. Burns, Jennifer (2012) "Ron Paul and the New Libertarianism," *Dissent* 59 (3): 46.
28. Paul, Ron (2017) "The Political Importance of Murray Rothbard," Ludwig von Mises Institute, March 1. At https://mises.org.
29. Young Americans for Liberty (2008) "YAL Mission Statement." At https://web.archive.org/web/20081206010303/http:/www.yaliberty.org/mission.php (last accessed July 2020).
30. Young Americans for Liberty (n.d.) "About." At https://yaliberty.org/about (last accessed December 2020).
31. Cliff Maloney (2019) "Young Americans for Liberty: A Dissenting Voice Amidst the Groupthink," *The Tom Woods Show*, February 13, Ep 1341 (21:25).
32. Young Americans for Liberty (n.d.) "Strategic Partners." At https://web.archive.org/web/20091017125233/http:/www.yaliberty.org/strategic partners (last accessed July 2020).
33. Windsor, Laura (2014) "Inside the Koch Brothers' Secret Billionaire Summit," *The Nation*, June 17.
34. See Appendix 1.
35. McCobin, Alexander (2015) "Letter From the President," *Students for Liberty Quarterly*, Fall, 3.
36. Young Americans for Liberty (n.d.) "Fight for Free Speech." At https://yaliberty.org/news/activism/fight-for-free-speech (last accessed October 2020).
37. Committee on Government Relations (2018) "Campus Free-Speech Legislation: History, Progress, and Problems," American Association of University Professors, April.
38. Franks, Mary Anne (2019) *The Cult of the Constitution*. Stanford: Stanford University Press, 109.
39. Young Americans for Liberty (n.d.) "YAL in Action." At https://yaliberty.org/news/tag/free-speech-ball (last accessed July 2020).
40. Young Americans for Liberty, "Fight for Free Speech." At https://web.archive.org/web/*/https://yaliberty.org/news/activism/fight-for-free-speech (last accessed May 2021).
41. Foundation for Individual Rights in Education (n.d.) "Modesto Junior College: Students Barred from Distributing Constitutions on Constitution Day," FIRE Case Files. At www.thefire.org/cases/modesto-junior-college-students-barred-from-distributing-constitutions-on-constitution-day (last accessed August 2020).
42. KCC Daily (2017) "KCC Responds to Political Organization's Lawsuit," Kellogg Community College, June 22. At http://daily.kellogg.

edu/2017/06/22/kcc-responds-to-political-organizations-lawsuit (last accessed July 2020).

43. Atlas Network (2018) "YAL's 'National Fight for Free Speech' Restores Rights to Over 100,000 Students in US in 2017," February 5. At www. atlasnetwork.org/news/article/yals-national-fight-for-free-speech-restores-rights-to-over-100000-students (last accessed July 2020). See also Chapter 8.

44. Cooley, Lauren (2018) "Young Americans for Liberty Scores 50 Pro-Free Speech Policy Changes on Campuses Across the Country." *Washington Examiner*, December 31. See Chapter 4 for connections between the *Washington Examiner* and Koch donor network.

45. Wasserman, *The Marginal Revolutionaries*, 278–83.

46. Wilson, Ralph (2018) "Academic White Supremacy," *UnKoch My Campus*. At https://tinyurl.com/yy9qrejo (last accessed December 2020).

47. Tanenhaus, Sam and Jim Rutenberg (2014) "Rand Paul's Mixed Inheritance," *The New York Times*, January 25.

48. Southern Poverty Law Center (2000) "The Neo-Confederates," *Intelligence Report*, Summer.

49. Southern Poverty Law Center (n.d.) "Identity Evropa/American Identity Movement," Extremist Files. At www.splcenter.org/fighting-hate/extremist-files/group/identity-evropaamerican-identity-movement (last accessed July 2020).

50. Holt, Jared (2019) "Young Americans for Liberty 'Officer' Identified as Member of Identity Evropa," *Right Wing Watch*, June 11. At www.rightwingwatch.org/post/young-americans-for-liberty-officer-identified-as-member-of-identity-evropa (last accessed July 2020).

51. Kotch, Alex and Jared Holt (2019) "Koch Network Alums Are Going Full-On White Nationalist," *Sludge*, May 30; Geva, Shoham (2014) "Student Group Settles Reimbursement Lawsuit with the University," *The Michigan Daily*, July 11.

52. For an overview of YAF, see: Andrew, John A. (1997) *The Other Side of the Sixties: Young Americans for Freedom and the Rise of Conservative Politics*. New Brunswick, NJ: Rutgers University Press; Viguerie, Richard A. and David Franke (2004) *America's Right Turn: How Conservatives Used New and Alternative Media to Take Power*. Chicago: Bonus Books, 65–6.

53. See back cover of YAF's publication *Libertas* 37 (3), Fall 2016.

54. Young America's Foundation (n.d.) "Historical Timeline." At www.yaf.org/about/history (last accessed June 2019); Hoplin, Nicole and Ron Robinson (2008) *Funding Fathers: The Unsung Heroes of the Conservative Movement*. New York: Simon and Schuster, 228.

55. Young America's Foundation (n.d.) "Our Mission." At www.yaf.org/about (last accessed June 2019).

56. Young America's Foundation (n.d.) "Notable Alumna." At https://alumni.yaf.org (last accessed June 2019). Steven Miller is known to

espouse white nationalist ideas. Rogers, Katie and Jason DeParle (2019) "The White Nationalist Websites Cited by Stephen Miller," *The New York Times*, November 18.

57. Ibid.

58. Holthouse, David (2007) "Neo-Nazi Preston Wiginton Joins Forces with Young Americans for Freedom at Michigan State University," *Intelligence Report*, Southern Poverty Law Center, December 1.

59. Young America's Foundation (n.d.) "Partnerships." Archived at https://web.archive.org/web/20170314060148/https:/www.yaf.org/partnerships (last accessed July 2020).

60. Kotch, Alex (2018) "Ben Shapiro 'Owns the Libs' ... But Who Owns Him?" *TYT*, July 31; Wong, Ashley (2017) "Young America's Foundation: Who is Funding UC Berkeley's Ben Shapiro Event?" *The Daily Californian*, September 14; Young America's Foundation (n.d.) "Reagan Ranch Board of Governors." At www.yaf.org/rr-board (last accessed December 2020).

61. See Appendix 1.

62. State Policy Network (n.d.) "Young America's Foundation." At https://spn.org/organization/young-americas-foundation (last accessed May 2021).

63. Saul, "The Conservative Force Behind Speeches Roiling College Campuses."

64. Young America's Foundation (n.d.) "Campus Activism." At https://students.yaf.org/campus-activism (last accessed June 2019).

65. Young America's Foundation (n.d.) "Speakers Bureau." At www.yaf.org/speakers (last accessed June 2019).

66. Wong, "Young America's Foundation."

67. Young America's Foundation (n.d.) "Censorship Exposed." At www.yaf.org/freespeech (last accessed June 2019).

68. Holthouse, "Neo-Nazi Preston Wiginton Joins Forces with Young Americans for Freedom"; Kunzelman, Michael and Dylan Lovan (2018) "Racist 'Alt-Right' Movement Reeling After String of Setbacks," *Associated Press*, May 15; Southern Poverty Law Center (n.d.) "Kyle Bristow." At www.splcenter.org/fighting-hate/extremist-files/individual/kyle-bristow (last accessed July 2020). For a fairly comprehensive overview of connections between YAF and the alt-right see: Hatemi, Peter (2021) "What Do You Do When Hate Knocks on Your Door?" *Medium*, February 10. At https://phatemi.medium.com/what-do-you-do-when-hate-knocks-on-your-door-2cfb99da7aed (last accessed May 2021).

69. Zupkus, Kara (2019) "Childish Leftist Professor Hangs Posters Claiming YAF Chapter is a Hate Group," Young America's Foundation, November 14. At www.yaf.org/news/childish-leftist-professor-hangs-posters-claiming-yaf-chapter-is-a-hate-group (last accessed July 2020).

70. Sommer, Will (2019) "Conservative Group Fires Michelle Malkin Over Support for Holocaust Denier," *The Daily Beast*, November 18.

71. Hatemi, "What Do You Do When Hate Knocks on Your Door?"
72. Ibid.; Baumann, Nick (2013) "Top Conservatives Run PAC That Funded White Nationalists," *Mother Jones*, January 29.
73. Turning Point USA (2019) "Turning Point USA." At www.tpusa.com (last accessed April 2019).
74. Mayer, Jane (2017) "A Conservative Nonprofit That Seeks to Transform College Campuses Faces Allegations of Racial Bias and Illegal Campaign Activity," *The New Yorker*, December 21.
75. Kirk, Charlie (2018) *Campus Battlefield: How Conservatives Can Win the Battle on Campus and Why It Matters*. New York: Post Hill Press.
76. López, Christina (2019) "A Short History of Turning Point USA's Racism," Media Matters, October 1. At www.mediamatters.org/charlie-kirk/short-history-turning-point-usas-racism (last accessed July 2020).
77. Owen, Tess (2019) "Leaked Chats Show White Nationalist Group's Plot to Infiltrate Turning Point USA," *Vice*, March 11.
78. Kotch, Alex (2020) "Koch Foundation Criticizes Turing Point USA Even as Koch Network Funds the Group," *PRWatch*. At www.prwatch.org/news/2020/04/13557/koch-foundation-criticizes-turning-point-usa-even-koch-network-funds-group (last accessed July 2020).
79. See Appendix 1.
80. Aronsen, Gavin (2011) "The Koch Brothers' Million-Dollar Donor Club," *The Nation*, September 6; Bykowicz, Julie (2015) "This Boy Wonder Is Building the Conservative MoveOn.org in an Illinois Garage," *Bloomberg*, May 7.
81. Thomas is no longer on the TPUSA board, but archived webpages demonstrate that she once was. Turning Point USA (n.d). "Advisory Council." At https://web.archive.org/web/20180228083216/https:/www.tpusa.com/aboutus/advisory-council (last accessed July 2020).
82. Vasquez, Michael (2017) "Inside a Stealth Plan for Political Influence." *The Chronicle of Higher Education*, May 7.
83. Mayer, "A Conservative Nonprofit That Seeks to Transform College Campuses."
84. Bauman, Dan (2019) "T-Shirts, Conferences, and Rising Salaries: Here's What's in Turning Point USA's Latest Financial Disclosure," *The Chronicle of Higher Education*, August 14.
85. Vasquez, "Inside a Stealth Plan for Political Influence."
86. Mayer, "A Conservative Nonprofit That Seeks to Transform College Campuses."
87. Turning Point USA (2019) "About Turning Point USA." At www.tpusa.com/aboutus (last accessed September 2019).
88. Ibid.
89. Ibid.
90. Ibid.
91. Turning Point USA (2018) "Professor Watchlist." At www.professorwatchlist.org/aboutus (last accessed April 2019).

92. Vasquez, "Inside a Stealth Plan for Political Influence."
93. Vasquez, Michael (2018) "5 Takeaways From Turning Point's Plan to 'Commandeer' Campus Elections," *The Chronicle of Higher Education*, April 6.
94. Ibid.
95. Ibid.

3 THE PROVOCATEURS

1. Powell, Jr., Lewis F. (1971) "Confidential Memorandum: Attack on American Free Enterprise System." Archived at https://archive.org/details/PowellMemorandum-AttackOnAmericanFreeEnterpriseSystem (last accessed June 2020).
2. Coppin, Clayton A. (2003) *Stealth: The History of Charles Koch's Political Activities*. For information on this text, see Chapter 1, fn. 44.
3. For example, Campus Reform and The College Fix (see Chapter 4) pay students to report on "liberal bias" on campus, TPUSA's "Professor Watchlist" targets faculty perceived to "discriminate against conservative students and advance leftist propaganda in the classroom," and the Middle East Forum criticizes faculty they see as insufficiently pro-American in their approach to American foreign policy and the Israel/Palestine conflict.
4. Bérubé, Michael and Cary Nelson, eds. (1995) *Higher Education Under Fire: Politics, Economics, and the Crisis of the Humanities*. New York: Routledge; Newfield, Christopher (2008) *Unmaking the Public University: The Forty-Year Assault on the Middle Class*. Cambridge, MA: Harvard University Press.
5. Lewis, Matt (2017) "The Insidious Libertarian-to-Alt-Right Pipeline," *The Daily Beast*, August 23.
6. Sheffield, Matthew (2016) "A History of Hate: Long Before Trump, White Nationalists Flocked to Ron Paul," *Salon*, December 9.
7. Lewis, "The Insidious Libertarian-to-Alt-Right Pipeline"; Siegel, Jacob (2016) "The Alt-Right's Jewish Godfather," *Table*, November 29.
8. Fausset, Richard (2017) "A Voice of Hate in America's Heartland," *The New York Times*, November 25.
9. See Appendix 1.
10. Jaschik, Scott (2017) "5 Suspended for Blocking Speech," *Inside Higher Ed*, July 18.
11. Creedon, Kathleen (2019) "Previously, on SGA: Tables Have Turned," *Trinitonian*, October 3. At www.trinitonian.com/previously-on-sga-tables-have-turned (last accessed July 2020).
12. Wiener, Don (2020) "Right-Wing Prager U Triples Revenue in Two Years," *PR Watch*, Center for Media and Democracy, January 16. At www.

prwatch.org/news/2020/01/13527/right-wing-prageru-triples-revenue-two-years (last accessed August 2020).

13. SourceWatch (2017) "Young America's Foundation," Center for Media and Democracy. At www.sourcewatch.org/index.php?title=Young_America%27s_Foundation (last accessed July 2020).

14. Saul, Stephanie (2017) "The Conservative Force Behind Speeches Roiling College Campuses," *The New York Times*, May 20.

15. Kotch, Alex (2017) "Discrimination 101: How Koch, DeVos Families Fund Hate Speech On U.S. College Campuses," *Salon*, April 20.

16. SourceWatch (2010) "Ann Coulter," Center for Media and Democracy. At www.sourcewatch.org/index.php?title=Ann_Coulter (last accessed July 2020).

17. Bauman, Dan (2019) "T-Shirts, Conferences, and Rising Salaries: Here's What's in Turning Point USA's Latest Financial Disclosure," *The Chronicle of Higher Education*, August 14.

18. Turning Point USA (n.d.) "Speakers Bureau." At www.tpusa.com/speakers bureau (last accessed July 2020).

19. Foster, Madelyn (2017) "Turning Point Founder Charlie Kirk Speaks on Socialism," *The Daily Illini*, October 5; Petersen, Anne Helen (2019) "Charlie Kirk and Candace Owens' Campus Tour Is All About the Owns," *BuzzFeed*, May 1; Denburg, Hart Van (2019) "Donald Trump Jr. and Charlie Kirk Lead a 'Culture War' Moment at Colorado State University," *CPR News*, October 23.

20. Wong, Ashley (2017) "Young America's Foundation: Who is Funding UC Berkeley's Ben Shapiro Event?" *Daily Californian*, September 14.

21. Young America's Foundation (n.d.) "Speakers Bureau." At www.yaf.org/speakers (last accessed November 2020).

22. Young America's Foundation (n.d.) "Censorship Exposed." At www.yaf.org/freespeech (last accessed June 2019).

23. Yiannopoulos, Milo (2015) "Birth Control Makes Women Unattractive and Crazy," *Breitbart*, December 8; Yiannopoulos, Milo (2017) "Trump Slims Down Lena Dunham. Is There Anything He Can't Do?" *Breitbart*, February 7.

24. Bernstein, Joseph (2016) "Top Conservative Writer Is a Group Effort, Sources Say," *BuzzFeed*, March 31.

25. Campuzano, Eder (2016) "Milo Yiannopoulos at the University of Oregon: 'I Don't Want Any Muslims in the Country,'" Oregon Live, *The Oregonian*, May 11; Guest Author (2016) "Milo Speaks Freely," Students for Liberty, June 13. Archived at https://web.archive.org/web/20160824193449/https://studentsforliberty.org/blog/2016/06/13/milo-speaks-freely (last accessed July 2020).

26. Boyer, Matthew (2016) "Blood Paint and Vandalism Greet Anti-Feminist Troll Milo Yiannopoulos at Rutgers," *The College Fix*, February 11.

27. Wolcott, R.J. (2016) "Protesters Arrested Prior to Milo Yiannopoulos Event at MSU," *Lansing State Journal*, December 7; Yiannopoulos,

Milo (2019) "Milo at MSU on 'Reclaiming Constantinople,'" *Breitbart*, December 7.

28. News Staff (2017) "Man Shot on UW Campus During Protest is Improving," KIRO 7, January 22.
29. Oppenheim, Maya (2017) "US Berkeley Protests: Milo Yiannopoulos Planned to 'Publicly Name Undocumented Students' in Cancelled Talk," *Independent*, February 3.
30. Tucker, Jill, Kimberly Veklerov, Lizzie Johnson, and Nanette Asimov (2017) "Yiannopoulos Visits Sproul for 15 minutes; UC Berkeley Spends $800,000," *San Francisco Chronicle*, September 24.
31. Lee, Madeleine (2016) "Yiannopoulos' Dangerous Faggot Tour Passes Through UCSB," *The Bottomline*, UC Santa Barbara, May 31.
32. The Collegian Editorial Board (2018) "Student Leaders Should Disaffiliate with Turning Point USA," *The Rocky Mountain Collegian*, April 4.
33. Sheeler, Andrew (2018) "Security for Milo Yiannopoulos' Cal Poly Event Cost More Than $86,000," *The Tribune*, May 4.
34. Bernstein, Joseph (2019) "Alt-White: How the Breitbart Machine Laundered Racist Hate," *BuzzFeed*, October 5.
35. Cadwalladr, Carol (2017) "Robert Mercer: The Big Data Billionaire Waging War on Mainstream Media," *The Guardian*, February 26.
36. Vogel, Kenneth P. and Ben Schreckinger (2016) "The Most Powerful Woman in GOP Politics," *Politico*, September 7.
37. Ibid.
38. SourceWatch (2018) "Robert Mercer," Center for Media and Democracy. At www.sourcewatch.org/index.php/Robert_Mercer (last accessed July 2020).
39. Breningstall, Jeremy (2017) "Mercer Family Potentially Funding Milo Yiannopoulos, 'Free Speech Week.'" *Daily Californian*, September 22.
40. Ibid.
41. Ibid.; Nguyen, Tina (2017) "'Holy S—T': Allies Shocked as Bob Mercer Renounces Milo, Dumps His Stake in Breitbart," *Vanity Fair*, November 2.
42. Nussbaum, Matthew and Alex Isenstadt (2017) "Milo Yiannopoulos Disinvited from CPAC Slot Amid Tape Controversy," *Politico*, February 20.
43. Gray, Rosie (2017) "The Mercers Wash Their Hands of Milo," *The Atlantic*, November 2.
44. Anonymous (n.d.) "More Milton Friedman, Less Milo Yiannopoulos: A Call for Real Liberty," Students for Liberty. Archived at https://web.archive.org/web/20190803190649/www.studentsforliberty.org/2017/02/24/more-milton-friedman-less-milo-yiannopoulos-a-call-for-real-liberty (last accessed July 2020).
45. Singal, Jesse (2019) "Explaining Ben Shapiro's Messy, Ethnic-Slur-Laden Breakup with Breitbart," *Intelligencer*, New York Magazine, May 26; Tavernise, Sabrina (2017) "Ben Shapiro, a Provocative 'Gladiator,' Battles to Win Young Conservatives," *The New York Times*, November 23.

46. Groypers are a loose group of alt-right, white supremacists, and neo-Nazis who follow podcaster Nike Fuentes, AIM leader Patrick Casey, and others. The Groyper Army has targeted TPUSA's Charlie Kirk, Ben Shapiro, and others on the right for being insufficiently "pro white" and Christian. Tanner, Charles and Devin Burghart (2020) "From Alt-Right to Groyper: White Nationalist Rebrand for 2020 and Beyond," Institute for Research & Education on Human Rights. At www.irehr.org/reports/alt-right-to-groyper (last accessed August 2020).
47. Tavernise, "Ben Shapiro, a Provocative 'Gladiator.'"
48. Shapiro, Ben (2004) *Brainwashed: How Universities Indoctrinate America's Youth*. Nashville, TN: WND Books.
49. Shapiro, Ben (2013) *Bullies: How the Left's Culture of Fear and Intimidation Silences Americans*. New York: Threshold Editions.
50. Tavernise, "Ben Shapiro, a Provocative 'Gladiator.'"
51. Ibid.
52. Young America's Foundation (n.d.) "The #1 Requested Speaker Partners with the #1 Conservative Youth Outreach Organization for the Spring 2020 Semester." At www.yaf.org/shapirotour (last accessed July 2020).
53. Nguyen, Tina (2018) "'Let Me Make You Famous': How Hollywood Invented Ben Shapiro," *Vanity Fair*, December 9.
54. Ibid.
55. Montgomery, Peter (2014) "Meet the Billionaire Brothers You Have Never Heard of Who Fund the Religious Right," *The American Prospect*, June 13.
56. Ibid.
57. Ibid.
58. Kotch, Alex (2019) "Ben Shapiro 'Owns the Libs' ... But Who Owns Him?" *TYT*, July 31.
59. Wong, "Young America's Foundation."
60. YAF, "The #1 Requested Speaker."
61. Garcia, Sid and Tim Rearden (2016) "Ben Shapiro Escorted by Police from CSULA Due to Angry Protesters," ABC 7, February 26.
62. Young America's Foundation (2016) "Ben Shapiro LIVE at University of Wisconsin–Madison," YouTube, November 16.
63. Johnson, Lizzie, Nanette Asimov, Kimberly Veklerov, and Jill Tucker (2017) "Ben Shapiro Takes Stage at UC Berkeley Under Extraordinary Security," *San Francisco Chronicle*, September 15.
64. Wong, "Young America's Foundation."
65. Turning Point USA, "Speakers Bureau."
66. Bandur, Michelle (2018) "Police Presence at Ben Shapiro Event on Creighton University Campus," KETV Omaha, March 5.
67. Ben Shapiro, "Turning Point USA Is An Indispensable Organization," Twitter, June 14, 2016. At https://twitter.com/benshapiro/status/742758853918347264?lang=en (last accessed December 2019).

68. Murray, Charles (1984) *Losing Ground: American Social Policy, 1950–1980*. New York: Basic Books, 219.

69. Deparle, Jason (1994) "Daring Research or 'Social Science Pornography'?: Charles Murray," *The New York Times Magazine*, October 9.

70. Herrnstein, Richard J. and Charles Murray (1994) *The Bell Curve: Intelligence and Class Structure in American Life*. New York: Free Press Paperbacks.

71. Lane, Charles (1994) "The Tainted Sources of 'The Bell Curve,'" *The New York Review of Books*, December 1.

72. Southern Poverty Law Center 2019 (n.d.) "Charles Murray." At https://www.splcenter.org/fighting-hate/extremist-files/individual/charles-murray (last accessed May 2021).

73. Murray, Charles (2012) *Coming Apart: The State of White America 1960–2010*. New York: Crown Forum.

74. Moskowitz, P.E. (2019) *The Case Against Free Speech: The First Amendment, Fascism, and the Future of Dissent*. New York: Bold Type Books, 49.

75. Institute for Humane Studies (2019) "Big Think Partnership Brings New Audience to IHS," *News from IHS*, Fall 2019, 3.

76. Gee, Taylor (2019) "How the Middlebury Riot Really Went Down," *Politico*, May 28.

77. DiGravio, Will (2017) "Students Protest Lecture By Dr. Charles Murray at Middlebury College," YouTube, March 2.

78. Moskowitz, *The Case Against Free Speech*, 43–64; Gee, "How the Middlebury Riot Really Went Down"; Hewitt, Elizabeth (2016) "Swastika Found on Middlebury Jewish Center," *VT Digger*, November 17.

79. Mayer, Jane (2016) *Dark Money: The Hidden History of the Billionaires Behind the Rise of the Radical Right*. New York: Doubleday, 111.

80. Moskowitz, *The Case Against Free Speech*, 50–1.

81. Deparle, "Daring Research or 'Social Science Pornography.'"

82. Schwarz, Hanna (2016) "Bradley Foundation Gives Grant to 'The Bell Curve' Co-author," *Milwaukee Journal Sentinel*, July 2.

83. Windsor, Lauren (2014) "Inside the Koch Brothers' Secret Billionaire Summit," *The Nation*, June 17.

84. Ha, Thu-Huong (2019) "The Koch Brothers' Summer Reading List for their Super Secret Conservative Millionaire Consortium," *Quartz*, August 1.

85. Gold, Matea and James Hohmann (2017) "Koch Network Could Serve as Potent Resistance in Trump Era," *The Washington Post*, January 30.

86. Murray, Charles (2012) "On the Cato-Koch Affair," *National Review*, July 29.

87. See Appendix 1.

88. AEI's Board of Trustees can be found at the institute's website (www.aei.org/about/board-of-trustees) and cross-referenced with a list of Koch network donors assembled by SourceWatch (www.sourcewatch.org/index.php/Koch_Network).

89. Murray, Charles (2015) *By the People: Rebuilding Liberty Without Permission.* New York: Crown Forum, 117.

90. Middlebury College (n.d.) "American Enterprise Institute Club." At https://middlebury.campuslabs.com/engage/organization/AEI (last accessed June 2019).

91. Indiana University's Tocqueville Program is funded by the Manhattan Institute and the Charles Koch Foundation, as per its website: http://web.archive.org/web/20160709134530/http://ostromworkshop.indiana.edu/tocqueville/welcome.php.

92. Verschoor, Sarah and Lydia Gerike (2017) "IUPD Costs Revealed for Charles Murray's Speech," *Indiana Daily Student*, April 27.

93. American Enterprise Institute (n.d.) "AEI Executive Councils." At www.aei.org/academic-programs/executive-councils (last accessed June 2019).

94. Commission on Free Speech (2018) "Report of the Chancellor's Commission on Free Speech," Office of the Chancellor, University of California-Berkeley, April 10, 2.

95. Ibid., 6 (emphasis added).

96. Franks, Mary Anne (2020) *The Cult of the Constitution: Our Deadly Devotion to Guns and Free Speech.* Stanford, CA: Stanford University Press; Batchis, Wayne (2016) *The Right's First Amendment: The Politics of Free Speech and the Return of Conservative Libertarianism.* Stanford, CA: Stanford University Press.

97. Franks, *The Cult of the Constitution*, 111.

98. Joo, Thomas W. (2014) "The Worst Test of Truth: The Marketplace of Ideas as Faulty Metaphor," *Tulane Law Review* 89: 387.

99. The Koch network privately acknowledges that its political ideas are held by a minority. As a result, the spread of disinformation has become an important strategy. MacLean, Nancy (2021) "'Since We Are Greatly Outnumbered': Why and How the Koch Network Uses Disinformation to Thwart Democracy," in *The Disinformation Age: Politics, Technology, and Disruptive Communication in the United States*, ed. W. Lance Bennet and Steven Livingston. Cambridge: Cambridge University Press.

100. Coppin, *Stealth*, 67.

4 THE MEDIA AMPLIFIERS

1. Some paragraphs in this chapter are used, or adapted, from Isaac Kamola (2019) "Dear Administrators: To Protect Your Faculty from Right-Wing Attacks, Follow the Money," *Journal of Academic Freedom* 10: 1–22. We would like to thank the AAUP for granting permission to republish this material.

2. Benkler, Yochai, Robert Faris, and Hal Roberts (2018) *Network Propaganda: Manipulation, Disinformation, and Radicalization in American Politics.* Oxford: Oxford University Press, 383.

3. Ibid.
4. Mayer, Jane (2016) *Dark Money: The Hidden History of the Billionaires Behind the Rise of the Radical Right*. New York: Doubleday, 55; MacLean, Nancy (2021) "'Since We Are Greatly Outnumbered': Why and How the Koch Network Uses Disinformation to Thwart Democracy," in *The Disinformation Age: Politics, Technology, and Disruptive Communication in the United States*, ed. W. Lance Bennet and Steven Livingston. Cambridge: Cambridge University Press, 123.
5. Mayer, *Dark Money*, 55–6; Kotch, Alex (2018) "Charles Koch Is Funding Rightwing, Pro-Trump Media, New Disclosure Reveals," *Sludge*, November 21.
6. Ibid.
7. Ibid.
8. Charles Koch Institute (n.d.) "Partner Organizations." Archived at https://web.archive.org/web/20171014022713/https:/www.charleskoch institute.org/educational-programs/partner-organizations and https:// web.archive.org/web/20190108205154/https:/www.charleskoch institute.org/educational-programs/partner-organizations (last accessed March 2020).
9. We place "stories" and "reporting" in quotation marks when referring to the writing done by Campus Reform and the College Fix, to convey that this material is not created to investigate or accurately report on the complexities of campus free speech issues. Rather these outlets produce partisan hackery and should be treated as such.
10. Kamola, "Dear Administrators," 3.
11. Gluckman, Nell (2020) "The Outrage Peddlers Are Here to Stay," *The Chronicle of Higher Education*, November 17; Bader, Eleanor (2020) "'Campus Reform' is Funneling Koch Money to Groom Right-Wing 'Journalists,'" *TruthOut*, November 15; Speri, Alice (2021) "A Billionaire-Funded Website with Ties to the Far Right is Trying to 'Cancel' University Professors," *The Intercept*, April 10; Tiede, Hans-Joerg, Samantha McCarthy, Isaac Kamola, and Alyson K. Spurgas (2021) "Data Snapshot: Whom Does Campus Reform Target and What Are the Effects?," *Academe*, American Association of University Professors (AAUP), Spring. At https://www.aaup.org/article/data-snapshot-whom-does-campus-reform-target-and-what-are-effects (last accessed May 2021).
12. Quintana, Chris and Brock Read (2017) "Signal Boost: How Conservative Media Outlets Turn Faculty Viewpoints Into National News," *The Chronicle of Higher Education*, June 22.
13. Campus Reform (n.d.) "About." At www.campusreform.org/about (last accessed January 2020).
14. Campus Reform (n.d.) "Alumni." At www.campusreform.org/Alumni (last accessed March 2020).

15. Leadership Institute (n.d.) "What's Going On in the National Field Program?" At www.leadershipinstitute.org/campus (last accessed April 2019).

16. Schmidt, Peter (2015) "Higher Education's Internet Outrage Machine," *The Chronicle of Higher Education*, September 8.

17. Ibid.

18. Campus Reform, "Alumni."

19. Tapper, Malanika K. (2020) "Inside the Conservative Media Outlet Feeding Harvard Students to Fox News," *Harvard Crimson*, March 5.

20. Leadership Institute, "What's Going On in the National Field Program?"

21. SourceWatch (2018) "The Leadership Institute," Center for Media and Democracy. At www.sourcewatch.org/index.php?title=The_Leadership_Institute (last accessed April 2020).

22. Leadership Institute (2010) "Leadership Institute-trained Freedom Fighters Gather In Washington, DC," January 22. At https:/www.leadershipinstitute.org/News/?NR=2276 (last accessed January 2020).

23. "Leadership Institute (n.d.) "Request a Speaker Grant." At www.leadershipinstitute.org/campus (last accessed January 2020).

24. Frumin, Ben (2010) "The Leadership Institute: The Group That Helped Launch The Conservative Careers of Two Alleged Phone Tamperers," *Talking Points Memo*, January 27.

25. James O'Keefe (n.d.) "The Left Wants to Ban All Conservatives," Leadership Institute. At https://secured.leadershipinstitute.org/james (last accessed August 2020).

26. Quintana, Chris (2017) "A Campus-Politics Whodunit: Who Invited James O'Keefe to Speak at Middlebury?," *The Chronicle of Higher Education*, December 13.

27. Holthouse, David (2007) "Neo-Nazi Preston Wiginton Joins Forces with Young Americans for Freedom at Michigan State University," *Intelligence Report*, Southern Poverty Law Center, December 1.

28. Vogel, Pam (2017) "The Conservative Dark-Money Groups Infiltrating Campus Politics," *Media Matters*, March 29. At www.mediamatters.org/research/2017/03/29/conservative-dark-money-groups-infiltrating-campus-politics/215822#cr (last accessed April 2019).

29. Quoted in Givas, Nick (2018) "Campus Reform Editor-in-Chief Blames College Culture for Current Mob Mentality," *The Daily Caller*, September 19.

30. See Appendix 1. Vogel, "The Conservative Dark-Money Groups Infiltrating Campus Politics."

31. Leadership Institute (n.d.) "Kevin Gentry—Volunteer Faculty at the Leadership Institute," "David Dziok—Volunteer Faculty at the Leadership Institute," "Reid Smith—Volunteer Faculty at the Leadership Institute," "Catherine Rodriguez—Volunteer Faculty at the Leadership Institute," and "Kasey Darling—Former Guest Speaker at the Leadership Institute." At www.leadershipinstitute.org (last accessed January 2020).

32. Fain, Paul, and Rick Seltzer (2017) "Family Ties," *Inside Higher Ed*, February 7.

33. The College Fix (2018) *Prospectus: 2018–19 School Year*, 3. At www.thecollegefix.com/wp-content/uploads/2018/11/SFPA-Prospectus-2018-FINAL-1.pdf (last accessed January 2020).

34. Schmidt, "Higher Education's Internet Outrage Machine."

35. Ibid.

36. The College Fix, *Prospectus*, 11.

37. Ibid., 2; The College Fix, "Student Reporters." At www.thecollegefix.com/about/authors (last accessed December 2020).

38. Student Free Press Association, "Mission." Archived at https://web.archive.org/web/20100830232912/http:/www.studentfreepress.net:80/about-2/mission (last accessed January 2020).

39. The College Fix, "About the Fix." At www.thecollegefix.com/about (last accessed January 2020).

40. See Appendix 1. Kotch, "Charles Koch Is Funding Rightwing, Pro-Trump Media."

41. The College Fix (n.d.) "Who We Are." At www.thecollegefix.com/about/who-we-are (last accessed March 2020).

42. Fain and Seltzer, "Family Ties."

43. The College Fix, *Prospectus*, 9.

44. Breitbart, "Campus Reform." At www.breitbart.com/tag/campus-reform (last accessed January 2020).

45. Breitbart, "YAF." At www.breitbart.com/tag/yaf. And "Turning Point USA." At www.breitbart.com/tag/turning-point-usa (last accessed March 2020).

46. Bernstein, Joseph (2017) "Here's How Breitbart and Milo Smuggled White Nationalism Into the Mainstream," *BuzzFeed*, October 5.

47. Kutner, Max (2016) "Meet Robert Mercer, the Mysterious Billionaire Benefactor of Breitbart," *Newsweek*, November 21.

48. Swenson, Kyle (2018) "Rebekah Mercer, the Billionaire Backer of Bannon and Trump, Chooses Sides," *The Washington Post*, January 5.

49. Mayer, Jane (2017) "The Reclusive Hedge-Fund Tycoon Behind the Trump Residency," *The New Yorker*, March 17.

50. Vogel, Kenneth P. and Mike Allen (2014) "Koch Donors Uncloaked," *Politico*, October 14.

51. Byers, Dylan (2012) "Foster Friess Celebrates The Daily Caller," *Politico*, January 23.

52. PEN America (2019) *Chasm in the Classroom: Campus Free Speech in a Divided America*, April 2. At https://pen.org/wp-content/uploads/2019/04/2019-PEN-Chasm-in-the-Classroom-04.25.pdf (last accessed March 2020).

53. Meares, Joel (2011) "The Great Right Hype: Tucker Carlson and his Daily Caller," *Columbia Journalism Review*, July/August; Eric Boehlert (2011) "Daily Caller Hyped O'Keefe's NPR Tapes, Now Won't

Acknowledge Doubts Surrounding Them," *Media Matters*, March 14. At www.mediamatters.org/tucker-carlson/daily-caller-hyped-okeefes-npr-tapes-now-wont-acknowledge-doubts-surrounding-them (last accessed March 2020); Leonning, Carol D. and Ernesto Londoño (2013) "Escorts say Menendez Prostitution Claims Were Made Up," *The Washington Post*, March 4.

54. Stephen Piggott and Alex Amend (2017) "The Daily Caller Has a White Nationalist Problem," Southern Poverty Law Center, August 16. At www.splcenter.org/hatewatch/2017/08/16/daily-caller-has-white-nationalist-problem (last accessed March 2020).

55. Tom Kludt (2017) "Fox News, Daily Caller Delete Posts Encouraging People to Drive Through Protests," CNN Business, August 15.

56. John Bowden (2017) "Daily Caller Drops Milo Yiannopoulos After First Column," *The Hill*, November 4.

57. Calvin Sloan (2017) "Tucker Carlson, His 'Charity,' and the Trump Campaign Cash He Didn't Tell FOX Viewers About," Center for Media and Democracy, June 1. At www.exposedbycmd.org/tucker-carlson (last accessed March 2020); Borchers, Callum (2017) "Charity Doubles as a Profit Stream at the Daily Caller News Foundation," *The Washington Post*, June 2.

58. Borchers, "Charity Doubles as a Profit Stream."

59. Armiak, David (2017) "Bradley Foundation Funds Right Wing Media Machine," Center for Media and Democracy, May 31. At www.exposedbycmd.org/2017/05/31/bradley-foundation-funds-right-wing-media-machine (last accessed March 2020).

60. See Appendix 1. Also Kotch, "Charles Koch is Funding Rightwing, Pro-Trump Media."

61. Sloan, "Tucker Carlson, His 'Charity,' and the Trump Campaign Cash."

62. Kotch, "Charles Koch is Funding Rightwing, Pro-Trump Media."

63. Timpf, Katherine (2019) "Help Us Fight Campus Craziness," *National Review*, May 25. At www.nationalreview.com/2019/05/spring-webathon-help-defend-free-speech-campus (last accessed March 2020).

64. National Review (n.d.) "George Leef." At www.nationalreview.com/author/george-leef (last accessed March 2020).

65. Michael Wolff (2019) "Can Students be Civil and Still 'Own the Libs'? National Review Writers Say Yes, Explain How," *The College Fix*, April 16.

66. Alliance Defense Fund (2010) "About David French." At https://web.archive.org/web/20101201085217/http://www.alliancealert.org/2010/03/01/about-david-french (last accessed March 2020).

67. French, David (2017) "Media Beware: The Southern Poverty Law Center Has Become a Dangerous Joke," *The National Review*, July 13.

68. Southern Poverty Law Center (2013) "Dangerous Liaisons," July 10. At www.splcenter.org/20130709/dangerous-liaisons (last accessed March 2020); Southern Poverty Law Center (2018) "American Anti-LGBT

Groups Battling Same-Sex Marriage in Romania," September 27. At www.splcenter.org/hatewatch/2018/09/27/american-anti-lgbt-groups-battling-same-sex-marriage-romania (last accessed March 2020).

69. Krutz, Stanley (2015) "A Plan to Restore Free Speech on Campus," *National Review*, December 7. For a list of Krutz's writing on campus free speech issues, see: National Review (n.d.) "Stanley Kurtz." At www.nationalreview.com/author/stanley-kurtz (last accessed March 2020).

70. Armiak, "Bradley Foundation Funds Right Wing Media Machine."

71. See Appendix 1.

72. National Review Institute (n.d.) "Board of Trustees." At https://nrinstitute.org/about-nri/board (last accessed March 2020).

73. Protect our Power (n.d.) "David M. DesRosiers, PhD." At https://protectourpower.org/advisory-panel/david-desrosiers (last accessed March 2020).

74. Buckley, F.H. (2018) *The Republican Workers Party: How the Trump Victory Drove Everyone Crazy, and Why It Was Just What We Needed.* New York: Encounter Books, 28.

75. Harden, Nathan (2019) "2019 Survey of Campus Speech Experts," *Real Clear Education*, October 24.

76. See Appendix 1.

77. Michael Calderone (2009) "Phil Anschutz's Conservative Agenda," *Politico*, September 16.

78. Nwanevu, Osita (2020) "Finding Neverland: The American Right's Doomed Quest to Rid Itself of Trumpism," *The New Republic*, March.

79. Qiu, Linda (2019) "Trump's Baseless Claim About Prayer Rugs Found at the Border," *The New York Times*, January 18.

80. Source Watch (2015) "Anschutz Foundation," Center for Media and Democracy. At www.sourcewatch.org/index.php?title=Anschutz_Foundation#cite_note-The_Two_Sides_of_Philip_Anschutz-2 (last accessed March 2020); Koch, Charles (2010) Agenda for "Understanding and Addressing Threats to American Free Enterprise and Prosperity," St. Regis Resort, Aspen, June 27 and 28, 12. Archived at https://ia801206.us.archive.org/34/items/2010KochSummit/2010%20KochSummit.pdf (last accessed March 2020).

81. Hogan, Marc (2018) "Coachella Co-Owner's Latest Charitable Filing Shows Deep Anti-LGBTQ Ties," *Pitchfork*, January 31.

82. Ari Melber (2008) "YouTube For Smart People," *The Nation*, March 31.

83. The Floating University (n.d.) "FAQ." At https://web.archive.org/web/20111007221016/http:/floatinguniversity.com/faq (last accessed March 2020).

84. Jordan Peterson (2019) "The Fatal Flaw Lurking in American Leftist Politics," *Big Think*, January 1.

85. Big Think (n.d.) "Charles Koch Foundation." At https://bigthink.com/charles-koch-foundation (last accessed March 2020).

86. The Atlantic (2018) "The Atlantic Begins 'The Speech Wars' Reporting Project," *The Atlantic*, November 28.
87. The Charles Koch Foundation (2018) "The State of Free Speech," December 17. At www.charleskochfoundation.org/story/the-state-of-free-speech (last accessed March 2020).
88. Institute for Humane Studies (n.d.) "How to Handle Controversial Speakers on Campus." At https://sponsored.chronicle.com/Controversial-Speakers/index.html (last accessed August 2020).
89. MacLean, "'Since We Are Greatly Outnumbered,'" 123.
90. Ibid., 121.
91. Kamola, Isaac (2017) "Crashing the Academic Conversation," *The Chronicle of Higher Education*, July 9.

5 THE LAWYERS

1. Cokorinos, Lee (2003) *The Assault on Diversity: An Organized Challenge to Racial and Gender Justice*. Lanham, MD: Rowman & Littlefield, 13.
2. Ibid.
3. Ibid.
4. Miller, John J. and Karl Zinsmeister (2015) "Agenda Setting: A Wise Giver's Guide to Influencing Public Policy," *Philanthropy Roundtable*, March, 49.
5. Project on Fair Representation (n.d.) "Project on Fair Representation: Legal Defense Foundation." At www.projectonfairrepresentation.org (last accessed August 2020).
6. Biskupic, Joan (2012) "Behind U.S. Race Cases, a Little-Known Recruiter," *Reuters*, December 4; Hartocollis, Anemona (2017) "He Took on the Voting Rights Act and Won. Now He's Taking on Harvard," *The New York Times*, November 19.
7. Students for Fair Admissions (n.d.) "About." At https://studentsforfairadmissions.org/about (last accessed August 2020).
8. Ibid.
9. Ibid.
10. Center for Individual Rights (2012) "Nix v. Holder," November 12. At www.cir-usa.org/cases/laroque-et-al-v-holder-et-al (last accessed August 2020).
11. Center for Individual Rights (n.d.) "Mission." At www.cir-usa.org/mission (last accessed August 2020).
12. Greve, Michael S. (1991) Letter to Louis V. Gerstner, Jr., RJR Nabisco Inc., May 3. Tobacco Institute Records; Master Settlement Agreement. At www.industrydocuments.ucsf.edu/docs/rfcp0059 (last assessed August 2020).
13. Stan, Adele M. (2015) "Who's Behind Friedrichs? The Right-Wing One-Percenters Who Are Funding a Mega-Attack on Unions," *The American Prospect*, October 29.

14. Cross, Theodore (1999) "African-American Opportunities in Higher Education: Racial Goals of the Center for Individual Rights," *Journal of Blacks in Higher Education*, Spring, 95. (Italics removed.)
15. Ibid., 94.
16. Center for Individual Rights (1997) "CIR: Annual Report 1996–97." At https://web.archive.org/web/20000818204455/http:/www.cir-usa.org/annual.pdf (last accessed August 2020).
17. Delgado, R. (2019) *Understanding Words that Wound*. New York: Routledge.
18. Batchis, Wayne (2016) *The Right's First Amendment: The Politics of Free Speech and the Return of Conservative Libertarianism*. Stanford: Stanford University Press, 69; Gould, Jon B. (2005) *Speak No Evil: The Triumph of Hate Speech Regulation*. Chicago: University of Chicago Press.
19. Lawrence, Charles R., Maria J. Matsuda, Richard Delgado, and Kimberlé Crenshaw (1993) "Introduction," in *Words that Wound: Critical Race Theory, Assaultive Speech, and the First Amendment*. ed. Maria J. Matsuda et al. Boulder: Westview Press, 14.
20. Ibid.
21. Teles, Steven M. (2008) *The Rise of the Conservative Legal Movement: The Battle for Control of the Law*. Princeton: Princeton University Press, 229–31.
22. Ibid., 232.
23. Quoted in ibid., 233.
24. Center for Individual Rights (n.d.) "Freedom of Speech and Religion." Archived at https://web.archive.org/web/20000304092158/http:/www.cir-usa.org/fa-pc.htm (last accessed August 2020).
25. Kors, Alan Charles and Harvey A. Silverglate (1998) *The Shadow University: The Betrayal of Liberty on America's Campuses*. New York: The Free Press, 9; Woolley, Wayne (1993) "Racial Harassment Charges Dropped Against Student," *Associated Press*, May 24.
26. Shea, Christopher (1993) "Outcome at Penn Leaves No One Satisfied," *The Chronicle of Higher Education*, June 2.
27. Kors and Silverglate, *The Shadow University*, 2, 4.
28. Ibid., 339–54.
29. Kors, Alan Charles (1999) "Did Western Civilization Survive the 20th Century?" *The National Interest*, December 1; Kors, Alan Charles (2000) *Did Western Civilization Survive the 20th Century?* Fairfax: Institute for Humane Studies.
30. Bradley Impact Fund (n.d.) "Foundation for Individual Rights in Education, Inc." At www.bradleyimpactfund.org/areas-of-impact-listing/foundation-for-individual-rights-in-education-inc (last accessed December 2020).
31. Kissel, Adam (2009) "FIRE letter to University of Chicago President Robert J. Zimmer," Foundation for Individual Freedom in Education,

February 23. At www.thefire.org/fire-letter-to-university-of-chicago-president-robert-j-zimmer (last accessed December 2020).

32. Encounter Books (n.d.) "Peter Collier, 1939–2019." At www.encounterbooks.com (last accessed October 2020); Sleeper, Jim (2016) "The Conservatives Behind the Campus 'Free Speech' Crusade," *The American Prospect*, October 19.

33. Lukianoff, Greg and Jonathan Haidt (2015) "The Coddling of the American Mind," *The Atlantic*, September.

34. PEN America (2016) "Diversity, Inclusion, and Freedom of Speech at U.S. Universities," October 17, 75. At https://pen.org/sites/default/files/PEN_campus_report_final_online_2.pdf (last accessed December 2020).

35. Sleeper, "The Conservatives Behind the Campus 'Free Speech' Crusade."

36. Ibid.

37. Sleeper, Jim (2016) "What the Campus 'Free Speech' Crusade Won't Say," *AlterNet*, September 4.

38. GuideStar (1999) "Foundation for Individual Rights in Education, Inc." At www.guidestar.org/profile/04-3467254 (last accessed August 2020). Relevant text is in dropdown on the page.

39. For an overview of this controversy, see PEN America (2016) "Diversity, Inclusion, and Freedom of Speech at U.S. Universities," 46–50.

40. Sleeper, "What the Campus 'Free Speech' Crusade Won't Say."

41. Ibid.

42. Ibid.

43. PEN America, "Diversity, Inclusion, and Freedom of Speech at U.S. Universities," 47.

44. Sleeper, Jim (2016) "The 'Blame the Campus Liberals' Campaign Targets Yale," *AlterNet*, February 14.

45. Hudler, Haley (2015) "Yale Students Demand Resignations from Faculty Members Over Halloween Email," Foundation for Individual Rights in Education, November 6. At www.thefire.org/yale-students-demand-resignations-from-faculty-members-over-halloween-email (last accessed December 2020).

46. Kors, Alan (2016) "Curriculum Vitae," University of Pennsylvania, March 28. Archived at https://ia601402.us.archive.org/8/items/alan-kors/Alan%20Kors.pdf.

47. See Appendix 1.

48. Foundation for Individual Rights in Education (2006) "Spotlight on Speech Codes 2006: The State of Free Speech on Our Nation's Campuses." At https://web.archive.org/web/20111125061902/http:/thefire.org/public/files/FINAL_FREE_SPEECH_REPORT_2006.pdf?direct (last accessed August 2020).

49. Majeed, Azhar (2009) "Defying the Constitution: The Rise, Persistence, and Prevalence of Campus Speech Codes," *Georgetown Journal of Law and Public Policy* 7: 530.

50. Gould, J. B. (2007) "Returning Fire," *The Chronicle of Higher Education* 53 (33), April 20. For a look at similar inflation in FIRE's database of uninvited speakers, see: Reichman, Henry (2019) *The Future of Academic Freedom*. Baltimore: Johns Hopkins University Press, 194–200.

51. FIRE (n.d.) "FIRE's Stand UP for Speech Litigation Project." At www. standupforspeech.com (last accessed May 2020).

52. FIRE (n.d.) "Search Results." At www.thefire.org/?s=young+americans+ for+liberty (last accessed August 2020).

53. FIRE (n.d.) "University of Cincinnati: Speech Code Litigation." At www. thefire.org/cases/university-of-cincinnati-speech-code-litigation (last accessed November 2020).

54. FIRE (n.d.) "DePaul University: In Multiple Acts of Censorship, DePaul Bans Political Chalking and Two Controversial Speakers." At www. thefire.org/cases/depaul-university-in-multiple-acts-of-censorship-depaul-bans-political-chalking-and-two-controversial-speakers (last accessed August 2020).

55. FIRE (n.d.) "University of New Mexico: Imposition of Excessive Security Fees for Controversial Speaker." At www.thefire.org/cases/ university-of-new-mexico-imposition-of-excessive-security-fees-for-controversial-speaker (last accessed August 2020).

56. FIRE (n.d.) "Search Results." At www.thefire.org/?s=TPUSA (last accessed August 2020).

57. FIRE (2017) *Bias Response Team: Report 2017.* At https://web.archive. org/web/20170506164707/www.thefire.org/fire-guides/bias-response-team-report-2017 (last accessed August 2020).

58. University of Kentucky (n.d.) "Bias Incident Report Form." At https:// cm.maxient.com/reportingform.php?UnivofKentucky&layout_id=20 (last accessed August 2020).

59. Parke, Caleb (2018) "University of Kentucky's Bias Response Team is a 'Literal Speech Police,' Group Claims," Fox News, May 24.

60. Harris, Samantha (2018) "Speech Code of the Month: University of Kentucky," FIRE, May 22. At www.thefire.org/speech-code-of-the-month-university-of-kentucky (last accessed August 2020).

61. Silverglate, Harvey A. and Jordan Lorence (2005) *FIRE's Guide to First-Year Orientation and Thought Reform on Campus.* Philadelphia: Foundation for Individual Rights in Education, 14.

62. Franks, Mary Anne (2019) "The Miseducation of Free Speech," *Virginia Law Review Online* 105, December, 231.

63. Speech First (n.d.) "About Us." At https://speechfirst.org/about (last accessed December 2020).

64. Bauman, Dan (2018) "Hate Crimes on Campuses Are Rising, New FBI Data Show," *The Chronicle of Higher Education*, November 14.

65. Moattar, Daniel (2018) "The Dark Money Behind Campus Speech Wars," *The Nation*, July 9; Fisher, Lauren (2019) "U. of Michigan Settles

with Free-Speech Group in Suit About Bias-Response Team," *The Chronicle of Higher Education*, October 29.

66. *Speech First, Inc. vs. Mark Schlissel* (2018) Eastern District of Michigan, May 8. At https://speechfirst.org/wp-content/uploads/2018/05/05–08–2018-Complaint.pdf (last accessed August 2020).

67. Fitzgerald, Rick (2018) "U-M Calls Free-Speech Lawsuit Allegations 'A False Caricature,'" *The University Record*, University of Michigan, June 15.

68. Parker, Linda V. (2018) "Opinion and Order Denying Plaintiff's Motion for Preliminary Injunction," *Speech First, Inc. vs. Mark Schlissel*, Civil Case No. 18–11451, Eastern District of Michigan, 32. At https://cases.justia.com/federal/district-courts/michigan/miedce/4:2018cv11451/329504/25/0.pdf?ts=1533639241 (last accessed August 2020).

69. Bauer-Wolf (2019) "See Hate Speech, Leave it Up," *Inside Higher Ed*, February 11.

70. Armiak, David and Ralph Wilson (2019) "Kochs' Dark-Money Network Bankrolls Campus 'Free Speech' Group," *PR Watch*, Center for Media and Democracy, June 11. At www.prwatch.org/news/2019/06/13476/kochs-dark-money-network-bankrolls-campus-free-speech-group (last accessed December 2020); Speech First. (n.d.) "Univ. of Texas Case." At https://speechfirst.org/category/univ-of-texas-case (last accessed May 2020).

71. Speech First (2018) "Speech First Files Federal Lawsuit Challenging Four University of Texas Policies that Chill Student Speech," December 13. At https://speechfirst.org/univ-of-texas-case/speech-first-files-federal-lawsuit-challenging-four-university-of-texas-policies-that-chill-student-speech (last accessed May 2020).

72. *Speech First, Inc. v. Fenves*, 384 F. Supp. 3d 732 – Dist. Court, WD Texas 2019. At https://scholar.google.com/scholar_case?case=14347996263090595354&q=speech+first+v.+fenves&hl=en&as_sdt=8006&as_vis=1 (last accessed May 2020).

73. Speech First, "Univ. of Texas Case."

74. Speech First (n.d.) "Membership Confirmation." At https://speechfirst.org/action-confirmation (last accessed May 2020).

75. Moattar, "The Dark Money Behind Campus Speech Wars."

76. Armiak and Wilson, "Kochs' Dark-Money Network Bankrolls Campus 'Free Speech' Group."

77. Moattar, "The Dark Money Behind Campus Speech Wars."

78. Armiak and Wilson, "Kochs' Dark-Money Network Bankrolls Campus 'Free Speech' Group."

79. Moattar, "The Dark Money Behind Campus Speech Wars."

80. Dezenhall, Eric (2001) "Appeasing Extremists Brings No Peace," *New York Post*, March 30. Republished by Nichols-Dezenhall. Archived at http://web.archive.org/web/20010418211913/http:/www.nichols-dezenhall.com/ndcurnyp301.html (last accessed August 2020). Dezenhall is also

a corporate sponsor of the American Legislative Exchange Council and has served on its Energy, Environment, and Agriculture Taskforce alongside Koch Industries. SourceWatch (2019) "Dezenhall Resources," Center for Media and Democracy. At www.sourcewatch.org/index. php?title=Dezenhall_Resources (last accessed August 2020).

81. Compiled from Speech First's 990 (2018) and Mauler's LinkedIn page.
82. Alliance Defending Freedom (n.d.) "Who We Are." At www.adflegal.org/about-us (last accessed May 2020).
83. Southern Poverty Law Center (n.d.) "Alliance Defending Freedom." At www.splcenter.org/fighting-hate/extremist-files/group/alliance-defending-freedom (last accessed November 2020).
84. Alliance Defending Freedom (2015) "Student Rights Regarding Religious and Conservative Expression at Public Colleges and Universities," 2. At https://tinyurl.com/yaupwch2 (last accessed May 2020).
85. Shea, Christopher (2014) "Controversy Heats Up Over Exclusionary Religious Groups," *The Chronicle of Higher Education*, October 6.
86. Wehe, Carol (2017) "ADF's Alan Sears and LI's Morton Blackwell Friends in Liberty," Leadership Institute, August 9. At https://leadershipinstitute. org/news/?NR=13222; Mattox, Casey (2017) "State Laws on Student Free Speech – How Does Your State Measure Up?" Alliance Defending Freedom, October 17. At www.adflegal.org/blog/state-laws-student-free-speech-how-does-your-state-measure (last accessed May 2020).
87. Alliance Defending Freedom, "Who We Are."
88. Wehe, "ADF's Alan Sears and LI's Morton Blackwell Friends in Liberty."
89. Alliance Defending Freedom (n.d.) "Allies." Archived at https://web.archive.org/web/20181119004720/http://adflegal.org/about-us/allies (last accessed May 2020).
90. Charles Koch Institute (n.d.) "Charles Koch Institute Welcomes Casey Mattox to Free Speech Team." At www.charleskochinstitute.org/blog/welcome-casey-mattox (last accessed May 2020).
91. Appendix 1. See also: SourceWatch (2019) "Alliance Defending Freedom," Center for Media and Democracy. At www.sourcewatch.org/index.php/Alliance_Defending_Freedom (last accessed April 2021).
92. Langhofer, Tyson (2017) "Take Your 'Free Speech' Beach Ball and Go Home, Michigan University Tells Students," Alliance Defending Freedom, October 18. At www.adflegal.org/press-release/take-your-free-speech-beach-ball-and-go-home-michigan-university-tells-students (last accessed May 2020).
93. Berrien, Hank (2017) "After Lawsuit From Shapiro and YAF, CSULA Now Will Let Conservatives Speak On Campus," *Daily Wire*, February 28; Alliance Defending Freedom (2018) "Univ. of Minnesota Sued for Banishing Conservative Event to Inadequate Venue," July 3. At https://adflegal.org/press-release/univ-minnesota-sued-banishing-conservative-event-inadequate-venue (last accessed August 2020).

94. Nardi, William (2018) "UMass Amherst Settles Free Speech Lawsuit Filed by Young Americans for Liberty," *Washington Examiner*, June 26; Davis, Janel (2015) "UGA Revises Freedom of Speech Policies, Student Group Drops Lawsuit," *The Atlanta Journal-Constitution*, March 6; Ernst, Douglas (2017) "Students Arrested During Constitution Giveaway; Lawsuit Filed Against Mich. College," *Washington Times*, January 2017; Geller, Ryan (2018) "UC Berkeley Settles Lawsuit Filed by Libertarian Student Group Young Americans for Liberty," *The Daily Californian*, May 25.

95. Alliance Defending Freedom (2017) "Student Club Supporters Arrested for Handing Out US Constitution at Michigan College, ADF Sues," October 18. At https://adflegal.org/press-release/student-club-supporters-arrested-handing-out-us-constitution-michigan-college-adf (last accessed August 2020); Agar, John (2017) "Kellogg Community College Rejects Conservative Youth Group's Speech Complaint," *MLive*, June 22.

96. Verges, Josh (2020) "Commentator Ben Shapiro Loses Free-Speech Lawsuit over St. Paul Venue Choice for UMN speech," *Twin Cities Pioneer Press*, August 28.

6 CHANGING THE LAWS

1. Powell, Lewis (1971) "Confidential Memorandum: Attack on American Free Enterprise System." Archived at https://archive.org/details/PowellMemorandum-AttackOnAmericanFreeEnterpriseSystem (last accessed June 2020).

2. SourceWatch (2021) "Atlas Network," Center for Media and Democracy.

3. Smith, Julia, Sheryl Thompson, and Kelley Lee (2017) "The Atlas Network: A 'Strategic Ally' of the Tobacco Industry," *The International Journal of Health Planning and Management* 32(4): 433.

4. Atlas Network (n.d.) "Global Directory: United States." At www.atlasnetwork.org/partners/global-directory/united-states(last accessed August 2020).

5. FIRE (2019) "Campus Free Expression Act." At www.thefire.org/presentation/wp-content/uploads/2019/09/18105224/Campus-Free-Expression-Act.pdf (last accessed May 2020).

6. Stone, Geoffrey R. et al. (2014) "Report of the Committee on Freedom of Expression," Office of the Provost, University of Chicago. At https://provost.uchicago.edu/sites/default/files/documents/reports/FOECommitteeReport.pdf (last accessed November 2020).

7. FIRE (2015) "Frequently Asked Questions: The Campus Free Expression (CAFE) Act," December 17. At www.thefire.org/frequently-asked-questions-the-campus-free-expression-cafe-act (last accessed May 2020).

8. *Good News Club v. Milford Central School* (2001) 533 U.S. Supreme Court 98. At https://supreme.justia.com/cases/federal/us/533/98 (last accessed December 2020).

9. *Widmar v. Vincent* (1981) 454 U.S. Supreme Court 270. At www.law. cornell.edu/supremecourt/text/454/263 (last accessed December 2020).

10. FIRE, "Campus Free Expression Act."

11. See Appendix 1.

12. Lacey, Marc (2011) "A Watchdog for Conservative Ideals," *The New York Times*, December 25. According to his family, Goldwater intended for the organization to focus on academic research and became disappointed when he saw it had become "a special-interest, big-business lobbying group." Goldwater died suddenly before he could finish establishing "checks and balances" on the misuse of his legacy. Ortega, Tony (1999) "Think Tank Warfare," *Phoenix New Times*, May 13.

13. ALEC Exposed (2013) "A Reporter's Guide to the Goldwater Institute: What Citizens, Policymakers, and Reporters Should Know," Arizona Working Families and the Center for Media and Democracy. At www. prwatch.org/files/Report_on_the_Goldwater_Institute_final.pdf (last accessed December 2020).

14. Stanley Kurtz, James Manley, and Jonathan Butcher (2017) *Campus Free Speech: A Legislative Proposal*. Phoenix: Goldwater Institute, January 30, 4. At https://goldwaterinstitute.org/wp-content/uploads/2019/03/ Campus-Free-Speech-A-Legislative-Proposal_Web.pdf (last accessed March 2020).

15. Kurtz, Manley, Butcher, *Campus Free Speech*.

16. Kurtz, Stanley (2015) "A Plan to Restore Free Speech on Campus," *National Review*, December 7.

17. Ibid.

18. Rowe, John Carlos (2004) "Edward Said and American Studies," American Quarterly, March, 56(1), 43.

19. Nolan, Lucas (2017) "'MILO Bill' Filed in Tennessee to Ensure Freedom of Speech on College Campuses," *Breitbart*, February 9.

20. Corporate Genome Project (n.d.) "Campus Free Speech Laws." At https:// www.corporategenomeproject.org/campus-free-speech-movement (last accessed August 2020).

21. Hertel-Fernandez, Alexander (2019) *State Capture: How Conservative Activists, Big Business, and Wealthy Donors Reshaped the American States—and the Nation*. New York: Oxford University Press.

22. Weyrich was also affiliated with the John Birch Society. A recent review of JBS archives shows him at meetings through the 1970s and 1980s and contributing columns for two JBS publications. Schlozman, Daniel and Sam Rosenfeld (2018) "The Long New Right and the World It Made," American Political Science Association Meeting, 54. At https://static1. squarespace.com/static/540f1546e4b0ca60699c8f73/t/5c3e694321c67

c3d28e992ba/1547594053027/Long+New+Right+Jan+2019.pdf (last accessed December 2020).

23. Cited in Edwards, Lee (1997) *The Power of Ideas: The Heritage Foundation at 25 Years.* Ottawa, IL: Jameson Books, 1997, 91.

24. State Policy Network (n.d.) "History." At https://spn.org/history (last accessed March 2020).

25. State Policy Network (n.d.) "The Network." At https://spn.org/directory (last accessed March 2020).

26. See Appendix 1.

27. Corporate Genome Project (n.d.) "Issue: Campus Free Speech Movement." At http://corporategenomeproject-dev.herokuapp.com/issues/425 (last accessed June 2021).

28. ALEC (2016) "ALEC Annual Report," American Legislative Exchange Council, Arlington, VA, 8 & 10. At www.alec.org/app/uploads/2017/05/2016-Annual-Report_WEB-FINAL.pdf (last accessed December 2020).

29. ALEC (n.d.) "Center to Protect Free Speech." At www.alec.org/policy-center/center-to-protect-free-speech (last accessed August 2020).

30. ALEC (2018) "Statement of Principles on Commercial Speech." December 26. At www.alec.org/model-policy/statement-of-principles-on-commercial-speech (last accessed August 2020).

31. ALEC (2017) "Forming Open and Robust University Minds (FORUM) Act." At www.alec.org/model-policy/forming-open-and-robust-university-minds-forum-act (last accessed August 2020).

32. ALEC (2017) "Education and Workforce Development Task Force—Higher Education Subcommittee." At www.alec.org/meeting-session/education-and-workforce-development-task-force-higher-education-subcommittee (last accessed August 2020).

33. ALEC (n.d.) "Jonathan Butcher." At www.alec.org/person/jonathan-butcher (last accessed August 2020).

34. Emmett, Shelby (2017) "Why Conservative Lawmakers Are Turning to Free-Speech Bills as a Fix for Higher Ed," American Legislative Exchange Council, June 8. At www.alec.org/article/why-conservative-lawmakers-are-turning-to-free-speech-bills-as-a-fix-for-higher-ed (last accessed August 2020).

35. ALEC (n.d.) "Campus Free Speech at a Glance." At www.alecaction.org/toolkit/campus-free-speech-at-a-glance (last accessed August 2020).

36. ALEC, "Forming Robust University Minds (FORUM) Act."

37. Americans for Prosperity (n.d.) "Tell Montana Lawmakers: Protect Free Speech on College Campuses." Archived at https://web.archive.org/web/20200321145616/https://americansforprosperity.ivolunteers.com/ContactOfficials/Tell-Montana-lawmakers-Protect-free-speech-on-college-campuses (last accessed March 2020; in the "Read More" tab).

38. ALEC, "Campus Free Speech at a Glance"; Moran, Dan (2017) "Proactivity and Partnerships: The Keys to Defending Free Speech,"

American Legislative Exchange Council, December 15. At www.alec.
org/article/proactivity-and-partnerships-the-keys-to-defending-free-
speech; Emmett, "Why Conservative Lawmakers Are Turning to
Free-Speech Bills."

39. Miller, Vanessa (2017) "Student Group Sues University of Iowa Over
Allegations it Rejected a Gay Student," *The Gazette*, December 13.

40. Emmett, "Why Conservative Lawmakers Are Turning to Free-Speech
Bills."

41. ALEC Exposed (2018) "Bills Related to Guns, Prisons, Crime, and
Immigration," Center for Media and Democracy. At www.alecexposed.
org/wiki/Bills_related_to_Guns,_Prisons,_Crime,_and_Immigration
(last accessed December 2020).

42. ALEC (n.d.) "Private Sector Executive Committee." At https://web.
archive.org/web/20110409132834/http:/www.alec.org/AM/Template.
cfm?Section=Private_Sector_Executive_Committee2 (last accessed
August 2020).

43. Cray, Charlie and Peter Montague (2014) *Kingpins of Carbon and their
War on Democracy*, Greenpeace, 55. At www.greenpeace.org/usa/
wp-content/uploads/legacy/Global/usa/planet3/PDFs/Kingpins-of-
Carbon.pdf (last accessed November 2020).

44. Derysh, Igor (2021) "Conservative Groups Are Writing GOP Voter
Suppression Bills — And Spending Millions to Pass Them," *Salon*,
March 27. At https://www.salon.com/2021/03/27/conservative-groups-
are-writing-gop-voter-suppression-bills---and-spending-millions-to-
pass-them; Wiener, Don and Alex Kotch (2021) "ALEC Members Lead
Voter Suppression Efforts in 2020 Battleground States," *Exposed*, Center
for Media and Democracy, April 13. At https://www.exposedbycmd.
org/2021/04/13/alec-members-lead-voter-suppression-efforts-in-2020-
battleground-states (last accessed May 2021).

45. MacLean, Nancy (2021) "'Since We Are Greatly Outnumbered': Why and
How the Koch Network Uses Disinformation to Thwart Democracy,"
in *The Disinformation Age: Politics, Technology, and Disruptive
Communication in the United States*, ed. W. Lance Bennet and Steven
Livingston. Cambridge: Cambridge University Press, 137.

46. Wilce, Rebeka (2012) "Six More Corporations Dump ALEC; 38 Companies
Have Now Cut Ties With Corporate Bill Mill," *PRWatch*, August 27. At
www.prwatch.org/news/2012/08/11724/six-more-corporations-dump-
alec-38-companies-have-now-cut-ties-corporate-bill-mil (last accessed
December 2020).

47. Almasi, David (2014) "Boycott of Florida Businesses Over Stand Your
Ground Criticized," *Project 21*, National Center for Public Policy
Research, March 11.

48. Emmett, Shelby (2014) "Eric Garner Was Killed by New York Tax
Collectors," *Project 21*, National Center for Public Policy Research,
December 31.

49. Emmett, Shelby (n.d.) LinkedIn. (last accessed August 2020).
50. See Appendix 1.
51. Powers, Scott (2018) "Group Supports Bob Rommel, Dennis Baxley for Bills on Campus Free Speech," *Florida Politics*, January 2.
52. Search for press releases via state at Americans For Prosperity (n.d.), https://americansforprosperity.org (last accessed August 2020).
53. Corey, Jamie (2020) "Ohio Senate Unanimously Passes ALEC Model Legislation Allowing Hate Speech on College Campuses," *Documented*, January 30.
54. Americans for Prosperity (2019) "Governor Reynolds, Lawmakers Protect Free Expression on Iowa Campuses," March 27. At https://americansforprosperity.org/governor-reynolds-lawmakers-protect-free-expression-on-iowa-campuses (last accessed October 2020).
55. For the lobbying activity on HF 276, HF 661, and SB 3120 see the lobbying reports compiled by the Iowa state legislature, available at: www.legis.iowa.gov/lobbyist/reports/declarations?ga=88&ba=HF276; www.legis.iowa.gov/lobbyist/reports/declarations?ga=87&ba=SSB3120; and www.legis.iowa.gov/lobbyist/reports/declarations?ga=88&ba=HF661 (all accessed August 2020).
56. CWALAC Staff (2017) "Capitol Hill Brief—Campus Free Speech," Concerned Women for America, May 15. At https://concernedwomen.org/capitol-hill-brief-campus-free-speech (last accessed August 2020).
57. Kansas Legislature (2018) "Follow up Written Opposition Testimony of SB 340," Kansas Senate Federal and State Affairs Committee, February 15. At www.kslegislature.org/li_2018/b2017_18/committees/ctte_s_fed_st_1/documents/testimony/20180215_03.pdf (last accessed December 2020).
58. Bisaha, S. (2018) "Bill Promises to Make Kansas Campuses Welcome the Left and the Right," KCUR, February 16.
59. Open Secrets (n.d.) "Sen. Orrin G. Hatch—Utah." At www.opensecrets.org/members-of-congress/contributors/orrin-g-hatch?cid=N00009869&cycle=2018&recs=100&type=C (last accessed December 2020).
60. FollowTheMoney.org (n.d.) "Q. Show me contributions to Brat, David Alan (DAVE) (within federal, state and local data)." At www.followthemoney.org/show-me?c-t-eid=24351695#%5B%7B1%7Cgro=d-eid (last accessed August 2020).
61. McIntosh, Robert (2018) "Campus Free Speech Bill Introduced in House of Representatives," Foundation for Individual Rights in Education, December 18. At www.thefire.org/campus-free-speech-bill-introduced-in-house-of-representatives (last accessed August 2020).
62. Binkley, Collin (2019) "Trump Orders Colleges to Back Free Speech or Lose Funding," *Associated Press*, March 21.
63. Tom Cotton's Office (2020) "Cotton, Colleagues Introduce Legislation Protecting Free Speech on College Campuses." At www.cotton.senate.gov/?p=press_release&id=1406. For a text of the bill see: www.

cotton.senate.gov/files/documents/Campus%20Free%20Speech%20
Restoration%20Act.pdf (all accessed August 2020).

64. Audio and transcript posted at: Lady Libertine (2014) "Exclusive
    Audio: Mitch McConnell at the Koch Brothers Donor Summit," August
    26. Archived at https://web.archive.org/web/20140904235327/http:/
    ladylibertine.net/2014/08/26/mmky (last accessed August 2020).

65. Bailey, Analis (2020) "Sen. Kelly Loeffler, Co-Owner of WNBA's Atlanta
    Dream, Says Black Lives Matter Threatens to 'Destroy' America," *USA
    Today*, July 10.

66. AAUP (2018) "Campus Free-Speech Legislation: History, Progress, and
    Problems," April. At www.aaup.org/file/Campus_Free_Speech_2018.pdf
    (last accessed August 2020).

67. AAUP (2017) "Legislation on Free Speech," May 11. At www.aaup.org/
    file/2017-free_speech_legislation.pdf (last accessed May 2020).

68. Ibid.

69. AAUP, "Campus Free-Speech Legislation: History, Progress, and
    Problems."

70. Ibid.

71. Ibid.

7 THE ACADEMICS

1. Koch, Charles G. (1974) *Anti-Capitalism and Business*. Menlo Park, CA:
   Institute for Humane Studies, Inc., 4–7. Archived at https://kochdocs.
   org/2019/06/07/charles-koch-anti-capitalism-big-business (last accessed
   December 2020).

2. Gentry, Kevin (2014) "Leverage Science and the Universities," Freedom
   Partners. Transcript by Alderson Reporting Company, June 15. At
   https://tinyurl.com/y54739dv (last accessed August 2020).

3. Ibid.

4. Wilson, Ralph (2017) "Universities Dumping Koch at an Exponen-
   tial Rate," *UnKoch My Campus*. At https://tinyurl.com/y5lg66nb (last
   accessed November 2020).

5. From the Charles Koch Foundation 990 Tax Forms, 2005–2018.

6. UnKoch My Campus (2021) "Increased Funding, Increased Influence:
   Koch University Funding Update," May. Report available at http://www.
   unkochmycampus.org/funding-report (last accessed May 2021).

7. Coppin, Clayton A. (2003) *Stealth: The History of Charles Koch's Political
   Activities*. For information on this text, see Chapter 1, fn. 44.

8. See Appendix 1.

9. Gentry, "Leverage Science and the Universities."

10. APEE is an academic association of scholars from "universities, public
    policy institutes, and industry" whose mission is "studying and support-
    ing the system of private enterprise" and "revealing the Invisible Hand
    through education." APEE claims to be "instrumental in establishing

[endowed] Chairs and Centers of Private Enterprise in colleges," which "in turn develop courses and programs reaching tens of thousands of students each year." This professional organization received $390,500 from Koch family foundations between 2006 and 2018. Association of Private Enterprise Education (n.d.) "Welcome to APEE!" At www.apee. org (last accessed August 2020). For funding numbers, see Appendix 1.

11. From the transcript of: Association of Private Enterprise Education (2016) "Successful Models of Programs in Private Enterprise (Session 3.F.7)," Annual Meeting, Bally's Casino, Las Vegas, NV, April 5. Archived at https://tinyurl.com/y5qdsmwa (last accessed August 2020).

12. Beets, S. Douglas (2019) "The Charles Koch Foundation and Contracted Universities: Evidence from Disclosed Agreements," *Journal of Academic Ethics* 17 (3): 223.

13. Wilson, Ralph, Jerry Funt, and Sydney Norris (2015) "A Student Review of FSU Gift Acceptance Policy: Undue Influence and Charles Koch Foundation," May. *FSU Progress Coalition* and *UnKoch My Campus*. At https://tinyurl.com/y3nszwgx; Wilson, Ralph (2017) "A Case Study in Academic Crime: The Charles Koch Foundation at Florida State University," Spring. *FSU Progress Coalition* and *UnKoch My Campus*. At https://tinyurl.com/y368dtj2; Wilson, Ralph (2018) "Violations of Academic Freedom, Faculty Governance, and Academic Integrity: An Analysis of the Charles Koch Foundation," December. *UnKoch My Campus*. At https://tinyurl.com/y6fcx9c2 (all last accessed December 2020).

14. Pienta, Allison and Ralph Wilson (2018) "Donor Influence at George Mason Finally Exposed," *UnKoch My Campus*. At https://tinyurl.com/ y65dgs3h (last accessed November 2020).

15. Woolsey, Angela (2018) "GMU President Calls for Review of Financial Donor Agreements," *Fairfax County Times*, May 4.

16. See Appendix 1.

17. Beets, "The Charles Koch Foundation and Contracted Universities," 239. Beets's findings are confirmed in Aaron Supple's study of 39 CKF contracts, including ones made public after the publication of Beets's article: Aaron Supple (2020) "Concealed Philanthropy," Political Science Thesis, Trinity College, Hartford, CT.

18. Reichman, Henry (2019) *The Future of Academic Freedom.* Baltimore: Johns Hopkins University Press, 105–34.

19. Doherty, Brian (2007) *Radicals for Capitalism: A Freewheeling History of the Modern American Libertarian Movement.* New York: Public Affairs, 430.

20. Stringham, Edward P. (2010) "Toward a Libertarian Strategy for Academic Change: The Movement Building of Peter Boettke," *Journal of Private Enterprise* 26 (1): 7 fn. 10.

21. Benson, Bruce (2007) "Koch Foundation Proposal for Supporting FSU Economics Department." Archived at: https://ia800509. us.archive.org/24/items/2015FSUKoch/KochCostsBenefits%20(1).pdf

(last accessed August 2020). Obtained in 2014 through public records requests by students with FSU Progress Coalition.

22. See Appendix 1.

23. Ad Hoc Committee (2011) "Koch Foundational Memorandum of Understanding: Ad Hoc Committee Review Report," Faculty Senate, Florida State University. Archived at https://ia800509.us.archive.org/24/items/2015FSUKoch/FSSC%20Report%20Standley.pdf (last accessed August 2020).

24. Gibson, Connor (2014) "Academic Pollution: Greenpeace Traces Koch Money on Campus," Greenpeace, September 17. At www.greenpeace.org/usa/academic-pollution-greenpeace-traces-koch-money-campus (last accessed November 2020).

25. Kochak, Jacque (2008) "Questions Raised About New AU Business Center," *The Auburn Villager*, September 18.

26. The text for *Stern v. Auburn University* is available at *Inside Higher Ed* (n.d.), www.insidehighered.com/sites/default/server_files/media/388 952067-Stern-v-Auburn-University_0.pdf (last accessed August 2020).

27. See Appendix 1; Kochak, "Questions Raised About New AU Business Center."

28. Sadasivam, Naveena and Jordan Sigler (2016) "Hostile Takeover," *Texas Observer*, September 26.

29. See Appendix 1.

30. Wilson, Ralph (2018) "Exposing the Association of Private Enterprise Education (APEE)," December. *UnKoch My Campus.* At https://tinyurl.com/yxok78fe (last accessed December 2020).

31. See Appendix 1.

32. Ad Hoc Committee (2017) "Report of the Ad Hoc Committee of the Senate of Wake Forest University on the Eudaimonia Institute," Wake Forest University, March, 15. At https://tinyurl.com/y3tsrt4o (last accessed August 2020).

33. See Appendix 1.

34. Faculty Senate (2016) "Agenda for the Faculty Senate Meeting," George Mason University, April 27. At www.gmu.edu/resources/facstaff/senate/AGENDA_FS_2015-16/FS_AGENDA_5-4-16-cont-4-27-16_FINAL.pdf (last accessed October 2020).

35. Johnson, Becky (2015) "WCU Leaders, Faculty at Odds over Koch-funded Free Enterprise Center," *Smokey Mountain News*, December 9.

36. Johnson, Becky (2016) "Blue-Ribbon Committee Seeks Balance in Push-and-Pull Over Koch-funded Center at WCU," *Smokey Mountain News*, February 10.

37. Ibid.

38. See Appendix 1.

39. Wilson, Ralph (2018) "Donor Intent of the Koch Network: Leveraging Universities for Self-Interested Policy Change," *UnKoch My Campus*,

December, 15. At https://tinyurl.com/y3zugtdb (last accessed August 2020).

40. IHS (n.d.) "IHS Grant for Free Speech & Open Inquiry." At https://theihs. org/ihs-grant-for-free-speech-open-inquiry (last accessed May 2020).

41. IHS (2017) "IHS FY17 Mid-Year Proposal to the Charles Koch Foundation." At https://tinyurl.com/y3saoxlq (last accessed May 2020). Leaked anonymously to *UnKoch My Campus*.

42. Ibid.

43. Ibid.

44. Downs, Donald A., Kristen Roman, George Waldner, and Emily Chamlee-Wright (2018) *The Framework for Campus Crisis Management*, Institute for Humane Studies. At http://openinquiryproject.org/ wp-content/uploads/2018/04/framework_final_revised_web.pdf (last accessed May 2020).

45. Donald A. Downs, George Waldner, and Emily Chamlee-Wright (2017) *A Framework for Campus Free Speech Policy*, Institute for Humane Studies. At http://openinquiryproject.org/wp-content/uploads/2017/04/ OpenInquiryBooklet_Web_Mar2017.pdf (last accessed May 2020).

46. Ibid.

47. Downs, et al., *The Framework for Campus Crisis Management*.

48. Downs, et al., *A Framework for Campus Free Speech Policy*.

49. Ibid.

50. Downs, et al., *The Framework for Campus Crisis Management*.

51. Ibid.

52. IHS, "IHS FY17 Mid-Year Proposal to the Charles Koch Foundation."

53. Chamlee-Wright, Emily (2018) "IHS Creates Free Speech Resources for Campus Leaders," *News from IHS*, Summer, 2.

54. Chamlee-Wright, Emily (2020) "Progress on Campus Free Speech?," *Forbes*, March 19.

55. Division of Student Affairs (n.d.) "Speech and Expression Policy," Georgetown University. At https://studentaffairs.georgetown.edu/ policies/student-life-policies/speech-expression (last accessed August 2020).

56. IHS (2018) "Promoting Free Speech on Campus," YouTube, February 12, min. 49–51.

57. Hasnas's CV is archived at https://tinyurl.com/ya3hnknw (last accessed June 2020).

58. See Appendix 1. Also compare the Charles Koch Foundation 990s for 2017 and 2018.

59. Flietner, Rudie. "Sr Director Corporate & Foundation Relations at University of Wisconsin Foundation." LinkedIn. At http://archive. is/9RwZw#selection-1323.13–1323.95 (last accessed May 2020).

60. Center for the Study of Liberal Democracy (n.d.) "History," University of Wisconsin, Madison. At https://csld.wisc.edu/history (last accessed May 2020).

61. Center for the Study of Liberal Democracy (n.d.) "2020 Summer Scholarships Available." At https://csld.wisc.edu/courses/2020-summer-class-scholarship (last accessed May 2020)
62. See Appendix 1.
63. Downs, Donald (2016) "The Wisconsin Fight for Academic Freedom," *Academic Questions*, Summer.
64. Downs, Donald Alexander (2004) *Restoring Free Speech and Liberty on Campus*. Oakland: The Independent Institute & Cambridge University Press, 216, 17.
65. Ibid., xv.
66. Ibid., 44.
67. IHS, "IHS FY17 Mid-Year Proposal to the Charles Koch Foundation."
68. Ibid.
69. Abrams, Samuel J. (2018) "Think Professors Are Liberal? Try School Administrators," *The New York Times*, October 16.
70. Ibid.
71. O'Mahony, Jerry (2018) "Students, Faculty, Administration Respond Following National Publication of SLC Professor's Op-ed," *The Phoenix*, October 18.
72. Abrams, Samuel J. (2018) "The Dangerous Silence in Higher Education," *Spectator*, November 10.
73. See Appendix 1.
74. IHS (n.d.) "Join Us at Our Exclusive Donor Events." At https:/theihs.org/supporters/join-us-at-our-exclusive-donor-events; Turner, Daniel and Michael Slabinsky (2017) "Free Speech a Major Theme at ALEC's States and Nations Policy Conference," American Legislative Exchange Council, December 18. At www.alec.org/article/free-speech-a-major-theme-at-alecs-states-and-nation-policy-conference; IHS (2018) "Threats to Academic Freedom and Free Speech," JW Marriott, Washington, D.C., February 7–8. At http://theihs.org/wp-content/uploads/2018/02/Threats-to-Academic-Freedom-PRS-Booklet_DIGITAL.pdf (all last accessed August 2020).
75. Villasenor, John (2017) "Views Among College Students Regarding the First Amendment: Results From a New Survey," Brookings Institution, September 18.
76. Villasenor, John (2018) "Views Among College Students Regarding Freedom of Expression: An Analysis in Light of Key Supreme Court Decisions." *Journal of Constitutional Law Online* 20 (1): 1.
77. Charles Koch Foundation (n.d.) "UCLA Professor John Villaseñor Finds College Students' Hostility Towards Free Speech." At www.charleskochfoundation.org/news/ucla-professor-john-villasenor-finds-college-students-hostility-towards-free-speech (last accessed August 2020).
78. Beckett, Lois (2017) "'Junk Science': Experts Cast Doubt on Widely Cited College Free Speech Survey," *The Guardian*, September 22.

79. Kisliuk, Bill (2020) "UCLA Launches Institute to Explore Legal, Policy Impact of Emerging Tech," *Newsroom*, University of California, Los Angeles, January 16; Charles Koch Foundation (n.d.) "UCLA Brings Together Engineering and Law Scholars to Study How to Harness Benefits of Emerging Technology." At https://charleskochfoundation. org/news/ucla-engineering-and-law-scholars-study-harness-benefits-of-emerging-technology (last accessed June 2021).

80. UCLA Law (n.d.) "First Amendment Amicus Clinic." At https://law.ucla. edu/academics/clinical-education/clinics/first-amendment-amicus-clinic (last accessed August 2020). For example, Volokh's clinic wrote a brief supporting FIRE's defense of a student who was institutionally reprimanded for advocating the idea that homosexuality is immoral. The amicus brief filed in *Jennifer Keeton v. Mary Jane Anderson-Wiley, et al.* (Eleventh Circuit Court of Appeals) can be found here: https://tinyurl. com/y2x350ex (last accessed August 2020).

81. Speech broadcast on ReasonTV (2017) "Eugene Volokh: Free Speech on Campus," Reason Weekend, Palos Verdes, CA, YouTube, April 4.

82. Simkovic, Michael (2018) "A Well-Organized Campaign to Bait, Discredit, and Take Over Universities is Exploiting Students and Manipulating the Public," Brian Leiter's Law School Reports, April 30. At https://leiterlawschool.typepad.com/leiter/2018/04/a-well-organized-campaign-to-bait-discredit-and-take-over-universities-is-exploiting-students-and-ma.html (last accessed August 2020).

83. IHS (n.d.) "Join Us at Our Exclusive Donor Events."

84. See Appendix 1.

85. IHS (2019) "People and Ideas Making a Difference for Liberty," *News from IHS*, Spring, p.4.

86. Sophia Buono (2018) "After Charles Murray Fiasco, Middlebury College Launches Civil Discourse Program," *Washington Examiner*, November 13.

87. Alexander Hamilton Forum (n.d.) "About Us." At http://sites.middlebury. edu/hamilton/about-us (last accessed August 2020).

88. Board, Riley (2019) "College Braces for Right-Wing Speaker Accused of Homophobia," *The Middlebury Campus*, April 16.

89. Ibid.

90. Kapp, Caroline (2018) "Students Took Koch Money to Fund On-Campus Lecture," *The Middlebury Campus*, May 2; Finn, James and Caroline Kapp (2020) "Charles Murray Invited Back to Middlebury by College Republicans," *The Middlebury Campus*, January 22.

91. School of Civic and Economic Thought and Leadership (n.d.) "Free Speech and Intellectual Diversity in Higher Education and American Society." Archived at https://tinyurl.com/yylh3r3w; School of Civic and Economic Thought and Leadership (2018) "2018 Spring Conference: Free Speech and Intellectual Diversity in Higher Education and Amer-

ican Society." Archived at https://tinyurl.com/y3ytl7te (last accessed August 2020).

92. See Appendix 1.
93. The Committee on Free Expression was chaired by John Arnold, Executive Director of the Arizona Board of Regents. The committee's charge is to ensure that the Arizona Board of Regents—representing Arizona State University, Northern Arizona University, the University of Arizona, and the state's community colleges—adopts policies that declare academic institutions public forums, prevent speakers from being disinvited, and creates a campus hearing procedure that can mete out punishment that includes "suspension or expulsion." The text of the charge, "HB 2563: Postsecondary Institutions; Free Expression Policies," can be found here: https://tinyurl.com/yyndtfj4 (last accessed August 2020).
94. Committee on Free Expression (2018) "Annual Report," Arizona Board of Regents, September 1. At www.azregents.edu/sites/default/files/public/2018_Free_Expression_Report.pdf (last accessed November 2020).
95. Goldwater Institute (n.d.) "It Takes a Team." Archived at https://web.archive.org/web/20111125154346/https:/goldwaterinstitute.org/people (last accessed August 2020).
96. See Appendix 1.
97. Strauss, Valerie (2018) "Professor: A Disturbing Story About the Influence of the Koch Network in Higher Education," *The Washington Post*, April 22.
98. Small, Jim (2018) "GOP Legislature Sending More Money to 'Freedom Schools,' Despite Existing Surplus," *Arizona Capital Times*, May 2.
99. McLeod, Harriet (2014) "Clemson University Fraternity Suspended Over Gang-Themed 'Cripmas' Party," *Reuters*, December 8; Schafer, Susanne M. (2007) "Clemson University Probes Racist Party," *The Washington Post*, January 30.
100. Thompson, C. Bradley, C. Alan Grubb, and Bradley S. Meyer (2015) "An Open Letter to Clemson Students," *Capitalism Magazine*, February 2.
101. Morey, Alex (2015) "Faculty Focus: How Three Professors Banded Together to Beat Back a Free Speech Threat at Clemson," Foundation for Individual Rights in Education, December 28; Keaveney, Stephanie (2016) "These Professors Are Working to Restore Free Speech on Campus," James G. Martin Center for Academic Renewal, August 15; Thompson, Miller and Kaitlyn Schallhorn (2015) "Clemson Professors Demand Criminal Prosecution of Social Media Posts," *Campus Reform*, January 29.
102. WeRoarClemson (2016) Facebook Post, June 13. At http://archive.ph/36w1W (last accessed August 2020).
103. Hussion, Patrick and Corey Davis (2016) "Controversial Trump Supporter Speaks to Clemson Students," WYFF4, October 19.

104. Association of Private Enterprise Education, "Successful Models of Programs in Private Enterprise."
105. Uhlmann, Rick (2018) "10 Young Minds Added to the Lyceum Scholars Program Family," *The Newsstand*, September 17.
106. See Appendix 1.
107. Wade, Jalen (2018) "Free Speech Advocates Weigh Banning Hate Speech, Making Students Feel Safe at UMD Panel," *The Diamondback*, November 30; Associated Press (2018) "Judge Asked to Postpone Trial for Man Charged with Hate Crime in University of Maryland Stabbing," *Baltimore Sun*, December 11.
108. Iyer, Kaanita (2017) "With Hate Symbol Ban Not Possible, UMD Senate Considers Alternatives," *The Diamondback*, November 12.
109. Wade, "Free Speech Advocates Weigh Banning Hate Speech."
110. See Appendix 1.
111. For example, members of AFA include Donald Downs, Michael Munger (Center for the History of Political Economy, Duke), Sam Abrams, Keegan Callanan, David Schmidtz, Colleen Sheehan (School of Civic and Economic Thought and Leadership, ASU), Tim Shiell (Center for the Study of Institutions and Innovation, UW-Stout), John Thomasi (Political Theory Project, Brown), Eugene Volokh, David Bernstein (Law & Liberty Center, GMU), as well as Alan Charles Kors, Jonathan Haidt, Victor Davis Hanson (*National Review*, Koch seminar attendee, Bradley Foundation board), and others. Those listed here without affiliation are discussed in greater detail throughout this chapter.
112. Academic Freedom Alliance (n.d.) "Mission of the Academic Freedom Alliance." At https://academicfreedom.org/about (last accessed April 2021).
113. Yang, Wesley (2021) "A New Group Promises to Protect Professors' Free Speech," *The Chronicle of Higher Education*, March 8.
114. See Appendix 1. This program's role in campus free speech was not discussed, and so it does not appear on the table. However, these numbers were calculated using the same method.
115. Doherty, *Radicals for Capitalism*, 409.
116. From the transcript of Association of Private Enterprise Education (2016) "Being an Intellectual Entrepreneur (Session 2.C.5)," Annual Meeting, Bally's Casino, Las Vegas, NV, April 5.
117. Polanyi, Michael (1962) "The Republic of Science: Its Political and Economic Theory," *Minerva* 1. Republished in *Minerva* 38 (1) (2000): 1–32.
118. Tankersley, Jim (2015) "'I Don't Like the Idea of Capitalism': Charles Koch, Unfiltered," *The Washington Post*, August 1.
119. We take the idea of knowledge cultivation from Robbie Shilliam, who argues that knowledge is not something simply manufactured by wage laborers in a factory but rather cultivated through deep, reciprocal

relationships. Shilliam, Robbie (2015) *The Black Pacific: Anti-Colonial Struggles and Oceanic Connections*. London: Bloomsbury Publishing.

120. State Policy Network (n.d.) "SPN 27th Annual Meeting." At https://web.archive.org/web/20191102111657/https://spn.org/meeting/spn-27th-annual-meeting (last accessed August 2020).

121. Atlas Network (n.d.) "Global Directory: United States." At www.atlasnetwork.org/partners/global-directory/united-states/4 (last accessed August 2020).

8 THE FREE SPEECH INTERNATIONAL

1. Cockett, Richard (1995) *Thinking the Unthinkable*. London: Fontana, 306–7; Hoplin, Nicole and Ron Robinson (2008) *Funding Fathers: The Unsung Heroes of the Conservative Movement*. Washington, D.C.: Regnery Publishing, 151–66.

2. SourceWatch (2021) "Atlas Network," Center for Media and Democracy. At www.sourcewatch.org/index.php?title=Atlas_Network (last accessed April 2021).

3. Atlas Network (2019) "2019 Annual Report." At www.atlasnetwork.org/assets/uploads/annual-reports/AR_2019_Revised.pdf (last accessed July 2020).

4. Fang, Lee (2017) "Sphere of Influence: How American Libertarians Are Remaking Latin American Politics," *The Intercept*, August 9.

5. See Appendix 1.

6. Drimonis, Toula (2018) "Did American Right-Wing Trolls Radicalize the Quebec Mosque Shooter?" *Huffington Post*, April 23.

7. Boutilier, Alex (2018) "Rise of Right-Wing Extremists Presents New Challenge for Canadian Law Enforcement Agencies," *The Star*, October 7.

8. Boutilier, Alex (2018) "CSIS Sees 'Significant' Jump in Far-Right Activity Online," *The Star*, October 8.

9. Friends of Simon Wiesenthal Center for Holocaust Studies (2019) "Rising Tide of White Supremacy in Canada," January. At https://tinyurl.com/y6k8u826 (last accessed August 2020).

10. Cernetig, Miro (1994) "Neo-Cons Young Buck of the New Right," *Globe and Mail*, February 5.

11. Ball, David P. (2012) "Sun News Host Ezra Levant Recalls 'Wonderful' Koch Foundation Summer," *Vancouver Observer*, May 1; Levant, Ezra (1996) *Youthquake*. Vancouver: The Fraser Institute (see "About the Author").

12. See Appendix 1.

13. Levant, *Youthquake*, 164.

14. Walker, Michael (2016) "If it Matters, Measure It: Teaching the Economics That is Always Relevant," Association of Private Enterprise Education (APEE), Annual Meeting, Las Vegas, NV, at 12:43. Archived by *UnKoch-*

MyCampus at: https://soundcloud.com/a-philadelphia-experiment/
apee-2016-michael-walker-frasier-institute-if-it-matters-measure-it
(last accessed 2020).

15. Campus Unmasked (n.d.) "Our Purpose." At https://campusunmasked.
com/our-purpose (last accessed July 2020).

16. Southern, Lauren (2015) "'There Is No Rape Culture in the West': She
Held Up That Sign at SlutWalk, and This is What Happened," *Rebel
Media*, June 9; Wilson, Jason (2018) "News Corp Australia's Promotion
of Lauren Southern is Disturbing," *The Guardian*, July 16.

17. Houpt, Simon (2017) "Rebel Media Co-Founder Quits Over Company's
Ties to Right-Wing Groups," *The Globe and Mail*, August 14.

18. Canadian Criminal Code (R.S.C., 1985, c. C-46). At https://laws-lois.
justice.gc.ca/eng/acts/C-46/section-319.html#docCont (last accessed
August 2020).

19. Campus Freedom Index (n.d.) "2019 Campus Freedom Index," Justice
Center for Constitutional Freedoms. At https://campusfreedomindex.ca
(last accessed July 2020).

20. Campus Freedom Index (n.d.) "Methodology," Justice Center for
Constitutional Freedoms. At https://campusfreedomindex.ca/
methodology (last accessed July 2020).

21. Justice Center for Constitutional Freedom (n.d.) "Student Free Speech
Grants." At www.jccf.ca/projects-media/student-projects/student-free-
speech-grants; Justice Center for Constitutional Freedom (2013)
"Building Free Speech Walls Across Canada," April 1. At www.jccf.ca/
building-free-speech-walls-across-canada (both last accessed July 2020).

22. Crowe, Kelly (2015) "PM's Charity Audits Look for 'Bias, One-sidedness,'"
CBC, February 4.

23. Rieger, Sarah (2018) "Calgary Lawyer Challenging Gay-Straight Alliance
Bill Compares Pride Flags to Swastikas," CBC, November 11.

24. Atlas Network (n.d.) "Global Directory: Canada." At www.atlasnetwork.
org/partners/global-directory/canada (last accessed July 2020).

25. Generation Screwed (n.d.) "About Us," Canadian Taxpayers Federation.
At www.generationscrewed.ca/about-us (last accessed July 2020).

26. North99 Staff (2018) "How American Far-Right Groups Influence
Canadian University Students: Generation Screwed," *North99*, February
26.

27. Tucker, Jason and Jason VandenBeukel (2016) "Are Universities Dying?"
C2C Journal, December 1.

28. Lott, Tim (2017) "Jordan Peterson and the Transgender Wars," *Spectator
Life*, September 20.

29. Peterson, Jordan B. (2016) "Professor Against Political Correctness:
Part 1: Fear and the Law," YouTube, September 27. Archived at https://
web.archive.org/web/20160930011644/https://www.youtube.com/
watch?v=fvPgjg201wo

30. Ibid.

31. Rebel News (2016) "Toronto Radicals Fight Free Speech," YouTube, October 13. At www.youtube.com/watch?v=-4RobWC41g4 (last accessed July 2020).

32. Savva, Sophia (2017) "Jordan Peterson's Federal Funding Denied, Rebel Media Picks up the Tab," *The Varsity*, May 1; McKeen, Alex (2017) "Controversial U of T Professor Making Nearly $50,000 a Month Through Crowdfunding," *The Star*, July 4.

33. PressProgress (2017) "Jordan Peterson Blasted By Alt-Right Fans For Banning Speaker From 'Free Speech on Campus' Event," November 27. At https://pressprogress.ca/jordan-peterson-blasted-by-alt-right-fans-for-banning-speaker-from-free-speech-on-campus-event (last accessed 2020).

34. Hutchins, Aaron (2017) "What really Happened at Wilfrid Laurier University," *Macleans*, December 11.

35. Booth, Laura (2018) "Faith Goldy Talk at Wilfrid Laurier University Shut Down by Fire Alarm After Protest," *The Star*, March 20; Husein, Safina (2018) "Indigenous Ceremony and Community Protests Held on Campus in Response to LSOI Event," *The Cord*, May 10.

36. Vescera, Zak (2019) "A Splintered Movement: How the Far-Right Found a Foothold on Campus," *The Ubyssey*, April 20.

37. Campus Freedom Index, "2019 Campus Freedom Index." Archived at https://web.archive.org/web/20191004035941/https://campusfreedom index.ca (last accessed November 2020).

38. Alphonso, Caroline and Simona Chiose (2018) "Ford Vows Changes to Ontario's Sex-Ed, Math Curriculums if PCs Win Election," *The Global and Mail*, May 8.

39. Ontario PC Youth Association (2018) Facebook Post, September 1. Archived at http://archive.is/tDMZ2 (last accessed July 2020).

40. PressProgress (2018) "Doug Ford Stands Behind This Photo He Took With a Group of Extremely Racist White Nationalists," September 24. At https://pressprogress.ca/doug-ford-stands-behind-this-photo-he-took-with-a-group-of-extremely-racist-white-nationalists (last accessed July 2020).

41. Crawley, Mike (2019) "Doug Ford Met Jordan Peterson, Appointment Calendar Reveals," CBC, January 28.

42. Friesen, Joe (2019) "Only One Event Cancelled for Safety Concerns after Ontario Postsecondary Free-Speech Directive: Assessment," *The Global and Mail*, November 4.

43. Canadian Constitution Foundation (2019) "Freedom to Express Controversial Political Views on Trial at Supreme Court of Canada," March 20. At https://theccf.ca/freedom-to-express-controversial-political-views-on-trial-at-supreme-court-of-canada; No Forced Speech (n.d.) "A Charter Challenge to the Law Society's Mandatory Statement of Principles." Archived at https://web.archive.org/web/20200222074751/www.noforcedspeech.ca (last accessed August 2020).

44. Runnymede Society (n.d.) "About Us." At https://runnymedesociety.ca/about-us (last accessed August 2020).

45. Fine, Sean (2019) "Libertarian Student Group Runnymede Society Seeks to Shake Up Canada's Legal Culture," *The Globe and Mail*, September 10; St-Hilaire, Maxime and Joanna Baron (n.d.) "Attacks on the Rule of Law From Within," Runnymede Society. At https://runnymedesociety.ca (last accessed August 2020).

46. Fine, "Libertarian Student Group Runnymede Society Seeks to Shake Up Canada's Legal Culture."

47. Smith, Evan (2020) *No Platform: A History of Anti-fascism, Universities and the Limits of Free Speech*. New York: Routledge, 4–10.

48. "NUS' No Platform Policy: Key Information, Background and FAQ" (n.d.) National Union of Students, London. At https://tinyurl.com/y3gaj6oa (last accessed July 2020).

49. Monbiot, George (2018) "How US Billionaires Are Fueling the Hard-Right Cause in Britain," *The Guardian*, December 7.

50. Smith, *No Platform*.

51. Spiked (n.d.) "How We Rank," Free Speech University Rankings. Archived at https://web.archive.org/web/20150213214902/http:/www.spiked-online.com/free-speech-university-rankings/how-we-rank (last accessed July 2020).

52. Spiked (2016) "Tackling the New Intolerance," February 19. At www.spiked-online.com/2016/02/19/tackling-the-new-intolerance (last accessed July 2020).

53. Small, Mike (2018) "US Oil Billionaire Charles Koch Funds UK Anti-Environment Spiked Network," DeSmog UK. At www.desmog.co.uk/2018/12/04/spiked-lm-dark-money-koch-brothers (last accessed April 2021). See Appendix 1.

54. Monbiot, "How US Billionaires Are Fueling the Hard-Right Cause in Britain."

55. Spiked (2017) "The Unsafe Space Tour 2017," September 8. At www.spiked-online.com/2017/09/08/the-unsafe-space-tour-2017; Spiked Magazine (n.d.) "Learn Liberty." At www.learnliberty.org/speakers/spiked-magazine (both last accessed July 2020).

56. Spiked (n.d.) "The State of Free Speech on Campus." Archived at https://web.archive.org/web/20150315024739/http:/www.spiked-online.com/free-speech-university-rankings#.VQTy1S2B5UM (last accessed July 2020).

57. Of the three Atlas Network annual reports that provide a full list of partner organizations, Policy Exchange was listed in two of them (2011 and 2014, not 2018). Annual reports are available at www.atlasnetwork.org/about/annual-reports (last accessed July 2020)

58. Transparify (2017) "Think Tanks in the UK 2017: Transparency, Lobbying and Fake News in Brexit Britain," February 8, 6. At https://tinyurl.com/y9pbf63a (last accessed July 2020). See also Policy Exchange

(2019) "Who Funds You?" October 22. At http://whofundsyou.org/org/policy-exchange (last accessed July 2020).

59. We arrive at this claim by comparing the list of think tanks receiving a "highly opaque" rating from Transparify against the list of UK think tanks appearing in the "Atlas Network Partner Directory" published in the 2018 Annual Report. Atlas Network (2018) "Annual Report 2018," 6. At www.atlasnetwork.org/assets/uploads/annual-reports/2018yearinreview.pdf (last accessed July 2020).

60. Hughes, Solomon (2019) "Group That Called Extinction Rebellion 'Extremist' Is Funded By Big Energy," *Vice*, August 19; Wilson, Tom and Richard Walton (2019) "Extremism Rebellion," Policy Exchange, July 13, 7.

61. Syal, Rajeev and Rowena Mason (2017) "Jo Johnson to Tell Universities to Stop 'No-Platforming' Speakers," *The Guardian*, December 25.

62. Legatum Institute (n.d.) "United Kingdom: Prosperity Score 80.7 (11th)." At https://prosperitysite.s3-accelerate.amazonaws.com/2115/7413/8858/United_Kingdom_2019_PIcountryprofile.pdf; DeSmog (n.d.) "Legatum Institute." At www.desmogblog.com/legatum-institute (last accessed August 2020).

63. See Appendix 1.

64. Carl, Noah (n.d.) *Lackademia: Why Do Academics Lean Left?* Adam Smith Institute, London. At https://tinyurl.com/y6qcw7sa (last accessed July 2020).

65. John Templeton Foundation (n.d.) "Magna Carta and the Revival of Freedom Today." At www.templeton.org/grant/magna-carta-and-the-revival-of-freedom-today-2 (last accessed July 2020). See also Appendix 1.

66. Joint Committee on Human Rights (2018) Freedom of Speech in Universities, House of Commons (HC 589) and House of Lords (HL Paper 111), March 27, 8 & 19–20. At https://publications.parliament.uk/pa/jt201719/jtselect/jtrights/589/589.pdf (last accessed July 2020).

67. Schraer, Rachel and Ben Butcher (2018) "Universities: Is Free Speech Under Threat?" BBC, October 23.

68. Policy Exchange (2019) *The First Hundred Days: How the Government Can Implement the Pledges in its 2019 Election Manifesto.* At https://policyexchange.org.uk/wp-content/uploads/2019/12/The-First-Hundred-Days.pdf (last accessed July 2020).

69. Simpson, Thomas and Eric Kaufmann (2019) "Academic Freedom in the UK," Policy Exchange. At https://policyexchange.org.uk/wp-content/uploads/2019/11/Academic-freedom-in-the-UK.pdf; Adekoya, Remi, Eric Kaufmann, and Thomas Simpson (2020) "Academic Freedom in the UK: Protecting Viewpoint Diversity," Policy Exchange. At https://policyexchange.org.uk/wp-content/uploads/Academic-freedom-in-the-UK.pdf (both last accessed June 2020).

70. Rawlinson, Kevin and Sara Luxmoore (2018) "Doubts Cast on DfE Claims of Toby Young's Qualifications for Watchdog Job," *The Guardian*, January 3.

71. Phipps, Claire, Kevin Rawlinson, and Rowena Mason (2018) "Toby Young Resigns from the Office for Students After Backlash," *The Guardian*, January 9.

72. Van Der Merwe, Ben (2018) "Exposed: London's Eugenics Conference and Its Neo-Nazi Links," *London Student*, January 10. At https://tinyurl.com/ydadcg2m (last accessed December 2020).

73. Commissioner for Public Appointments (2018) "The Commissioner for Public Appointments Report on the Recruitment Campaign for the Office of Students." At https://tinyurl.com/y732mmbl (last accessed December 2020).

74. Free Speech Union (2020) "Statement of Values." At https://freespeechunion.org/about/statement-of-values; Free Speech Union (2020) "About Us." At https://freespeechunion.org/about (both last accessed December 2020).

75. Free Speech Union (2020) "Who We Are." At https://freespeechunion.org/about/who-we-are (last accessed December 2020).

76. Ahmed, Nafeez (2021) "'Free Speech' Czar Role Linked to Toby Young's Free Speech Union and US Right-Wing Funding Network," *Byline Times*, February 16.

77. Quinn, Ben (2020) "Cambridge University Urged to Re-Invite Rightwing Academic Jordan Peterson," *The Guardian*, December 10.

78. Maitra, Sumantra (2020) "Toby Young Leads Rebuke to Leftist Censorship With Free Speech Union," *The Federalist*, March 5. At https://tinyurl.com/yb342bts (last accessed December 2020).

79. Ahmed, Nafeez (2020) "Alt-Right Pseudoscience: Lockdown Sceptics," *Byline Times*, December 4; Ahmed, Nafeez (2020) "Alt-Right Pseudoscience: 'Free Speech' and Scientific Racism," *Byline Times*, December 8.

80. Main, Ed (2019) "The Battle Over Britain's Newest Student Movement," *BBC Trending*, February 9.

81. Quoted in Spence, Alex and Mark Di Stefano (2019) "Days After Its Disastrous British Launch, Turning Point Has Already Lost One of Its Star Recruits," *Buzzfeed*, February 8.

82. Turning Point UK (n.d.) "Chapter Directory." At https://tpointuk.co.uk/chapter-directory (last accessed July 2020).

83. Turning Point UK (n.d.) "Education Watch." At https://tpointuk.co.uk/education-watch (last accessed July 2020).

84. Hazell, Will (2020) "Right-Wing Student Group Turning Point UK Accused of 'McCarthyism' for Plan to Film and Publish Lecturers' 'Political Bias,'" *iNews*, March 2.

85. Smith, James A (2019) "The Turning Point Saga Shows How Easily US Money Can Infiltrate and Influence British Political Discourse," *Independent*, February 7.

86. Atlas Network (n.d.) "Global Directory: Australia and New Zealand." At www.atlasnetwork.org/partners/global-directory/australia-and-new-zealand (last accessed July 2020).
87. DeSmog Blog (n.d.) "Institute of Public Affairs." At www.desmogblog.com/institute-public-affairs; SourceWatch (2020) "Institute of Public Affairs," Center for Media and Democracy. At www.sourcewatch.org/index.php?title=Institute_of_Public_Affairs (both last accessed July 2020).
88. Atlas Network (2015) "Institute of Public Affairs' Repeal the Carbon Tax Finalist the Prestigious Templeton Freedom Award," August 31. At www.atlasnetwork.org/news/article/institute-of-public-affairs-repeal-the-carbon-tax-finalist-for-prestigious- (last accessed July 2020).
89. Lesh, Matthew (2016) "Free Speech on Campus Audit 2016: The State of Intellectual Debate at Australian Universities," Institute of Public Affairs, May, 2. At https://ipa.org.au/wp-content/uploads/2016/12/18May16-ML-FreeSpeechonCampusAudit2016-May2016.pdf (last accessed July 2020).
90. Lesh, Matthew (2018) "Free Speech in Decline: IPA Free Speech on Campus Audit 2018," Institute of Public Affairs, December 10. At https://ipa.org.au/publications-ipa/media-releases/free-speech-in-decline-ipa-free-speech-on-campus-audit-2018 (last accessed July 2020).
91. Ibid.
92. Center for Independent Studies (n.d.) "Mission & History." At www.cis.org.au/about/mission (last accessed July 2020).
93. Sammut, Jermey (2018) "University Freedom Charters: How to Best Protect Free Speech on Australian Campuses," Culture, Prosperity and Civility Society and The Center for Independent Studies, no. 10, October. At www.cis.org.au/app/uploads/2018/10/pp10.pdf (last accessed July 2020).
94. Ibid., 2.
95. Zhen, Alan (2019) "Two Bettina Arndt Protesters Cleared from Misconduct Proceedings," *Honi Soit*, June 4.
96. See Appendix 1.
97. French, Robert (2019) "Report of the Independent Review of Freedom of Speech in Australian Higher Education Providers," Ministry of Education, March. At https://docs.education.gov.au/system/files/doc/other/report_of_the_independent_review_of_freedom_of_speech_in_australian_higher_education_providers_march_2019.pdf (last accessed July 2020).
98. Lesh, Matthew (2019) "IPA Welcomes Free Speech Review, Time For Universities To Act," Institute of Public Affairs, April 9; Hargreaves, Scott (2019) "Looming Crisis of Free Speech," Institute of Public Affairs, April 29. At https://ipa.org.au (last accessed July 2020).
99. French, "Report of the Independent Review of Freedom of Speech," 13.
100. Ibid., 54, 38.

101. Human Rights and Equal Opportunity Commission (1991) *Racist Violence*, Australian Government Publishing Service, Canberra. At https://humanrights.gov.au/our-work/race-discrimination/publications/racist-violence-1991 (last accessed August 2020).

102. Berg, Chris et al. (2016) "The Case for the Repeal of Section 18C," Institute of Public Affairs, December. At https://ipa.org.au (last accessed August 2020).

103. Berg, Chris (2012) "The Soviet Origins of Hate-Speech Laws," Institute of Public Affairs, August 12. At https://ipa.org.au/ipa-review-articles/the-soviet-origins-of-hate-speech-laws (last accessed August 2020).

104. PressProgress (2017) "Rebel Media's Ezra Levant Received Foreign Funding from 'Anti-Muslim' Think Tank," August 17. At https://pressprogress.ca/exclusive_rebel_media_ezra_levant_received_foreign_funding_from_anti_muslim_think_tank; Middle East Forum (2018) "MEF Organizes 25,000 Strong Protest in Support of Tommy Robinson; Plans Additional Rallies," July 8. At https://web.archive.org/web/20181124124308/https:/www.meforum.org/articles/2018/mef-organizes-25,000-strong-protest-in-support-of (both last accessed August 2020).

105. Drury, Colin (2018) "Tommy Robinson Protest: Police Release Pictures of Nine People Wanted After Violence at London Rally," *The Independent*, July 23.

106. Fang, "Sphere of Influence."

107. Ibid.

108. MacLean, Nancy (2021) "'Since We Are Greatly Outnumbered': Why and How the Koch Network Uses Disinformation to Thwart Democracy," in *The Disinformation Age: Politics, Technology, and Disruptive Communication in the United States*, ed. W. Lance Bennet and Steven Livingston. Cambridge: Cambridge University Press, 138.

CONCLUSION: REFUSING THE PLUTOCRATIC
FREE SPEECH NARRATIVE

1. Bauer-Wolf, Jeremy (2019) "Free Speech Laws Mushroom in Wake of Campus Protests," *Inside Higher Ed*, September 16.

2. SourceWatch (2017) "Chris Kapenga," Center for Media and Democracy. At www.sourcewatch.org/index.php/Chris_Kapenga (last accessed September 2020).

3. For example, equal access to education is enshrined in the 1964 Civil Rights Act and Title IX of the 1972 Education Amendments Act. Baer, Ulrich (2019) *What Snowflakes Get Right: Free Speech, Truth, and Equality on Campus*. Oxford: Oxford University Press, xvii.

4. Ibid., 105.

5. Fish, Stanley (2019) *The First: How to Think About Hate Speech, Campus Speech, Religious Speech, Fake News, Post-Truth, and Donald Trump*. New York: Simon and Schuster, 106.

6. Baer, *What Snowflakes Get Right*, 26.

7. Scott, Joan W. (2017) "On Free Speech and Academic Freedom," *Journal of Academic Freedom* 8, 4.

8. Ibid, 4.

9. Baer, *What Snowflakes Get Right*, 23.

10. Good Jobs First (n.d.) "Subsidy Tracker Parent Company Summary (Koch Industries)." At https://subsidytracker.goodjobsfirst.org/parent/koch-industries (last accessed October 2020).

11. Skocpol, Theda and Alexander Hertel-Fernandez (2016) "The Koch Network and Republican Party Extremism," *Perspectives on Politics* 14 (3): 695.

12. Leonard, Christopher (2020) *Kochland: The Secret History of Koch Industries and Corporate Power in America*. New York: Simon & Schuster, 392–461.

13. Ibid., 401.

14. Ibid., 445.

15. Ibid., 446.

16. Flynn, Meagan (2020) "Chanting 'Lock Her Up,' Michigan Protesters Waving Trump Flags Mass Against Gov. Gretchen Whitmer's Coronavirus Restrictions," *The Washington Post*, April 16; Mogelson, Luke (2020) "Nothing to Lose But Your Masks," *The New Yorker*, August 24, 34–5.

17. Mogelson, "Nothing to Lose But Your Masks," 35.

18. Stanley-Becker, Isaac and Tony Romm (2020) "The Anti-Quarantine Protests Seem Spontaneous. But Behind the Scenes, a Powerful Network is Helping," *The Washington Post*, April 22.

19. Ibid.

20. Armiak, David (2020) "Operatives Tied to Council for National Policy Organizing Protests Alleging Voter Fraud," Exposed, the Center for Media and Democracy, November 6.

21. Skocpol, Theda and Vanessa Williamson (2016) *The Tea Party and the Remaking of Republican Conservatism*. Oxford: Oxford University Press; Fang, Lee (2012) *The Machine: A Field Guide to the Resurgent Right*. New York: The New Press; Nesbit, Jeff (2016) *Poison Tea: How Big Oil and Big Tobacco Invented the Tea Party and Captured the GOP*. New York: Macmillan, 2016.

22. Sutter, Daniel (2019) "Is Climate Policy Debatable?" *Alabama Today*, April 24.

23. Mayer, Jane (2021) "Inside the Koch-Backed Effort to Block the Largest Election Reform Bill in Half a Century," *The New Yorker*, March 29. McKenzie quote from the 6:50 minute mark in the recording published alongside the article.

Index

AAUP (American Association of
University Professors), 113–114
Abrams, Samuel, 125–126, 216n111
absolutism, free-market, 19–20
absolutism, free speech: and
academic freedom, 153, 154, 155;
in Canada, 138–139; legislation
of, 105, 109–110; in litigation, 80,
86, 88–89, 91–92, 97
academic freedom: contrasted
to free speech narratives, 150,
153–157, 161–162; of Koch-
funded academics, 118, 124–125,
129–130; and legislation, 113; in
litigation, 96–97; of right-wing
faculty in the UK, 142
academics: in donor strategy, 11–12,
20–23; Koch-funded, 15–16,
116–130; in manufacturing the
free speech crisis, 150; in strategy
for social change, 20–23, 115–116.
See also centers, academic; faculty
access to higher education: in donor
strategy, 5, 7–8, 19–20, 22, 28;
equality of, 36–37, 83–84, 86,
153–154, 157, 224n3; in legislation, 7–8, 99, 103; litigation in,
7–8, 83–84; for provocateurs, 45,
49–51, 62–63, 103, 153–154, 156
activism/activists: anti-fascist,
in protests, 52–53; anti-racist,
46, 128–129, 134; compared
to climate deniers and anti-
lockdown protesters, 159–160;
corporate-funded, in legislation,
110–114; punishment of, in IHS
manuals, 122–123; resources

for, 169–173; resurgence of, 46;
in revealing Koch donations
to GMU, 117–118; of student
groups, 31–32, 36, 40–41,
44, 68–69. *See also* protests/
protesters; punishment for
activism and protests
Adam Smith Institute, 141–142
ADF (Alliance Defending Freedom),
67–68, 74–75, 76, 93, 94, 95–96,
109, 111
admissions policies, 82, 83–84
Aegis Strategic, 10–11
AEI (American Enterprise Institute),
59–60, 74, 151–152
AFA (Academic Freedom Alliance),
129–130, 216n111
affirmative action policies, 38, 64,
81–82, 84–85
AFP (Americans for Prosperity)/
AFP Foundation, *22,* 24,
110–111, 112–113, 158–159.
See also GenOpp (Generation
Opportunity)
Agarwal, Rajshree, 129
agendas, right-wing/libertarian:
academic centers funded by,
118–119; access to universities
in, 7–8; in challenging academic
community standards, 6; in
donor strategy, 11; government
as threat to, 160–161; legislative,
98, 105; litigation in, 87–88; and
media amplifiers, 68–69, 78;
provocateurs pushing, 53–54
AIM (American Identity
Movement), 38, 42–43

ALEC (American Legislative
Exchange Council), 10–11, 26, 27,
98–99, 105–110
Alexander Hamilton Forum, 127
alt-right groups and ideology:
Brietbart as platform for, 72;
and campus YAL groups, 33, 38;
international, 133–136, 145, 149;
and media amplifiers, 72–73,
134–136; and provocateurs,
46–47, 49, 51–52, 54–55,
135–136; provocateurs in pipeline
to, 48–51; and student groups, 30,
33, 38; TPUSA as, 42–43. *See also*
far-right groups and personalities;
white supremacists/supremacy
Alumni for Liberty, 35–36
American Center for Law and
Justice, 74–75
American Civil Rights Institute, 81
American Conservative Union, 54
American Energy Alliance, 10–11,
158–159
America's Frontline Doctors, 159
anarcho-capitalism, 20–21, 33–34,
48
anecdotes: in campus policy change,
123; in debating legislation,
98–99; in "empirical research,"
125; as evidence of crisis, 152;
in free speech international,
146; lawyers' use of, 86–88; in
manufacturing the free speech
crisis, 1–2, 151–152
anonymity of donors, 13–14, 27, 144
Anschutz, Philip, 65–66, 76
Anschutz Foundation, 76
anti-communism, 17
anti-government sentiment, 33, 34,
37–39, 48
anti-immigration positions and
rhetoric, 42–43, 49, 50, 51–52,
138–139
anti-racism, 46, 128–129, 134

anti-regulation organizations, 25,
133
antisemitism, 38, 54–55
anti-union laws, Canadian, 135
APEE (Association of Private
Enterprise Education), 116,
120–121, 135, 209–210n10
Arizona, 127
Arizona State University (ASU),
127–128
Arndt, Bettina, 146
Arnold, John, 215n93
Asness, Cliff, 121
astroturf groups, 10–11, 63, 93–94,
108, 110–111, 112, 148, 159.
See also grassroots support,
appearance of
The Atlantic, 77–78, 87–88
Atlas Network, 98–99, 132, 133–134,
136–137, 139–140, 141–142,
145–149
Auburn University, 34, 119
Australia, 145–147
autonomy: of academic centers,
120; individual, free speech in,
61–62; institutional, 113 (*See also*
governance: institutional); in the
republic of science, 131–132; of
UK student unions, 142

Baer, Ulrich, 156–157
Ball, Whitney, 13–14, 70–71
Bannon, Steve, 53–54, 72
Beck, Glenn, 65–66
Beets, Douglas, 118
Bell Curve, The (Murray), 57–58
Benkler, Yochai: *Network
Propaganda,* 65
Benson, Bruce, 118–119
Bernstein, David, 216n111
Big Think, 77
Black Lives Matter, 49–50, 52, 110,
112–113, 129
Blackwell, Morton, 68–69
Blum, Edward, 82

Boettke, Peter, 118
Bradley, Harry, 17
Bradley Foundation: academic
centers funded by, 116–120,
124–125, 127, 128–129; AFP
funded by, 110–111; Atlas
Network funded by, 133; Austrian
economics on campus funded by,
19; donations by, 165–168 A1;
litigation funded by, 81, 82, 87,
90; media amplifiers funded by,
69–70, 71, 73, 75; provocateurs
funded by, 59; Rebel News funded
by, 134–135; SPN funded by, 106;
and YAF, 40
Brandon, Adam, 43
Brat, David: "Student Rights Act of
2018," 112
Brazil, 147–148
Breitbart News, 53–54, 65, 71–72
Brexit, 144
Bristow, Kyle: Foundation for the
Marketplace of Ideas, 41–42
Brown, Brennan, 130–131
Brown v. Board of Education, 15–16
Buchanan, James McGill, 15–16
Buckley, F. H., 75–76
Buckley, William F., 39
Butcher, Jonathan, 104, 107

CAFAR (Committee for Academic
Freedom and Rights), 124–125
CAFE (Campus Free Expression)
Act (FIRE), 100–102
California State University, Los
Angeles, 56–57
Callanan, Keegan, 127, 216n111
Cal Poly, San Luis Obispo, 53
Cambridge Analytica, 53–54, 72
Cambridge University, 144
campus-as-culture-war narrative,
1–2, 27–28, 145
Campus Disorientation (SFL), 32–33
Campus Freedom Index (JCCF),
138–139

"Campus Free Speech Act"
(Goldwater Institute), 102–105
Campus Reform (LI), 66–70,
128–129, 187n3
Campus Unmasked initiative (Rebel
News), 135–136
Campus Victory Plan (TPUSA),
44–45
Canada, 134–140
cancel culture narrative, 1, 86, 148,
150, 164
cap-and-trade legislation, 158–161
carbon divestment and regulation,
43, 102–103
Carlson, Tucker, 72–73
Cato Institute, 27, 33–34, 77, 93. *See
also* think tanks
"cause of action" provisions, 112
CCF (Canadian Constitution
Foundation), 139–140
censorship, 73–74, 88–89, 99,
135–136, 142, 146, 155–156
Censorship Exposed program (YAF),
41, 50–51
Center for Enterprise and Markets
(U MD, College Park), 129
Center for Equal Opportunity, 81
Center for Growth and Opportunity
(Utah State University), 132
Center for the Study of Free
Enterprise (Western Carolina
University), 120
centers, academic: academic
freedom in, 156–157; APEE in
establishing, 209–210n10; in the
campus free speech machine,
4, 6–7; contracts in funding of,
119–120; "deliverables" by, 120;
and donor controlled giving,
116–117; in donor strategy,
10–11, 18–20, 115–116; exposure
of, 163; free speech focused,
120–130; GMU as model of,
116–118; pattern of, 118–120; in
political strategy, 161; and the

CSLD (Center for the Study of
Liberal Democracy) (University
of Wisconsin-Madison), 123–124
curriculum, 11–12, 80–81, 104, 119,
124, 128, 156–157
CWA (Concerned Women for
America), 110–111

The Daily Caller, 72–73
Daily Caller News Foundation
(DCNF), 73
The Daily Wire, 54–55, 56
Darling, Kasey, 69–70
David Horowitz Freedom Center, 56
Defenders of Property Rights, 21–22
demonstrations. *See* protests/
protesters
Dennis, Kimberly, 81–82, 94
deregulation, 11, 22–24, 36–37, 45,
91, 98–99, 133–134
DeSanctis, Alexandra, 74
designated forums, 101–102, 103
DeSmog Blog, 8–9
DesRosiers, David, 75–76
DeVos, Betsy, 14, 50, 71, 112–113,
159
DeVos, Richard, 75
DeVos family, 40, 43
Dezenhall, Eric, 94
Dezenhall Resouces, 94
discipline. *See* punishment for
activism and protests
discourse, academic: culture war
outrage in, 152–153; free speech
and civil rights balanced with,
96–97; at Koch-funded centers,
121, 122–123, 124–125; legislat-
ing, 99; provocateurs' hostility
toward, 47–48; sabotage of, 24–25
disinformation, 25, 78–79, 144, 145,
148–149, 163–164, 192n99
Disinformation Age (MacLean), 78
disruption of speakers: academic
centers on, 122–123; alternatives
for, in demonstrations, 171–172

A2; in international free speech
movements, 136, 142, 146;
in legislation, 100–101, 102,
103–105, 108; of provocateurs, 46,
48, 52–53, 56–57, 58–59, 60–61,
138. *See also* protests/protesters
diversity/diversity policies: in
academic centers, 124–125,
130–131; and academic freedom,
153; intellectual, 124–125,
130–131, 139–140; in the international free speech movement,
139–140, 143; litigation of,
81, 84–85, 92, 96–97; media
amplifiers on, 66–67, 73–74;
provocateurs on, 49, 56; training
in, 92, 105
donor control, 5, 80–81, 116–117
donor strategy: academic centers in,
10–11, 18–20, 115–116; access
to higher education in, 5, 7–8,
19–20, 22, 28; anonymity in,
13–14, 27, 144; desegregation in
origins of, 15–17; free-market
economics in, 11, 13–14, 16–17,
18, 19–20; Koch donor network
in, 12–15; manufactured public
opposition in, 24–25, 158–160;
political action in, 10, 16–17;
political organizations in, 10–11;
provocateurs in, 62; social change
in, 10, 11–12, 20–23; weaponization of free speech in, 23–28.
See also Koch donor network;
strategies, Koch network
DonorsTrust/Donors Capital Fund
(DT/DCF): academic centers
funded by, 116–120, 123–124,
126, 127, 128–129; in coronavirus
lockdown protests, 159; donations
by, 165–168 A1; in donor strategy,
13–14, 26; in the international
free speech movement, 133,
141–142; in legislation, 106,
110–111; in litigation, 81–82, 90,

96; and media amplifiers, 69–70, 71, 73, 75–76; student groups funded by, 40, 43

Downs, Donald, 122, 124–125, 216n111; *Restoring Free Speech and Liberty on Campus,* 124–125

Down with Campus Censorship campaign (Spiked Online), 140

Ducey, Doug, 127

Dziok, Dave, 69–70

echo chambers, 42, 65, 158–159, 163

economics, Austrian school of: in academic centers, 118, 119; American subset of, 177–178n33; anti-democratic nature of, 179n46; in donor strategy for social change, 21; in the international free speech movement, 133–134; in Koch campus investments, 17–20; in the libertarian to alt-right pipeline, 48; in the Republic of Ideas, 131; and student groups, 30, 32, 33–34, 35, 37–38. *See also* Hayek, Friedrich; Mises, Ludwig von

economics, free-market: in creation of academic centers, 116, 119, 121, 130–131; in donor strategy, 11, 13–14, 16–17, 18, 19–20; fundamentalism in, 5–6; in the international free speech movement, 133, 134–135, 137, 145; in legislation, 107, 109–110; libertarian/ultra-free market right, 11, 13–14, 19–20, 116, 156–157; and the marketplace of ideas, 60–61, 62, 130–131, 156–157; mythology of, 36–37; values of, and student groups, 43–45, 60

Education and Workforce Development Taskforce, 107

"Education Watch" (TPUK), 144

egalitarianism/anti-egalitarianism, 30, 34, 48, 51, 137

1851 Center for Constitutional Law, 90–91

elections: campus, student groups in, 30, 43–45, 91; in donor strategy, 10–11, 26–27, 28; election reform package (HR1), 164; funding of academics in capabilities for, 115–116; legislation on, 109–110; media amplifiers in, 76

Eleventh Amendment, 108

Ellison, Keith, 25

Emmett, Shelby, 107, 108, 110

Encounter Books, 87–88

Equality Act of 2010, UK, 143

equity on campus, 48, 85, 114

Estes, Bud, 111–112

ethics, 2, 96–97, 150

Eudaimonia Institute (Wake Forest), 119–120

eugenics/eugenicists, 57–60, 142–143

Evergreen State College, 1

extremism, 134, 141, 157–158

faculty: academic freedom of, 142, 153–157; in developing speech codes, 84; in donor strategy, 16–17; FSOI grants to, 121–122; harassment of, 2–4; Koch-funded, 62, 115–116, 117–118, 120–123, 128–130; monitoring of, 44, 69, 104, 144; plutocratic libertarian funding of, 6; political pressure on students by, 2–3; protests of, 1; provocateurs targeting, 187n3; in the republic of science, 131–132. *See also under* name of faculty member; scholars

Faris, Robert: *Network Propaganda,* 65

far-right groups and personalities: campus protests of, 1; in the international free speech movement,

"Free Speech Box" (YAF), 40–41
Free Speech Champions, 143
free speech crisis narrative, 1–2
free speech international: and the
    Atlas Foundation, 133–134;
    Australia, 145–147; Canada,
    134–140; United Kingdom,
    140–145
Free Speech on Campus Audit (IPA),
    145
Free Speech Project (Georgetown
    University), 2–3
"Free Speech Quick Action Plan"
    (YAF), 40–41
Free Speech Union, 141–144
Free Speech University Rankings
    (Spiked Online), 140, 142
"Free Speech Week" (Yiannopoulos),
    52–53
free speech zones, 36–37, 45, 85,
    90–91, 101–102, 112–113
French, David, 74–75
French, Robert, 146–147
French Report, 146–147
Friess, Foster, 43, 55–56, 72–73
FSOI (Free Speech and Open
    Inquiry) initiative (IHS), 121–122,
    125
funding, public, 1–2, 104, 112–113,
    128, 133–134

Garner, Eric, 110
Geller, Pam, 52–53
GenOpp (Generation Opportunity),
    10–11, 35–36, 110–111. See also
    AFP
Gentry, Kevin, 69–70, 115–116
George, Robert, 129–130
George Mason University (GMU),
    11–12, 83, 89–90, 116–118,
    119–120, 177–178n33
Georgetown University, 2–3,
    123–124
Glittering Seal (Mercer and
    Bannon), 54

Goldwater Institute, 89–90, 93,
    98–99, 102–105, 151–152
Goldy, Faith, 135–136, 138
Gorsuch, Neil, 25–26
Gottfried, Paul, 48
governance: faculty, 5, 99, 104,
    113–114, 118–120; institutional,
    80, 96–97, 99, 103, 113–114,
    119–120
grassroots support, appearance of,
    4–5, 10–11, 23–24, 29, 148, 159,
    160–161. See also astroturf
    groups
Greve, Michael, 83, 85
Groypers/Groyper Army, 54–55,
    190n46

Haidt, Jonathan, 77, 87–88, 216n111
Hanson, Victor David, 216n111
harassment, 2–3, 70, 80, 84, 93, 95,
    129, 143
Harper, F. A., 19
Harry Lynde Bradley Foundation.
    See Bradley Foundation
Hasnas, John, 123–124
Hatch, Orrin: "Free Right to
    Expression in Education Act," 112
hate groups, 30, 38–39, 41–42,
    74–75, 95
hate speech/hateful rhetoric: Atlas
    Group in international protection
    of, 139–140; in the international
    free speech movement, 135–136,
    145, 147; in legislation, 109–110;
    litigation in protection of, 80,
    84–85, 91, 92–93, 95, 96–97;
    policies/laws on, 36–37, 84–85,
    91, 92–93, 109–110, 135–136; by
    provocateurs, 46–47, 51–52, 53,
    54–55
Hayek, Friedrich, 17–19, 30–33;
    Road to Serfdom, 18; "The
    Intellectuals and Socialism," 18.
    See also economics, Austrian
    school of

Thanks to our Patreon Subscribers:

Lia Lilith de Oliveira
Andrew Perry

Who have shown generosity and
comradeship in support of our publishing.

Check out the other perks you get by subscribing
to our Patreon – visit patreon.com/plutopress.
Subscriptions start from £3 a month.